Bryant Acres

A Love Story

1781-1854

By: Ann L. Patterson Early, Ph.D., CSW

& Quinn Early

Bryant Acres

A Love Story

Ann L. Patterson Early / Quinn Early

ISBN (Print Edition): 978-1-54393-962-0

ISBN (eBook Edition): 978-1-54393-963-7

DEDICATION

In the memory of Ann's mother, Vernita Wilks
and her grandmother, "Big Mama" for keeping
the story of Sherrod Bryant alive.

And to Big Mama's sisters, Lovie Lee, Barbie Lee and
Dovie Lee. And to the memory of all the named and
unnamed Bryant's who died trying to survive in a
climate of race, hate and health deprivation.

To my mom, Dr. Ann L. Patterson Early Thank you for being a role
model in my life. Thank you for showing me that no matter how
hard life gets, and no matter how many people believe that you will
fail, always believe in yourself and you can accomplish anything.

A devoted wife and mother, you found yourself alone with no job.
You rolled up your sleeves and worked two jobs while going back
to college. You earned your bachelor's degree, your Master's degree
and finally, your PhD. All while trying to raise me. You were and
always will be my role model and the person that I aspire to be.
Thank you for passing down the life lessons that I instill in my
children. And thank you for loving me and always being there.

Thank you for being the amazing woman, mother
and friend that you were. I love you.

Quinn

BRYANT ACRES

A SPECIAL THANKS

A special thanks to my grandchildren, for their inspiration and input. Thank you to Dr. Dorothy Smith who was my spiritual guide, researcher, and travel partner. Without her support and encouragement, this book would have been more troubled labor. Thanks to my sister, Mosetta Pearson, for her technical assistance and who not only shared some of my experiences with Big Mama, but endured hours upon hours of conversations about the past. Thanks to Sally Huss for her technical assistance and marketing input. Thank you, Artha Drew, who became our guide in Tennessee. And my cousin Mary Watkins who not only chauffeured us around but led us to Bryant Acres while supplying some wonderful moments of humor. To Greedly and Westbrook who gave us lodging and stimulating conversation. To my Aunt and Uncle Sam Ella and Walter Patterson who took us into their home, fed us, and loved us during our trip to Tennessee. To my cousin Jonny Martin Patterson, who allowed us to turn his house into our Tennessee office. Thank you to Nelvinie and Lawrence for the pictures, the history lesson, and lunch. To my cousin, Dr. James Hammons, for the late-night calls, the pictures, and emotional support. And to all of the Bryants who showed up in the picture of the tombstone at Bryant Town Cemetery. Also, to the personnel in many state archives who didn't look at us as if we had two heads when we discussed researching history about free people of color in the late 1700s.

And a special thanks to Dr. John Seelig who helped both my mother and I navigate through her diagnosis of Alzheimer's. His friendship and guidance has been invaluable.

BRYANT ACRES

Prologue

William Cullen Bryant immortalized Thomas Jefferson's twenty-year affair with Sally Hemmings. The relationship is said to be one of the great interracial romances in American history. There are many interracial love stories in American history greater than Thomas Jefferson and Sally Hemmings'. However, they have gone unnoticed as neither of the partners, like Thomas Jefferson, wrote the declaration of independence nor became the president of United States. These couples were ordinary people who battled the odds, had families, and built towns. They contributed to the growth of education, industry, medicine, and religious beliefs as well as other factors that have gone into making this country what it is today. Bryant Acres is about such a couple. It is about a young, free Native American lad by the name of Sherrod Bryant who in 1800 came out of the hills of North Carolina, went to Virginia, and became an indentured servant to the Cole family. And how Sherrod bonded with the plantation owner's married daughter, Mary Polly Cole, and built her a cotton dynasty in Virginia. Sherrod and Mary Polly had an affair. She became pregnant, and Sherrod had to leave town before the return of her husband, Robert. He had spent the year in England doing business for his father in-law, Mr. Jesse Cole.

The story is based on fact. It was taken from an accumulation of data collected during two years of research and a recall of incidents told to me by my grandmother, Big Mama, during my growing up years as well as some recall by elderly relatives that I recently met in my travels south to Tennessee.

What has been uncovered is that once upon a time acres and acres of Nashville were once called Bryant Town. This town and thousands of acres of outland areas owned by Sherrod were called Bryant Grove and Bryant Hill. The settlements were parcels of Bryant Acres, Big Mama's family community.

Big Mama's great-great grandfather, Sherrod Bryant, was a pioneer who owned and settled Bryant Acres in the early to mid-1800s. At this writing, two hundred sixteen years have passed since Sherrod's birth. Unlike those of his white counterparts and neighbors, contributions that Sherrod made have gained little notice from historians and public institutions. A historical marker on Lebanon Road acknowledges the fact that Sherrod existed and it attests to his character. What it doesn't attest to are his historical contributions. This act of omission contributes to the myth that blacks and Native Americans were invisible during the building of the American frontier. This book, Bryant Acres, aims to set the record straight and fill the void that haunted Big Mama all of her life. Her family, the Bryants, were free blacks, whites, and Native Americans. They owned and resided for generations on large parcels of land that in general made up the Southeast section of Nashville, Tennessee, the airport, Highway 55, and especially Long Hunter State Park and the Percy Priest reservoir.

My earliest recollections are of Big Mama's passionate recall, her response to a family that she loved deeply, and her crusade for documentation that she said would correct the silence that had denied her family its rightful place in history.

At Long Hunter State Park's inception, Big Mama's cousin, Artie Adams, lobbied Congress for Tennessee legislation to name to the park as Bryant State Park. The legislators agreed that as much as there should be some sort of commemoration recognizing the Bryants who had a long history of owning and living on the land where the park was located, naming the park Bryant State Park was inconceivable. Rather, they elected three actions, which they carried out: They identified Bryant Creek that already existed. They left Bryant Groves trail and the Bryant Recreation Center areas intact as part of the Long Hunter State Park. They placed a historical marker on the side of the road at Lebanon Pike where Wilson County and Rutherford County meet.

Even though the legislators denied Artie Adams her wish to have the park named after the family, Big Mama would be proud of Artie Adams' effort and the historical marker. But like Artie Adams and the rest of the family, she would know the marker was just the beginning. Adjacent to the eastern boundary of the undeveloped area of Percy Priest is the Bryant Grove cemetery where Sherrod's son, Henderson, his sons, their wives, and children are buried. The family cemetery is overgrown, and the frontage is occupied by a section of houses with sprawling lawns that leave the cemetery with no access road.

Artie Adams, one of Big Mama's grand nieces, wrote a thesis detailing some of the Bryant history with phrases and pictures of commemoration for varied family members. Big Mama would also be proud of Artie Jones' sense of family and her fight to preserve the family history.

Several years ago, just before one of the Bryant family reunions, Artha Drew and Marty Adams took an old picture of Henderson, his wife, and his seven sons, and made carryall bags that were given to the family members who attended the reunion.

I wasn't at the reunion but when I went to visit, I was given one of the bags along with some good Southern hospitality: a warm bed, a home cooked meal, and a grand tour of Bryant Acres. Big Mama would also be proud of Artha Drew for serving as a resource for this book, supporting and helping those of us who are busy investigating leads and trails of Bryant history.

Hopefully, Bryant Acres will live up to Big Mama's expectations. She was hard to please.

INTRODUCTION

Big Mama used to set us children down and talk to us about what it was like when she was a little girl. Most of us listened intently to what she was talking about until someone moved and put his or her foot in the other's space and a fight would ensue. At that point, Big Mama would get mad and tell us how glad she was that our great grandfathers and mothers couldn't see what heathens she had to contend with and how we didn't appreciate all that our forefathers had gone through to keep us from being like the rest of the trash in the world. At that time, it was not clear why Big Mama thought people were trash or why she felt that she had to keep us from becoming trash, when all we ever did was try to be good and look out for one another like she asked. She didn't understand how living in the house with seventeen siblings and cousins was a lot of getting along, especially when you didn't always like everybody, relative or not. As hard as it seemed, sitting and listening to Big Mama's family history was easy compared to believing that one of her brothers was a lawyer and another was a doctor like she said. It was enough of a stretch for my imagination to accept that she was once a little girl with her mother and father and brothers and sisters. If two of her sisters and one of her brother's children were not making annual visits every summer and I wasn't getting to see them in a flash, I would have thought that she was telling one of those old wives' tales that I kept hearing the old folks accuse each other of.

Sometimes when Big Mama talked about her eleven siblings and her family and how all but six died before they were grown, she would become all choked up. Her voice would crack and that would make me sad and scared. I loved my two brothers and five sisters, and I couldn't bear the thought of anything happening to them. I asked my mother about it and told her what Big Mama said. She assured me that times were different then and explained how the world had gotten safer and that doctors were doing a better job because they were more educated now. I liked talking to my mother about things. She always made me feel better. She knew what she was talking about because she was a teacher once. Besides, there was proof. My mother's father died from pneumonia when she was sixteen, and my father got pneumonia when I was two and he got well. He was still alive. I always felt sorry that my mother lost her father. Every time she and Big Mama talked about Grandpa Sam, Mama would get this faraway look on her face. Grandpa Sam loved Mama; I could tell by the way she talked about their times together. He cared about what she thought, and he was always asking her opinion.

Big Mama said he was the finest man there ever was. She described him as a tall, handsome, brown-skinned man. She crooned when she talked about him. Her face would light up, and she took on this little girl look.

"He dressed so!" she would say with a toss of her head and smile. "He looked like he had just stepped out of a bandbox. He turned every woman's head in Bryant Town when he moved to the area from Polasky. The church hired him to play the organ, but his favorite instrument was the violin as well as the drums. He played them all, you know. Yes ma'am, he could play them all!"

To hear Big Mama tell it, Samuel Brown Wilkes was a man of means. He was the first free African American male born to his slave bred parents, Brownlow and Mary Wilkes. His aim was to make them proud. He worked hard, and he drove a fine leather buggy that was pulled by two striking Arabian horses with shining harnesses and bells that jingled as they pranced around the little one-lane dirt road that winded up and about the countryside.

"Samuel Brown married me when I was twelve," Big Mama would say, and every time she said it, those of us over eight years old would make a face and repeat the number with disbelief, "Twelve!"

"Twelve," she would say, rolling the number off of her tongue to emphasize the significance of what she was trying to tell us. "I was twelve, and he was twenty-six."

Afraid to let her hear what we were thinking, we would sit there, roll our eyes at each other, and snicker our disapproval. That didn't bother Big Mama. She would keep on talking. Every time she told the age part of the story, she would get a faraway look on her face. Then, as if she had caught herself with dealing something she wasn't sure she was supposed to disclose, she would hurriedly say, "He was the only man in town that wasn't kin to me. The other girls didn't mind marrying their cousins, but I held out. He had his pick. He could have had any girl in Bryant Town that he wanted. And he chose me."

Once Big Mama got into one of these history-telling modes, it was like she didn't want to stop. She would skip from one phase of her life to another. "The week after Sam and I got married, cousin Dora invited the single cousins and us to dinner. She was known for cooking, and that day she cooked a hearty meal. The conversation centered on Sam and me. The group mostly teased us about being newlyweds. Sam and I didn't mind. Everyone was having a good time. The teasing was being done in good taste. Sam's favorite dessert was apple cobbler. Dora had made several fancy apple pies, and she served him first. Everyone expressed how nice it was for her to be so welcoming. After Sam, she served the next person and the next. When there was no one left but me, she walked in my direction with this one piece of pie on a plate. She set it down in front of me and a strange smile came over her face.

Dora had told me that she liked Sam when he first came to town a year-and-half before. He had never paid any attention to her, and I had forgotten about that until that moment. I looked down at the pie, and my mind told me to take my fork and roll back the crust before I bit into it. Luckily I did, because when I rolled that crust back, there on top of the apples lay a large green caterpillar as alive as it could be."

"Big Mama!" we exclaimed, horrified that anyone could be so mean to Big Mama.

"What did you do to her?" we asked in anger.

"Nothing," Big Mama said. Then she would straighten her back in her chair, purse up her lips, and with all the dignity she could muster, she would say, "I got up from that child's table, turned to the other guests, and said, 'Mr. and Mrs. Samuel Le Brown Wilkes are leaving.' Without an inkling of what was happening, Sam pushed his chair back, stood up, and threw his napkin in his place. He took my arm and put it through his and we walked out the door." With that said, Big Mama smiled triumphantly. "You all's grandpa was something to behold."

Sometimes when Big Mama talked, she made us feel like winners. That was one of those times. When Big Mama was in a good mood, she would let me sit and watch her get dressed. Our family had more people in it than other families living in the flat. We had fewer clothes and oftentimes less to eat. Big Mama would try to compensate by giving us little chores to do and rewarding us with a new blouse, skirt, watermelon, or an ice cream. Daddy was prideful, and he hated it when Big Mama fed us in anyway. Most of the time, she would arrange to do it when he was at work. If he happened to come home from work and saw either one of us cutting grass, hoping to plant flowers, or sweeping the yard, he would rush upstairs and yell at Mama.

Mama would get mad and ask him why he hadn't yelled at Big Mama as he passed her in the yard. Daddy would then say something about running his own house and scream at us to come inside and go to bed. Enough of these incidents taught us that if we were going to get treats from Big Mama, we had to keep our business to ourselves. Along with that arrangement, however, came more storytelling and more family history. We eventually came to realize that Big Mama's storytelling was an important part of our contact with her. She was a woman who had very defined values and aspirations. She was clear about the way she expected us to carry ourselves as young ladies and young man.

Sometimes her conversations on the subject were not age-appropriate, and we must have shown it because every now and then in the middle of her dialogue, she would become irritated as if we had admonished her in some way. "Your old grandmother was not always fat and round," she would say. "I was something to look at in my day. I have a lot of white and Indian blood in me. Believe it or not, I once had a nice body. Even today, white folks can't tell if I'm white or not white. Many times, they have to ask me. It tickles me watching them trying to figure it out."

When she got into her narrative, we learned not to interrupt her. She knew where she was going with the conversation, and it didn't matter that she was confusing us with her prideful boasting about her white looks. It didn't matter that she had shared the many ways that white folks had hurt her and the rest of the colored people in her family throughout her years. Yes, she was pretty. Her silver hair was thin and straight. Her nose was not as broad as ours. Her cheekbones were high. And yes, her parents were white and Indian, but she married an African American and that made her colored. The question was, what was happening to Big Mama during those outbursts? Whatever it was became less of a question when I became a teenager and went off to high school. Actually, it was about that time that the transition of not having Big Mama in our day-to-day life started to happen. It started when my family joined the M.L. Franklin Church.

It was the 50s, and M.L. and C.L. Franklin were the ministers of note in Detroit. M.L. had relocated from the East side of Detroit to our community on the West side. Everyone in the community was excited. That is, everyone except Big Mama. She felt threatened by M.L.'s popularity, and she called him a shyster. She said ministers were not movie stars, and it was a sin for people to carry on about them the way they were doing. It didn't matter that my aunt and their families stayed with her in her church; she felt us moving away and she didn't like it.

The good thing about Big Mama was that she didn't hold a grudge. She said what she felt, and then she was finished with it until the next incident occurred. She never made you feel like you couldn't come to her with a problem. When I was in the eleventh grade, I took a creative writing class and the teacher asked us to write our family history. I went to Big Mama and asked her for help.

For the first time, I was asking her to tell me about the family instead of her forcing me to listen to her tell me about them. She must have taken that into consideration because she added new facts to the history that day.

She divulged that her great-great grandfather, Sherrod, was on her mother's side, and that he was of mixed heritage. He was an Indian/white man that fell in love with a wealthy white plantation owner's daughter. This was at a time when white people of color were being sold into slavery. This Sherrod was extremely wealthy, and he owned slaves long before the Civil War. I had grown up hearing how bad slavery was and how white folks had initiated slavery to keep black folks from succeeding. And here Big Mama was telling me that one of my forefathers had owned slaves.

I didn't want the other kids in my class to know that a member of my family had done such things, but I couldn't wait to get to school to see what the teacher thought about it. The teacher read the report, and then read it again. She called me up and read it to me out loud. When she finished reading, she asked me where I had gotten the information. I told her it was a true story and that my grandmother had told it to me. She laughed and said it was a good notion but that's all it was, a notion. I went home and told Big Mama what she said. Big Mama got really angry. I could always tell when she was real angry because her face turned red.

"What color is she?" she asked.

"She is white," I said. "A white teacher," I replied, wanting her to know that I knew why the teacher said what she said.

"It's just like that business at Fisk University," Big Mama went on to say. "William Ross doing all that work on the family and them giving him his grade pretending not to know what happened to the manuscript."

"Who is William Ross?" I asked.

"Your second cousin," she said and kept talking. "Many a time I have regretted not having an education. But things like this happened, and I asked myself, what can they teach me when they themselves can't handle the truth?" She was becoming more upset as she spoke. "It seems that no one will ever know the breadth and depth of our family's deeds, their education, their faith, and their hope. Did they do it all for nothing? Is there anybody to carry on? You children don't care. What I'm saying doesn't amount to nothing. The teacher just told you what you already believe."

I had never heard Big Mama sound so dejected. "I'm listening to you, Big Mama," I said. "Don't you worry, I'll write that book. I don't care what that old teacher said. I promise you, I will write the Bryant story." Big Mama seemed surprised by my response. She looked at me for a long time and then smiled. "I'm not one for hugging," she said, "but I feel like hugging you." With that, I got up and ran out of her house. Big Mama just laughed. I couldn't imagine her hugging me after all these years. As I went upstairs, I could still hear her laughing. She stopped hugging her grandchildren on their sixth birthday. We all knew it. We would warn all the five-year-olds and tease them about it so when she stopped hugging them it wouldn't hurt so much.

ANN L. PATTERSON EARLY

I meant what I said when I promised I would write the story, but life happened. I got married and had children. Big Mama didn't like my husband much. She had a funny way of relating to in-laws. The only way she was congenial to dark-brown-skinned men was if they had a high income and shared some of the proceeds with her. It's strange how she looked at it, because four of her six children, except Mama and the youngest boy, married dark-brown-skinned men. And for that matter, Grandpa Sam was brown skinned, but he was talented and successful so she forgave his color.

Like she forgave her youngest daughter's husband who was self-employed and did quite well in business. He knew Big Mama wanted to be fussed over, so he did. He bought her gifts and took her places. He ran her errands, and for that, she idolized him. My husband was brown skinned, too, and he had a high income. The first thing Big Mama said to him when she met him was, "I'm your grandmother. How much allowance do I get a week?"

He had heard stories about how Big Mama had three husbands and how they had all died and left her money. He had also heard how she had not worked in years and depended on her sons-in-law for financial support. When she approached him the way she did, he just looked at her and said, "I have a grandmother, thank you. I'm just starting my family. I should be asking you for money."

Big Mama had very little to do with me as a wife and mother after that. When I went to visit her, I usually went alone. My actions contributed to the distance that had arisen between us. And to add to it, my husband and I moved with my three sons to New York and only visited the family in Detroit once a year. During those visits, I came to see Big Mama for the nag that she was. She complained and acted like a victim and nobody reacted. Children and grown-ups alike acted as if her behavior was her right to do. She berated them and rarely had anything positive to say. In her eyes, the family members smoked, drank hard liquor, or sinned. They didn't go to church or just plain didn't live to suit her. Finally, there came a time when her treating me like a child was intolerable. I didn't like her doing it to my mother, my aunts, my sisters, and my brothers. I was so disgusted by it that when I returned to New York after a visit, I wrote her a letter and asked her who had appointed her God.

"Who gave you the permission to disrespect and dictate to us? If you spend as much time telling everyone that you love them as often as you rebuked them for all kinds of nonsense, maybe you would get your desired results."

Big Mama never responded to the letter. I heard from other family members, however, that she circulated it throughout the family. The next time I went to Detroit to visit, she called everyone to my mother's house for a family gathering. When we all arrived, she turned to me and said I love you. Just like that, she said it. Then she turned to the person sitting next to me, called them by name, and repeated it going around the room. She went person by person. One to the next one and so on; "I love you," is what she told everyone. I was overwhelmed by her gesture and ashamed. Instead of telling her what I felt, I played it off. I continued to engage her about perceived past indiscretions. For that I am sorry, because she died before my next visit. I never saw her alive again.

Days and months folded into years, and before I knew it, my sons were all grown up. To my surprise, my middle son married a white woman. After much confusion and dismay expressed by myself and his in-laws, their marriage was accepted, and as they had done from the beginning, they went about their business of living together as a couple. Then, my youngest son married a white woman. I found myself constantly drawn into conversation with friends both black and white, as well as relatives, about the racial aspects of my sons' relationships. More often than not, I found myself almost defending their marriages.

When I became a grandmother, these friends and relatives moved from discussing issues concerning the couples to race issues that they predicted for the children. My stance was like my over-all philosophy. Don't get baited into a problem. Wait until there is a problem, and then deal with it. That worked for the most part for my sons, their families, and for me.

Not so recently, I was babysitting for my youngest son and his wife while they went away for a few days. Part of my function was to take the oldest child, seven, to school. I was to introduce myself to the teacher and let her know who I was. When I explained to my grandson what I was to do, he became upset. He said he didn't want me to meet his teacher. I asked him why and he said he couldn't tell me because he didn't want to hurt my feelings.

I told him that he could talk to me. I was his grandmother and he could tell me anything. He became irritated. "I can't tell you," he said somewhat annoyed.

"Does it have to do with my being brown, having wooly hair, and being fat?"

"You don't know what I go through."

"Your daddy is brown. I am brown, your mama is white, and your other grandpa is white. You have two colors in your family. Do you know how lucky you are? When children talk about your brown side of the family, it's because they only have one color in the family."

He didn't say anything. I wasn't sure I had reached him. When we got to school, his teacher was standing at the curb greeting parents and children, as is the custom at his school. When the car came to a stop, he jumped out and ran towards the teacher.

"This is my grandmother," he called as he ran. "This is my Grandma Ann."

Even though it appeared that he had reached some resolve, his dilemma struck me. It made me question my participation in his life. I asked myself if I was a good enough grandmother doing everything that I could do to impact my grandchildren's learning. Was I helping them gain a sense of themselves? The conclusion was that it was time for me to keep my promise to Big Mama. Time for me to write the history and let my grandchildren know that their lives are not so unlike the lives of their ancestors. Proper choices will help them live productive lives in ways that will contribute to the world that is too often filled with hate and self-loathing.

AUTHOR'S NOTE

During the early 1700s to the 1900s, first names came from a limited list of names found in the Bible, heard in the community, or from the name of a relative or friend.

In this book, you will find that it was not unusual for members of three generations of a family to have the same name, an example being William. Sherrod had a brother, William; a son, William; a grandson, William; two nephews named William; and a host of grand-nephews named William. These persons named William all lived in Bryant Town at the same time. Other names that are often duplicated in this story are Henry, Mary, Missouri, Nancy, Thomas, and Silas. And, among people of color, it was quite common. In some states, freemen were not allowed to fraternize or marry slaves. Inasmuch as the number of freemen living in one area was limited, these free people of color followed the example of the white settlers and married family members, usually cousins, sometimes aunts and uncles. These marriages allowed any accumulation of worldly goods to stay in the family.

BRYANT ACRES CHAPTER I

I'm Going to Be a Gentleman Farmer

On May 20, 1781, when George Washington was beginning to meet with the French to finalize his plan to end the Revolutionary War, Sherrod Bryant was born in an unknown white and Indian settlement sequestered in hills that began at Pearson and ran to Granville Territory, straddling the North Carolina border.

In the early 1700s, several white settlers wandered into the hills away from what is known today as Roxboro. They came upon a tribe of Indians whom they found friendly and congenial, so they stayed. They helped the tribe establish a colony, intermarried, shared their cultures and their values, and lived together as one group.

Everyone in the settlement took part in the demands of the day-to-day living. The Indians had been longtime residents of the area, and they knew it well. They shared their knowledge, and the settlers shared theirs. A school was established and the Indians were taught to speak English, which became the primary language.

The wildness and the distance made traveling to the towns below difficult. It was a two-to-four-month journey. The only hill residents that ventured away were the white ruling elders who had relatives and friends that lived in Virginia and the surrounding area of Halifax and Mecklenburg, Virginia, as well as Granville and Pearson, North Carolina. These towns below were quite different from the hills where the Indian and white settlement thrived.

Occasionally, the white elders would sneak away and secretly make contact with a relative or friend who knew of their whereabouts and their lifestyle. The purpose of going to one of these towns was primarily to educate themselves on changing technology and to collect new educational and religious materials. The townspeople looked upon the occasional strangers as wanderers and eccentrics. They sometimes called them squaw men. Relatives and friends, however, knew their purpose and were careful to share all relevant news and modern technology.

If and when one of the young males ventured away from the hills and moved into town, relatives living in town would serve as their mentor and helped them learn the ways and customs of town folks.

Because none of these relatives had ever visited or seen the colonies in the hills, they often referred to them as "the lost colonies." The reference "lost colony" or "lost colonies" became code between the relatives of the varied settlers. They used the terms among themselves to let one another know it was time for a visit from one of the colony's elders.

By the time Sherrod was born, Indian rituals and customs were all but extinct. English was the dominant language; rarely was the language of the natives spoken.

Members of the colony varied in color. There were blonds and redheads, with gray, gray/blue, and light brown eyes. There were also brunettes with hazel, brown, and black eyes. Some of the people had straight black or wavy hair. The group as a whole was proud, handsome, friendly people with happy spirits that showed in their dresses. They wore bright colors and beautiful hand-stitched styles.

During that period between 1780 and 1790, North Carolina was essentially a rural state. It was unlike its neighboring colonies in that its isolation and lack of navigable rivers drew an influx of working class absent a proportionate number of aristocrats.

The racial and cultural characteristics of the people who lived there were major factors in the colony's development. Quakerism, Lutheranism, and Morovionism culturally influenced public policy and helped adopt a point of view towards free Negroes that was relative of its people rather than that of the Crown, the Council, or the Assembly.

Approximately 289,000 whites settled in the area, of which 83 percent were English, 11 percent Scottish, 3 percent German, 2 percent Irish, 3/10 of a percent French, 1/5 of a percent Dutch, and 1/10 of a percent were of undisclosed nationality. The aborigines consist of Tuscarora, Catawba, Cherokee, and some suspect varied derivatives of the Sioux.

By the time the members of the lost colonies became recognized as a group, the Indians had assimilated. Their traditions, customs, and language had been forgotten.

Sherrod's father, like his grandfather, had European white features. Sherrod's mother, like his grandmother, had Indian features. Sherrod was a stringy youngster, always tall for his age. Like his mother, his complexion was olive brown. He had straight black hair, a high forehead with deep-set light brown eyes, and a broad bridged prominent Indian nose.

He was a bright, inquisitive youngster. His community was like an extended family. It was a farming community that was self-sufficient and prosperous. He knew every family and every family knew him. His father, Silas, was one of the elders that from time to time ventured into town carrying news and well wishes.

Sherrod's father recognized Sherrod's talent for grasping information and applying it to everyday life. Unlike his brothers, he was interested in his environment. He cared about how things worked and what he could do to improve his lot. He attended the community school in the morning and worked the fields with his father and brothers until early evening. At night, his father worked with him on a trade of choice. Sherrod chose husbandry. When he first said it, his father laughed.

"Where did you learn such a fancy word," he asked, "and what does it mean?"

Sherrod was quite serious. He said his teacher talked about the larger picture and that the larger picture of farming was called husbandry. It had to do with the financial workings of the farm; how it made and lost money; cultivation, sowing, and reaping; growth and harvest; and the many different types of farming like range, dairy, stock, sheep, and cattle. It also had to do with the types of tools and their use. It had to do with the varied methods of farming and the different types of farmers, sharecroppers, tenant farmers, gentleman farmers, and small landholders.

From the early age of seven, Sherrod wanted to experience the varied jobs the farm offered: the farm hand, the plower, sower, reaper, harvester, mower, thresher, barnsman, and the pitcher. Like his father, he loved the land and wanted to know all there was to know about it.

Silas impressed upon his children they needed to be the best at whatever they decided to do. Even though the family lived in the hills where they were safe, he was aware of the danger of his children getting caught up in the race conflict that he heard was beginning to flare up in town.

As long as Silas could remember, he had heard about how blacks were bought and sold as slaves. He had seen it in the towns he visited. Even though he had been born free and had white skin, his father had warned him of the dangers of being of mixed blood. Now that he had his own children, some of whom were brown skinned, he fretted. Even though all of his children were born free, he was aware that there were dangers in their making any presumption about their free status. Whether one was a slave or a freeman in certain situations depended on the person's skin color and his features.

Two years before Sherrod was born, the first act against the stealing of free Negroes was passed. It was the Act of 1779, and it stated that *****no penalty would be annexed to the stealing, carrying off, and selling of free Negroes and mulattos within the limits of the state of North Carolina. The law stated that anyone who knowingly stole or sold a free Negro or persons of mixed blood and was legally convicted would be fined not less than fifty pounds, nor more than five hundred pounds, and be imprisoned not less than three months, nor more than eighteen months.

At the turn of the century, strong denunciation of the stealing of free Negroes was openly expressed. In 1802, the State Supreme Court gave the benefit of doubt to a person of mixed blood but made it clear that people with dark brown or black complexions would be excluded from the benefit and considered a slave.

It was around this time that Sherrod reached the age of twenty-one. He went to his father and told him he was ready to leave home. His father asked him where he wanted to go.

"I have done well with my husbandry, father," Sherrod replied. "You said so yourself. You said I was as good as you are at some things and better than you at others."

His father smiled. "So I did," he said. "My concern is not how you are going to support yourself, but rather where you are going to live while you are supporting yourself."

Sherrod laughed. "I am relieved," he said and laughed some more. "I thought my problem was going to be convincing you how important it is for me to leave here."

Silas looked at his son. He had never loved him more. "I have always known that we couldn't keep you," he said. "Your quest for life reaches far beyond these hills, Son. My concern is the race issue. You have been brought up in an environment that sees no color. This is not true on the outside. People living below do bad things to people who have dark skin. They buy and sell them like cattle, make them work in the fields, steal their babies, and separate mothers and fathers."

"I have medium dark skin," Sherrod laughed.

"You are of mixed blood," Silas reproached. "Because of your skin color you may be considered a Negro, a free Negro probably, but free Negroes are often hounded by slave thieves."

"I learned a lot about slaves at school, Daddy, you're not to worry. I'm grown now. You have taught me well. I can take care of myself."

Silas wasn't convinced. "Give me a few days. Let me see if I can find you something to do in Virginia."

"Why Virginia?" Sherrod asked.

"Thomas Cole has some relatives in Virginia that he will be visiting at the end of the week. Let me see what I can arrange."

Sherrod waited two days and just when he thought his dad had forgotten his promise, his dad called him in to talk.

"The only job that Mr. Cole's cousin in Virginia could offer was that of a state coach driver. The job would require you to be indentured to the Cole family for six months. Are you interested?"

"What is indenture?" Sherrod asked.

"An indentured servant is one who is bound to another in a work type capacity. The Master or Mistress of the servant provides for the servant's diet, clothing, lodging accommodations, and all education that is necessary for the servant to do his job. If you take the job, you will receive the same allowance that the other paid servants receive. You will have to work for the agreed upon six months, without question or attempts to change your mind."

"What is six months when you have a lifetime?" Sherrod smiled.

"Mr. Cole will issue you an apprenticeship certificate," Silas said, more to himself. "That will alleviate some of the concerns about color. White men honor contracts; they don't dare intrude on another man's property, unless they're looking for a fight."

Sherrod listened anxiously to his dad. He knew his dad had to get it straight in his own mind before he could give total approval. Finally, Silas looked at him, searched his face to be sure. Then he spoke.

"Do you think you can handle the job, Son?

Sherrod could no longer contain his excitement. "If I'm to be a gentleman farmer, I better handle it," he replied.

"A gentleman farmer," his dad laughed. "You don't want much, do you?"

Virginia, here I come, Sherrod thought and became all filled up inside. He knew he would miss the hills and the people, his brothers and his dad. He wished he could take them all with him but he knew he couldn't. The one person he could take was Nancy Johnson. She liked him as much as he liked her, she was pretty, and she wanted to leave the colony.

He thought about it for a minute and decided he would go by and tell the Johnsons goodbye before he left. That way, Nancy would know that she was special to him. He couldn't tell her directly because if he told her too much she would get ideas about marriage and that would take his mind off the work that was waiting for him.

BRYANT ACRES CHAPTER II

You Can Count on Me

On June 10, 1802, Sherrod arrived in Virgilina County. He was wide-eyed and extremely sensitive to the street noises and the people around him. The country store, blacksmith shop, community church, and dress shop that made up the town were not unlike his own colony, but there were more people milling about than he had ever seen before. The ones that stood out most clearly were the African people. There were dark people in his colony, but not as dark as those scampering about the street in Virgilina.

These people's skin was a deep black with a purple hue to it. They had large purple lips and purple gums. The texture of the men's hair for the most part was cotton like, miniscule rings of wool, that they wore matted to their head or under a hat or cap. Most of the African women wore their heads tied in bright-colored bandanas. Their bright colors made them look somewhat more presentable than the men, who appeared downtrodden and shabbily dressed.

All the Africans seemed light on their feet. They moved swiftly about, doing small tasks, driving wagons, or following behind white townsmen, who Sherrod assumed were slave masters.

Everyone who passed Sherrod looked at him. The Africans walked with their heads down until they came toe to toe with him in passing. At that point, their heads came up and their eyes met for a moment. Sherrod felt bad not offering them a greeting but he knew not to speak or initiate any conversations. His instinct told him to keep his eyes straight and to move quickly so as not to draw any attention to himself.

Mr. Thomas had prepared him, on the three-week journey down from the hills, for the onslaught of slaves that he was encountering.

Thomas had made many trips to Virgilina, and he was able to describe to Sherrod what he would encounter when they arrived in the city. He explained how the State of Virginia was the largest slave supplier in the South. Baltimore was the center for the slave trade and Alexandria the port of debarkation for slaves and free blacks who were transported by boats South on the Mississippi River.

He helped Sherrod understand how significant planters were to the economy. Because of their importance, they enjoyed enormous wealth, prestige, and power. He also made Sherrod aware of the slaves' role in the Southern whites' economic scheme and how any antagonism among planters was mostly along racial lines.

When Sherrod learned that a cousin of Thomas had slaves, he wasn't surprised. He suspected that men who lived outside the hills would live and think different than the people back home. It was a different way of thinking and being that he had come to Virginia to explore. His desire was to progress and acquire a higher level of thinking and working.

He was only a few hours away from becoming an indentured servant, yet Sherrod didn't identify with the slaves he encountered on the street. He perceived the slaves as poor, unfortunate people who, because they were uncivilized and poor, found themselves in a situation that they had no control over. And, even though his dad thought some whites would equate him with slaves because of his skin color, his servitude was by choice. He trusted his dad; therefore he would accept his dad's concern and presume that there were racial factors that could trap him. As a defense against such unforeseen incidents, he promised himself that he would never impulsively make a decision. He would consider all issues carefully and weigh his options before he acted on them.

The way Mr. Thomas explained it to him was that Thomas' cousin, Jesse Cole, would be his Master for six months. At the end of that time, he could either remain in Jesse's employ or be free to move on. Thomas then described Jesse's place. He said it was a large plantation that was functional because of slave-driven crops. The land had been in the Cole family for over thirty years. Jesse's three daughters and two sons were raised on it. He explained how one of his daughters, Mary Polly, was the only one of the married children who remained on the property. The others had left as young adults to live in neighboring colonies in the North Carolina, Tennessee, and Kentucky territories.

Thomas asked Sherrod if he knew what a plantation was. Sherrod thought about it for a moment and then explained: "The word derived from the word planter, it refers to a large spread that raises cotton, tobacco, sugar, and rice."

Thomas laughed. "Silas said you were ready," he said and patted him fondly on the shoulder. "I certainly hope everything works out for you. I'm setting you up for a driver's position; it's a lot of responsibility."

"A stage coach driver!" Sherrod exclaimed. "I thought I was going to be farming."

Thomas smiled. "A driver is a manager, Son. You will work closely with Jesse, supervising and disciplining field hands."

Sherrod perked up. "These field hands, who are they? Where did they come from?"

"Slaves like yourself," Thomas replied and waited for a reaction. When none was forthcoming, he added, "Sherrod, for six months you are going to be an indentured slave. Most often the position is referred to as an indentured servant, but in actuality, the indentured person is bonded and that makes him a slave. If you have any doubts the time to say them is now. You must be honest with me and tell me. If you don't think you can handle giving up your freedom, I want to know, Sherrod. Do you think you can handle it?"

"Sure thing," Sherrod said and nodded his head. "You just caught me unawares. I didn't understand where the driving fit in."

"On some of these plantations, overseers are called drivers because that's what they do. They push the field hands, supervise, and delegate responsibilities. You will be under the supervision of Jesse, of course, but you handle yourself like I know you can and Jesse will do right by you."

Sherrod liked the way the role of manager felt. "You can count on me, Mr. Cole," he said.

Thomas gave him a knowing smile.

Sherrod's mind drifted to a story Nancy had told him about one of her ancestors, a man named Anthony Johnson. It seemed that Anthony had arrived in America aboard a Dutch slave ship in

1619. An English vessel captured the ship. Anthony and some of the other slaves helped the English take the ship from the Dutch and was rewarded with a six months' indentured position and then set free. As a freeman, Anthony became a wealthy gentleman farmer with slave hands just like the white plantation owners.

As they walked, Sherrod thought about Anthony; he thought long and hard. Finally he decided that getting to work with slaves was a good thing, that it was time for him to understand where the business of slavery fit.

He went over his first encounter with the slaves and decided that acknowledging their presence without getting involved was a good first step.

In his colony at home, he had teased and played as young men do. Now it was time to get on with adult business and put to use the things he had spent so much time learning.

When they arrived at the stable, where they went for a horse and buggy, the talk was about the president's death. Six months before, in December 1799, George Washington had died. The news had just reached the city, and it was the topic of conversation wherever they went.

Jesse Cole was anxiously waiting for Thomas' arrival. He wondered what the traveling Thomas did would do to him if he tried it. The occasional trip to Alexandria to make purchases for Big Mary and Mary Polly and the occasional ride to neighboring plantations to spend the day with friends was about all he could handle.

He had never had an indentured slave before, and he wasn't quite sure how an indentured slave was any different than any other slave. Like most wealthy planters of the South, Jesse generally respected his slaves. He regarded them as little better than cattle, but he took no particular pleasure in punishing them unnecessarily. They were generally well provided for. They had sufficient food to eat and water to drink. Their clothes were not the best, but they were decent. For the most part, they were not overworked.

Jesse took great pride in the thrifty and sleek appearance of his slaves. He loved to show off all of his property, especially to his houseguests. He took pride in his large oxen, the superior appearance of his horses, and the excellent breed of his sheep and hogs.

There was equal pride in the superior quality of his crops of sugar, rice, grain, and cotton. Even the state of his utensils, the condition of his barn, stable, wagon, and slave huts. All his worldly goods served to heighten his pride and feelings of self-esteem. Sure, his wife Big Mary had financed their beginnings, but he had done well with the mere pittance of her meager inheritance.

Big Mary was also a descendant of the Cole family, but unlike the branch of Coles that Jesse was born into, her branch of Coles was able to improve their lot and rose to become a valuable part of King George's army. She considered her family to be of a higher station than most, but in actuality, hers was a reduced family from England.

Big Mary, as she was called, was a celebrated beauty before she followed Jesse to Virgilina. The wear and tear of the settlement wore her down, diminished her charm, and left Big Mary with little more than great pretentiousness. She felt she had married down and managed quite well to upstage the dominance Jesse held over his little empire.

From the outside, she was perceived as a good Southern planter's wife. She kept every department of her establishment that came under her observation in excellent order. She loathed the slaves, however, and had many quarrels with Jesse about keeping them in lock and chain. Old Black Tisha was the only one that Big Mary halfway warmed up to. Tisha had won her over by her ready seeming obedience to Big Mary's whims.

When Thomas and Sherrod turned on the path to the house, just clear of the forest, Tisha saw them and went inside to tell her Master, who had been waiting with Big Mary in the sitting room since early morning.

Big Mary ran to the window and looked out.

"Give Cousin Thomas my welcome," she said once her curiosity had been satisfied. "I don't feel well. I will be having my dinner in bed." With that, she left the room and Tisha followed her.

Jesse went out on the porch and waited for the arrival of his guests.

When Thomas and Sherrod stepped from the carriage, Jesse motioned for one of his slaves to come and retire the horse and buggy. Jesse hugged his cousin and told him how glad he was to see him. They exchanged a few more courtesies and, as they climbed the steps to the house, he said, "Tell me man, did you bring further news about poor George Washington's death?"

"Where would I get such news from, Jesse?" Thomas teased. "Where I come from is not like Virginia. Presidents and first ladies don't drop in at will."

Jesse laughed, and then they both laughed. Sherrod had a sense of who George Washington was, but the men were not talking to him so there was no need for him to participate in their graces. Like the servant that he was about to become, he stood behind Thomas, to be sure to convey to Mr. Jesse that he was aware that he was not part of the conversation and that he knew his place.

It was the first time he had ever been on a plantation, and he was overwhelmed by the size of it. There were rows and rows of fields and what seemed to be herds of black people plowing and sowing on land that stretched out as far as the eye could see, and for what turned out to be a three-day ride.

Jesse and Thomas continued to talk as they made their way into the sitting room. Sherrod quietly followed. The two men sat and continued their conversation while Sherrod stood and let his eyes wander around the room.

The house had a nice feel to it. The room was oversized, with two wide, large floor-to-ceiling windows that overlooked the meadow. There was a high, hand-carved ceiling that peaked in the middle where the beams came together. It held a circle of lanterns that he figured needed a pole, of some kind, to light. The walls were nicely papered with a print of small blue and white flowers that he decided was imported. The furniture was also oversized and light in color. He liked the way the room looked. He concluded Mrs. Cole or her daughter had done the decorating. His mind then took him to the next thought. What kind of people were these Coles? What kind of family were they?

Sherrod's gaze piqued Jesse Cole's curiosity. He turned and looked at him long and hard. Finally he said, "Sherrod, you are going to do fine here at Cole Manor. You have quite a presence. Come, let me show you your quarters before Tom and I settle down."

"Yes, Sir," Sherrod said and started towards his new master. Before he reached him, Jesse turned to Thomas as if he and Sherrod had not had an exchange.

"You must be tired, dear cousin. Three weeks is a long time to sit on a horse. Then again, them heathen ways you have learned up there in the hills probably give you a different strength than those of us living down here in Virginia."

With that said, Jesse chuckled and beckoned for Sherrod to follow him out.

Heathen indeed, Sherrod thought to himself as he followed Jesse down a narrow passageway to the back of the house. *I bet any man back home could teach him and the rest of the stuffies running these farms a thing or two about living.*

"Well, this is home," Jesse said, and showed him a wooden couch in the corner of a tiny room that also had a bench with drawers and a bench for sitting.

"Thank you for giving me a chance, Sir," Sherrod said.

Jesse ignored his gesture of appreciation.

"There is a stream out back where the Niggers bathe, and plenty of trees and bushes for your private use," Jesse said and headed towards the door.

"Will Mr. Thomas be spending the night?" Sherrod called after him.

"That's white man's business," Jesse snapped and without turning around said, "I don't know what goes on up in those hills, but here in Virginia, colored folks don't get into white man's business unless they're invited."

"Yes, Sir," Sherrod replied. "I'm a fast learner, Sir."

"That's good to hear," Jesse said and walked out of the room.

I have six months to play your silly colored game, Sherrod thought to himself, took off his shoes, and stretched across the bed as if he didn't have a care in the world.

The next thing he heard were female voices coming in from the outside. He opened his eyes and realized he had been asleep. If not for the moon shining into the room, he wouldn't have been able to see his hand in front of his face.

He stretched his legs and felt tiredness from his knees down thorough his feet. He turned over on his back and closed his eyes again. The giggling outside became louder. He got up from the bed and walked to the window, careful to stay in the shadows so as not to be observed.

Across the way, leaning with her back against the tree situated in front of the window to his room, stood a white woman laughing and talking to two young black girls. It seemed that the white woman was teasing them, and they were enjoying her attention.

He stood watching them until he heard the door to his room close. He turned and Mr. Thomas said, "I came to look in on you."

Mr. Thomas had a plate of food in his hand, which he took and placed on the bureau. He then walked to the window to see what had Sherrod's attention. "I'll be gone when you wake up in the morning," he said. "Do you have any regrets?"

"No regrets," Sherrod said and moved closer to where Thomas stood.

"Tell Dad he's not to worry about me. Mr. Jesse says what's on his mind. We will get along."

Thomas put his hand on Sherrod's shoulder. "Jesse likes you," he said. "His ways are different. You will get used to him." He started towards the door and then turned back. "Mixed couples are not looked upon favorably in Virginia, Sherrod."

"You don't have to worry about me," Sherrod laughed; he knew Thomas was referring to the white woman outside his window. "I don't have time for women."

Thomas smiled. "You will be working for Jesse's daughter, Mary Polly. She and her husband live on the road on the southeast corner of the property. Her husband is not much for farming. Jesse is going to find something else for him to do." He looked at Sherrod long and hard and then said, "What I have just said about Jesse's intentions is between you and me. You are not to ever repeat it. Is that clear?"

"I aim to make you proud, Sir," Sherrod said and held out his hand.

Thomas took the hand in his and gave it a hearty shake. He liked Sherrod. He always had. "You are more family to me than Jesse is," he said. "But I know how Coles think. Listen to what Jesse says. Take his words seriously, but not to heart. He'll be fair."

Sherrod felt his eyes well up. "Have a safe trip home, Mr. Cole," he said.

Thomas gave him a knowing wink of an eye, walked out of the room, and closed the door.

Sherrod felt an inner tug deep inside. It took effort for him not to cry out to Thomas, to let him know that he wanted to go home. He took a deep breath and held fast, reminded himself of the reason why he was in Virginia. He was there by choice. He had come of his own free will. And, as scared as he was, he was satisfied that the choice he made was his to make.

About daybreak, Sherrod heard voices outside his room in the passageway. He rose slowly and reached down beside the bed to the carpetbag he had dropped there the night before. He opened it and fetched an empty canning jar that once held Nancy's mother's best pears. He took off the lid, crawled from the bed to the floor, and relieved himself. He hurried to the window with the jar. The sun was busy trying to make its way up between the trees. He could see shadowy figures of men and women moving swiftly about in the slave camp at the edge of the site where the trees began. He poured the warm liquid on the bushes below. He then walked in his bare feet to the other side of the room and put his ear to the door. The voices were coming from the kitchen across the hall. He recognized one as that of Jesse Cole. The other was the voice of a white woman. He assumed it was Jesse's wife.

"Mary Polly is determined she is going to take over this spread," he heard her say.

Jesse appeared to be taking offense at what she was saying. "Why do you begrudge her?" he asked. Then, without waiting for a reply, he said, "Your precious Jesse took his stubborn self and moved off to North Carolina, you ran Joel away, and Missouri is not interested; someone has to carry on the Cole business."

"If she and Robert were doing it together as a couple, I would not question it."

"Oh, it's Cousin Robert that you're worried about," he said sarcastically and then laughed. "Mary Polly married him because you and Lavonia wanted it. She loves the land, and she is right. There is no reason why Robert's disdain for it should affect her."

"There is more to life than land, Jesse," she said somewhat irritated.

"More to life," Jesse snapped back and without hesitation broke into a tirade. "Your spineless, no good Cousin Robert definitely carries your hatred for the animals and the Niggers."

"Robert was bred different," she said. "He likes to use his mind reading and studying. He should be a teacher."

"He doesn't like animals; how could he teach children?" he mumbled, and then said, "You are trying to justify bringing Robert into this family. Lavonia obviously didn't know what to do with him. As for the rest of your kin, I don't think they like dear Cousin Robert any more than I do."

"A woman is supposed to support her husband, not lead him," she argued.

"And, if he can't lead?" Jesse snapped. He got up and started to pace. "I don't know why I am discussing this with you." He took a deep breath. "I took on a driver for Mary Polly. She wants to try her hand at farming. We gave her the land, and by golly she is going to have a chance to make a go of it. I am going to see to that!"

"Sherrod . . . Sherrod," he called.

Sherrod heard his footsteps coming towards his room. He ran quickly and scampered back into bed, under the covers, and pretended to be asleep.

"Sherrod!" he yelled and slammed open the door.

"Yes, Sir," Sherrod said and sat up in bed as if he were hearing his name called for the first time.

"It's a work day, Sherrod," Jesse said, and as he turned on his heels to leave, he added, "and you're already late!"

Sherrod reached and grabbed his pants, scrambled into them, with shoes in hand, and hurriedly put them on running after Jesse calling, "I don't know, Sir."

Without turning around, Jesse responded. "From here on in, you are to meet me outside on the front porch at sunrise. If you eat breakfast, you can work something out with Lizbeth. She lives in the place down there with smoke coming from the chimney."

Sherrod glanced over his shoulder but Jesse was moving so fast he barely saw anything except the barn that they had entered. A horse and buggy were ready and waiting for them when they arrived.

A tired-looking, elderly black man wearing patched pants and a cotton shirt helped Jesse aboard. He hardly noticed Sherrod. Jesse continued talking as if the man wasn't there.

"This is not your place of work. However, you will be living here. Today, I am going to give you an overview of what you will be dealing with. In the evening, just before sunset, we will come back here so you can become familiar with the surroundings and figure out what your personal routine will be."

Sherrod climbed into the buggy and settled down for the ride. The plantation was too large to cover in one day. A lot of the land was undeveloped with forests and creeks and lakes. That part of the tour, he was told, he would have to take on his own.

Around midday, Jesse and Sherrod pulled up in Mary Polly Cole's yard. Sherrod didn't think it odd that her married name was the same as her maiden name. He was aware that families intermarried in Virginia the same as they did in the hills.

Mary came running when she saw them coming. "Something is eating my tomato plants," she said. "They are not bothering the beans or peas, just the tomatoes."

Jesse jumped down from the wagon. "This is Sherrod," he said. "Cousin Tom brought him in from the hills. Tom says he knows his way around a farm; he is to be your driver."

"You mean it, Daddy!" she exclaimed and hugged him.

Somewhat embarrassed by her open show of affection, he patted her gently on top of the head.

"Is this any away to act in front of the help?"

"You said Sherrod was going to be part of the farm. We might as well give him a quick start," she said and laughed. She then took her dad's hand and led him towards the house.

Sherrod recognized her as the same woman that had stood under the tree in front of his window the night before. He wondered why Thomas didn't tell him who she was. He thought about Thomas' warning and smiled to himself. She was the most beautiful woman he had ever seen. Her long straight black hair flowed down her back and sparkled in the sunlight. Her eyes were like perfectly shaped ovals of coal. Her skin was clear and thin. She had a cute little nose and perfect teeth.

"Sherrod," she said without looking at him, "Esther and Mamie have your lunch waiting around on the back porch. We will discuss the work when Daddy and I finish eating."

With that said, she and Jesse went in the house and closed the door, her beauty tarnished.

On the ride over to Mary Polly's, Jesse had told Sherrod that he expected him to be the man that both he and Mary Polly could come to, to find out what was going on with the slaves, conditions of the crops, the animals, and the overall well-being of the whole operation. He asked Sherrod to control and discipline the slaves and to help Mary Polly maintain order on her part of the estate. He had explained that he wanted weekly reports and the reports were to include all changes, disruptions, and incidents.

Sherrod was feeling the weight of those expectations as he walked around the side of the house to the back porch where he was sent for lunch.

He saw Esther and Mamie standing on the steps talking. He recognized them as the girls that were visiting with Mary Polly near his room the night before. As he approached them, they started giggling.

"Is giggling all that the two of you do?" he asked. They giggled some more. "I was told my lunch was back here," he said, trying to estimate the girls' age.

Esther moved closer to Mamie and said in a loud whisper, "Is there an uppity Nigger on our porch trying to act important, Mamie?"

Mamie, carefully avoiding his eyes, replied with a loud sniffing noise, "Seems like I can smell one."

"When is the last time you had a bath, Uppity Nigger?" Esther turned and spat at him.

Sherrod grabbed her and put her under his arm like a sack of potatoes.

"Put me down," she cried, beating against his leg with her fist.

"How old are you, little girl?"

"I am not a little girl!" she spat.

"Oh, so you're a woman, are you?" he said and took off running with her head first towards the stair rails.

"You hurt her and Missus Mary will whip you bloody," Mamie cried, no longer playful.

"Maybe so." Sherrod laughed, and began swinging Esther back and forth as if she were a log that he hadn't decided how to use. "I will get whipped, and she will have a busted head."

"Twelve, she is twelve. Put her down," Mamie pleaded.

"I want to hear it from her," he said, moving with her closer to the rails.

"Twelve," Esther said. "I'm twelve. Are you satisfied?"

"Actually, I'm not," Sherrod said. "I'm your lunch guest, and I don't think you showed good manners calling me out of my name."

Esther began to cry. "Missus is going to beat me if I don't give you lunch, and I can't get lunch unless you put me down."

"Set plates for yourselves too," Sherrod said, standing her down on her feet. "I can't stand people watching me eat."

Mamie reached under the table and took out three plate tins and sat them on the table. Esther took the cloths off the biscuits, preserves, side of pork, and iced tea that were waiting there.

The three of them sat and ate in silence. Maybe the girls were right. Maybe he did smell, Sherrod thought to himself sitting there. He had hurried to bed out of fear of doing and saying the wrong thing. He hadn't bathed since he and Thomas had made the river stop long before they hit town and set their sights on Jesse Cole's house.

Sherrod looked out across the field. The air was still, and the sounds of slaves weeding and hoeing could be heard. A fly lit on his hand. The sting of it caused him to look down and smile. It was the first time he had felt anything since he left home, except for the occasional relief of his bladder and bowel. *I'm alive*, he said to himself. *This is me, Sherrod Bryant, standing here in Virginia, and I'm alive. A month has passed, and I'm still here.*

He smiled and got up from the table and strolled vigorously down the steps to the barn. Behind the barn were two rows of wooden log huts, which he assumed were where the slaves lived. He went inside the barn, and there against the wall lay several bales of cotton and hay. Long twists of tobacco hung from the rafters at the end of long pieces of rope. Oats and grain for the animals filled several barrels that sat by the door. Other goods were stored in wooden boxes and tins.

There was an old loom and spinning wheel that he assumed had fallen into disrepair. He checked the supply of tallow in the jar to assure himself there would be candles if he had to make his way in the dark one night. Under an old bench, he saw materials for dyeing cotton and linen. He also saw new coppers that were to be used to "set the colors."

He wandered over to a closed door and opened into what he knew to be the smoke house. Slabs of smoked ribs, hams, sides of beef, and chops were also suspended from the rafters at the end of a rope. He hurriedly closed the door so as not to let too much light into the room.

Back home, the same supplies were available but only on an as-needed basis. He was impressed.

He went out the back door of the barn and two rows of shabby log huts stood before him. He counted them. There were twenty, ten on each side of a narrow dirt strip that was obviously used as a common walkway. Centered in the middle of the strip was a fire pit, used for boiling water and cooking. At the far end was a well with a second barn situated next to it.

Sherrod started towards the second barn and heard female voices. They were singing. He opened the door and quietly stepped inside. The women of various ages were sitting in a circle quilting. They continued to do what they were doing and sang without a sign of knowing or caring that he was present.

"*I'm so tired of this thing called color,*" they crooned.

"*Weigh me down . . . weigh me down*

I wanna be free

I wanna be free

Just free . . . just free

From sun up

To sun down

Bad luck

Burdens

And frown

Let me be

Let me be

Let me be free . . ."

When Sherrod had heard enough, he went back out the door and closed it. The enormity of what he was dealing with hit him. Tears came to his eyes. How was he supposed to stay separate from all that pain?

He started back up towards the direction from which he came and heard his name being called. Mary was waiting for him.

"I told Daddy I would have someone show you the way home later on," she said to him as he approached. "Come on up to the house so we can talk." Then, she turned and walked to the house with him in tow. "This is all new to me too," she said as she walked. "Some things we can figure out together."

"Yes, Ma'am," he replied, feeling somewhat awkward in his effort to think of her as his Master.

He liked the fact that she was going to be working with him; that way, he was sure to do things the way she wanted them. It appeared that she was only a few years older than he. That and his ability to read and write were going to serve him well. It put him in good conversation order. His step hastened, and he felt some of the tiredness leave his body.

Mamie, who was dusting the hall furniture, flittered her eyes as he entered with Mary.

"Hi, Mr. Sherrod," she smiled.

"Well, I can see you have made one friend," Mary said knowingly. "Have a seat and let us try to figure out what it is you are going to be doing." She studied his face a moment and then asked, "What do you know about slaves?"

Her question seemed odd so he decided to play it safe. "Nothing, except they are people and they are black, Ma'am."

"Miss Mary, Miss Polly," she laughed. "Anything but Ma'am. Please."

"Yes, Ma—" he started to say and corrected himself, "yes, Miss Polly."

She continued, "There are two kinds of slaves. The indentured servants, which is what you are. Then, there are the bought-and-sold kind, which include Mamie and Esther and all the rest of the Negroes you will see living on this property. These slaves can be bought and sold. Presently, they are owned by me, forever and ever, if I choose it to be. The only rights they have are the ones I give them. Their stay here is not time limited like yours. You and I have a six-month agreement, after that you are free to go.

"The total number of slaves I own is thirty-five. Thirty-three of the Negroes were given to me as a wedding present three years ago. Mamie and Esther are the grandchildren of Mama's house slave, Old Black Tisha, who helped raise me. The children's mother was sold when Mamie was a baby and Esther was two. Daddy agreed to let Tisha keep them if she agreed not to raise a fuss when their mommy was sold.

"Tisha realized that she was getting up in age and sent Mamie and Esther to live with me as a wedding present. Mama and Daddy say I spoil them. They are my children. I wouldn't love them any more if I had birthed them." She paused and waited for a reaction from Sherrod, and when none was forthcoming, she continued, "Do you know anything about cotton?"

"I sure do. We raised a lot of cotton at home," he replied. He wasn't altogether pleased with his responses, but he was staying in the conversation and that is the way, he told himself, it had to be at the moment.

"Good," she said, "because I understand a man named Whitney has invented a cotton gin that is supposed to increase the cotton market from mere thousands of bales to millions of bales. Sherrod, I want us to take part in that growth. Over a half million slaves have been brought to America to date. People are preparing for the growth of cotton. You and I are going to be in the forefront.

"Our thirty or so field workers will be enough to get us started. My husband, Robert, has gone to England to establish a company there. He will be away for the duration of your servitude. Dad has made contact with a ship captain that deals in cotton. All that's needed is a unit that can do the sowing, the harvesting, and the packing. You and I, Sherrod, are in charge of building that unit." She took a deep breath. "Plantation owners are going to dominate this country even more than they do now. My father is getting to the place where he is not as open to trying new things the way he used to be. But, he's willing to take a chance on me. What I am telling you is, if you help me build it, I promise the experience and firsthand knowledge you gain will allow you to go anywhere in the country and be successful. You will be powerful and rich. You will never have to worry about your freedom."

Sherrod couldn't believe what he was hearing. She was offering him everything he had dreamed of. He felt excitement. His mind drifted, and he went up inside his head, the way he always did when he didn't trust himself to speak. *The tasks she wants to undertake are doable*, he told himself. *I have done what she is asking hundreds of times, and I am good at giving out jobs.* He thought about the conversation he had overheard between Big Mary and Jesse that morning and smiled to himself. I am sure glad I don't have to deal with that cracker husband of hers.

Mary Polly saw him smile and asked, "Sherrod, is there anything you want to say?" She could see that he was looking at her, but he wasn't responding. "Sherrod," she said, raising her voice slightly.

Sherrod realized the voice he heard was Mary Polly talking to him. "I was trying to digest all that you were saying," he said apologetically.

"Is there anything you want to add?" she asked.

"Do you have a plan of action?" he asked her.

"That is why you and I are sitting here," she laughed. "By the time we finish, we will know where we are. But first, I want to hear what kind of personal time you will require each morning. What will your mornings look like?"

"Well . . ." he stammered, not knowing how to answer. He watched the expression on her face, hoping it would give him guidance. "I will get out of bed just before the rooster crows at sunrise, take a drink from the pitcher of water that I have brought to the room the night before, put some salt in a glass, pour some water on top of the salt and rinse out my mouth. I will then grab a rag from some place, go out to the forest near the slave camp, and find a safe place for private duty.

"When that is finished, I will then take a bath in the creek and finish waking up my body. I will then put on a clean shirt and underwear, slip into my britches, put on my shoes, take a piece of fruit from the nearest tree, call for a horse, and ask someone for directions over here."

Mary Polly struggled not to laugh while he described his routine. When he finished, she burst into a hearty laugh. "You are thorough," she said.

He looked perplexed. Not wanting to give the impression that she was laughing at him, she cleared her throat and turned the conversation back to business.

"Let's go back to your question about the plan. On small plantations, it is convenient for owners to manage their own land. On large plantations, which is what you and I are building, the plan we set up will put an operation in motion larger than most of the people in this town have ever seen."

"When do you want to get started?"

"At daybreak. Is that too soon?"

"Not for me," he said.

"Good. Tomorrow, I want to call the slaves together and tell them that we are separating our agriculture from our cotton. The Armstrongs, the Carters, the Ruckers, and the Shines are couples that are elderly and sickly. What do you propose we do with them?"

He thought for a moment. "Let's see. It's early April. The early crop is just about planted . . ." he paused and then said, "I propose that we use the elderly men for weeding and doing household and equipment repairs. Their wives to do household chores, weave wool, spin cotton for jeans, socks, stockings, blankets, and flannels, as well as make the clothes. Slaves are deprived people. If we feed them well and dress them warmly, they will work long and hard."

Mary Polly was trying not to take in Sherrod's person but rather to see him as just another worker. *I wish he was as black as the slaves, then I wouldn't have to know that he was a good-looking man or that his eyes danced when he talked*, she thought as she sat listening to him. *His skin is almost bronze. The way he tosses his head when he talks even provokes the sunlight. And, how could the ends of a man's hair glitter when he is wearing a hat?* As long as Sherrod was quiet, Mary Polly had felt safe talking to him. When he spoke, she believed the thoughts behind his words, and that was different for her. She rarely ever believed anything anybody said, especially grown-ups.

"How do you know all that?" she asked him.

"We all want to feel safe, Miss Polly. When we are safe, we feel happy, and we respond well."

"How old are you, Sherrod?"

"Twenty-one."

"Well, by the time you are twenty-five, you are going to be known in these parts, I can tell."

"No disrespect meant, but when my time is up at the end of the year, I plan to move either to Granville Territory or to Kentucky."

She smiled. "You do right by me, and I will be doing everything in my power to change your mind," she warned.

That frightened Sherrod. Fear surged to the core of him. He stared at her for a long while. *She speaks different than her father*, he thought. *Her treatment of me is different, but she is still white.*

She had not meant to be as candid with him as she was, and when he didn't respond, she became worried. "I trust you will continue to be a man of few words and keep our discussions private," she said.

"Yes, Ma'am," he said, and she lashed out at him.

"What did I say about 'Yes, Ma'aming' me?"

Her anger caught both of them by surprise. She realized she was making much ado about nothing and she softened.

"What I have been trying to tell you, Sherrod, is that I am depending on you to help me make a dream come true. I don't want our plans known. I want everyone to wake up one day and it will all be in place. Am I clear?"

"Yes, Miss Polly."

"Now, that's better," she said, letting out a sigh and continued, Fifteen of our young men are between the ages of sixteen and twenty-two. As far as I know, they are without women that live on the property. What do you propose we do with them?"

"Do they know anything about cotton?"

"Yes, they all have planted, chopped, harvested, and baled it."

"Good. Then those are our field workers. Do you have any men that are thirty-five to forty years old?"

"Three."

"Good. Each will be a crew captain, responsible for five field hands. The group of six is to be free of people that are related."

"Okay," she said beginning to get the picture. "That leaves us with about seven women."

"Three of the seven women will be the crew captain's right hand. The other four women will be responsible for the overall camp. We can turn one of those old barns out there into a combination camp: dining room, general store, meeting place, court, and church."

"Great," she said, "just great."

Her enthusiasm made him smile. "It will be, if I can remember it all," he said.

"Esther," Mary Polly called.

"Yes, Ma'am," Esther said, entering from behind the doorframe with a long piece of coal in one hand and a wooden marking board in the other.

"Did you get the plan down?"

"Yes, Miss. I did."

"Then you can go," Mary Polly said.

"Bye Sherrod," Esther said and held the board up for him to see.

Mary Polly laughed. "That's a first. Esther usually doesn't like strangers."

Sherrod was impressed by Esther's drawings. The clusters of stick figures were centered in the designated area as per the plan; they were clear and to the point. Her ability was impressive. It helped ease the shock of Mary Polly planting her behind the door.

Still, the action served as a reminder of the need for him to always remember where he was, to give only what was asked of him, and to move cautiously.

BRYANT ACRES CHAPTER III

Every Thing ain't What it Seems

On the way from Mary Polly's place, Jesse started thinking. He had seen the way Mary Polly looked at Sherrod, and he was concerned. Her eyes lit up when she saw him. He remembered the way she jumped up around his neck and hugged him. Why, she had not hugged her daddy's neck since she was ten years old. Not since the time she walked in and caught him with Tisha in the barn.

He wasn't much of a drinking man, but when he did drink, it was with reckless abandon. Some thing, person, or incident had to upset him before he would want to tie one on. This was one of those times. He had a stash in the barn and he was looking forward to going up in the loft, away from the prying eyes of Big Mary, and think.

He had had some good times in that barn. It was his secret. Old Tisha knew, but that was like nobody knowing as far as he was concerned. He had confided in Old Tisha soon after Mary Polly was born and asked her to help him to protect Mary Polly from Big Mary's wrath. He had hated going to Tisha telling her his business, but she was safe. She was a slave and had very little contact with the outside. Besides, Big Mary would have her beaten and thrown off the place.

He let his mind wander and thought for a minute. What if someone found out that he was banging Tisha? It frightened him. Who would care? His daughter had some sense, enough not to make anything out of it. Besides, it was public knowledge that Carter had been banging his slave wench for years, even had a couple of half-white, bastard children running around in the store for everyone to see.

He pulled into the yard and saw Tisha sitting on the porch with the basket of socks in her lap. She was darning. He rode by without acknowledging her, pulled to the back of the barn, and began unhitching the horse instead of calling for Eatoe like he usually did. When he was satisfied that the horse could graze on its own, he went inside, took out his stash, and began to drink and converse with his thoughts.

He had serious doubts about what Mary Polly was getting into but he couldn't let on because Big Mary was critical of everything Mary Polly tried. He thought about Big Mary and wondered what she was doing. He prayed that she didn't hear him come in. *She is the last person I want to see this evening*, he thought, and he felt guilty for thinking it. He switched to nice thoughts of her as he always did when he had ill feelings towards her.

She tries, he said to himself. *She is a good soul. Where would I be without her? She could have pulled up the stakes and run off when I was having it so hard in the beginning, but she stayed. I don't like going against her, but I have to when it comes to Mary Polly because she don't treat the girl right.*

He took a fourth and fifth drink and thought back and remembered how things changed when Mary Polly was born.

"Take her away!" Big Mary had screamed when the midwife showed her. "I don't want to see a wench that can cause that much pain."

He took another swig. He had thought when Jesse II, Missouri, and Joel were born, Big Mary would bond with Mary Polly bring her into the family like she did the boys and Missouri. It hadn't happened. Big Mary was still finding ways to force Mary Polly to act in ways that were not in Mary Polly's best interest.

More than once he told himself, *If that fool Jesse II had stayed, he wouldn't have met that girl and let her trap him into marrying her the way he did. Then, maybe, just maybe, the notion of Eli Whitney and millions of bales of cotton wouldn't have piqued Mary Polly's interest the way it did.* He regretted the day Mary Polly had overheard the talk of cotton in Carter's store. Even though the store was abuzz with cotton talk, they could have gotten around it if Old John hadn't tried to get a rise out of him.

He looked at the bottle. It was half empty. He took a shorter drink.

The nerve of John Carter asking me to invest in a company that he knew he wasn't going to establish, a company in England of all places. I tried to fluff the nonsense off, see it for what it was. But, no, Carter wouldn't leave it alone.

He set his bottle aside, twisted his mouth, and mocked Carter. "It seems that our town is slower than others getting into the rhythm and tides of new events. But Jesse, I always thought, you would be part of the new frontier."

He wished his sons hadn't left him. He started to feel sad, turned his bottle up again, and took a long swig. *I wasn't even going to respond to Carter's hogwash, but Mary Polly butted in.*

He reflected and allowed Mary Polly's words to materialize in his mind. "My Daddy is the new frontier," he heard her say. And then he heard nothing. The whole damn store came to a standstill.

He remembered and became even angrier. He took another drink and asked himself, *After making that claim in front of the whole town, what was I supposed to tell Carter? That I was satisfied with things the way they were?*

He finished the bottle and threw it aside. His children, all but Mary Polly, made their statement when they married and moved out of the territory. Sure, they would inherit their share of his and Big Mary's goods, but as far as he was concerned, the land was Mary Polly's to expand and develop the way she saw fit.

As for the cotton, it would be a moneymaker. There were over ten thousand slaves in America and an increase in the cotton market would surely bring more. He had been relieved of the responsibility of thirty-five of his fifty slaves when Mary Polly, to Robert's dismay, had agreed to take all but the fifteen he needed to keep his lifestyle intact.

To take it a step further, he said to himself, *There has never been any real justification for slavery.* He thought about his own deeds and argued with himself. *Yes, I bought and sold them the same as my neighbor. It was about money. I needed to support my family and get ahead. Now that I am ahead, there is no need for me to continue to be responsible for people who can work and think as good as me.*

He heard a twig crackle outside. He knew he was about to have company. He lay down in the loft and waited. After a moment, Tisha entered carrying the sock basket. She looked around, then looked up, and smiled.

"Jesse Cole, you show yourself."

He was quiet for a while. She crossed to the steps and sat on the bottom rung. He knew she wasn't going away.

"Where is Big Mary?" he asked.

"She went to Lavonia's a while ago. Said she was gonna be gone the night."

"And what are you doing out here? What did you come for?"

She giggled, reached under the socks, and took out a bottle of corn liquor. He started down the steps towards her.

"You bring any tins?"

She took two tin cups from the socket basket and sat them on the steps. He reached down and grabbed the back of her neck.

"How do you always know what I need?"

She pulled away from him and stood up. She turned the bottle up to her mouth and took a long drink.

"Our baby girl has a new toy," he said to her. "This one ain't no Robert." Tisha could tell he was concerned. She filled the tins and passed him one.

"She is a high natured woman, Master Cole, that no count husband don't know what she like."

Jesse drank from the tin; whiskey dribbled from his lips. "You watch your mouth."

Tisha giggled and gulped down the rest of her liquor in one shot. She then meandered to a bale of hay sitting in front of him, pulled her skirt up to where it straddled her hips, and sat open legged to be sure he could see that she didn't have on any underpants.

Jesse, with more than a pint of liquor in him, hooked into what she was doing and allowed himself to get caught up in her giggles. They took him back to the beginning, when he and Tisha were young and daring.

"Have you ever wanted to sleep in Big Mary's bed?" he asked.

"Talk, talk, talk," she said, took his hand, and laid it on her breast. "Old saddle bags," she laughed. The liquor had him; she could see it in his eyes.

"I like it that you can laugh at yourself," he laughed and started to tug at her clothes.

"So what's the worst thing that can happen? Mary Polly makes the cotton work for her and she sleeps with the heathen." With that said, he slid to the floor and came to rest in front of her.

"You hush. Stop worrying yourself silly," she said gently and led his head to her lap. "Mary Polly has your ways. She ain't gonna let no heathen man wreck her life."

"You're right, Tisha," he said, and ran his hand up her leg, under her dress. Her nipples stiffened and began to swell. He reached up with his free hand and stroked her breast. He closed his eyes and imagined dark ripe raspberries blistering in the sun. She arched her back and helped him up to his knees.

"You are my special baby," she whispered.

Her words caressed him and made him hurt. He rested his head in her lap and moved his hand from her breast to her thighs. He inhaled the smell of her heat. Then he reached for her crotch and pried her legs apart. When he arrived at her center, she locked his hand in place with a vengeance. He moaned and his member, old and wrinkled as it was, started to harden. He pushed against her thighs and she opened her legs. He felt her button. It was wet and damp. He stroked it gently and she sighed, pulled her dress up, and pushed his head down. He feverishly buried his face where his hand had been.

For twenty years, he had wanted to know what was under that dress. All she had ever let him do was push his way into her in a tight corner somewhere. He was in his glory, thrashing, swallowing, and sucking.

Then he heard a cry. He opened his eyes and looked up.

"Mr. Cole. Mr. Cole, please," Tisha said, contempt showing clearly on her face.

He got up from the floor. The front of his pants was soiled. He tried to brush off the wet spots. When he saw he couldn't, he snatched her hand and pulled her to her feet. "Pour me another drink."

Tisha hurried across the floor and filled his tin. He drank in silence. After a moment, he took off his shirt and folded it across his arm, careful to place it to hide the spots on his pants.

"Call Armstrong. Tell him to put the buggy away and tie up the horse. Then you come to the house and do a wash." He tossed the few drops that remained in his tin onto the dirt floor and left the barn.

Tisha spat where the liquor landed as the door slammed shut.

"That old moldy peeper done struck Tisha for the last time," she said, and took another swig from the bottle, packed the sock basket, and broke into a song.

"*Control my presence*

But you can't control me

Control my whereabouts

But you can't control what I see."

She put the darning basket on her arm and danced towards the door.

"*White man, white man*

Leave me be . . .

Lest

I control thee."

She giggled, went out the door, and headed up to the house to get ready for the Master's week. It was almost dark. The Missus would be home directly.

BRYANT ACRES CHAPTER IV

Strings That Bind

Big Mary left the plantation as soon as she felt sure that she wouldn't run into Jesse and Sherrod on the road. The path to Lavonia's house was the same as the one to Mary Polly's, except it veered off to the right about twenty poles before Mary Polly's entrance. She was anxious to get to her sister's house. She wanted to confirm that, yes indeed, Sherrod had arrived and that he was a tall, muscle-bound man as they had surmised. She would have to admit that she hadn't spoken to or seen him up close. The window view had satisfied her curiosity. However, she had overheard him whispering to Cousin Thomas late the night before, long after heading to bed. Then he was up and ready to leave with Jesse at daybreak. He was obviously the epitome of what everyone said savages were, because not once did he leave his quarters to clean up or go to do private duty.

She agreed with Thomas Jefferson that he was indeed a heathen. Jefferson said, "They secrete less by the kidneys and more by the glands of the skin which gives them a strong disagreeable odor." And her stomach was clearly in no condition to deal with any strange smells that early in the day.

She felt smart for not telling Jesse that she was leaving. He would have found something to keep her at home. She didn't want to think ill of him because he was a good man, and she believed that he was just simple minded. He had no idea of what good taste was. He thought that fine dining was boiling an egg instead of frying it. And as for music, she wasn't even sure that he listened to it. As far as dancing went, moving to the rhythm of his heat was as close as he got. She sure put a stop to that. Mounting her like she was a dog.

Her mother had tried to warn her that the Cleo Cole branch of the family was different from the Joe Cole branch that her father came from.

Poor Jesse, she thought. She loved him anyway. He had made the best of her inheritance, and he was still around. At least he wasn't like his cousin Tom who went off to live in the hills with the Native Americans or Cousin Robert who shipped Lavonia and little Robert off to America so he could stay in England and plot with the British against General Washington and the French.

What a strange bird old man Cleo was, she thought to herself and laughed. Lavonia was waiting for her on the porch when she arrived. "Sister, I thought you would never get here."

Big Mary refused old Henry's hand and let herself out of the carriage. When he tried to help her down, she put her head up in the air and moved her nose way as far from him as she could. She then looked up at her sister and made a face. "You would think that you're not used to seeing slaves!" Lavonia said and laughed.

"My Africans know that they are to keep themselves away from me," she said as she followed Lavonia into the drawing room of the house where the table was set with biscuits and a pitcher of ice tea.

She was the oldest, and she took it upon herself not to let Lavonia forget. "Did you tell Clarissa to put more starch in those cable dollies like I told you to?"

"Clarissa worked all morning on these dollies. I told her that you were coming."

"Well, you spoke out of turn. I wasn't even sure what I was going to be doing this morning."

"You come here every Saturday morning, Mary. Stop playing with me and tell me about the new driver."

Big Mary rose from her seat, walked over to the dollies, and shifted them around on the table. "They could stand a bit more starch. Starch is what makes them fluff up and stand like petals on a flower."

Lavonia poured herself a glass of tea. She knew that it was better to ignore Mary at this point, because she didn't want to talk about the old heathen. It was all right with her that Robert wasn't worried about Sherrod working with Mary Polly. "I wonder how Robert's cruise is going," she said. "He was so looking forward to getting away. He wants to see his dad's grave."

Big Mary helped herself to a biscuit. "What in the world for? We are his parents, the only ones he ever had."

"His dad is a hero in England."

"Yes, a dead one."

"You are nasty today. Did you have a fight with Jesse?"

"I can't stand the thought of Mary Polly out there all day with that heathen, working and talking to him like he's a white man."

"Jesse and Robert feel okay about it."

"Jesse doesn't count, and Robert just wants to be away from farming," Big Mary snapped, shook her head, and wrung her hands together. "Robert is too good for Mary Polly, Lavonia. He is a delicate man, not in a feminine sort of way. He's delicate like fine china. He's artistic and educated. Look at this house. How he's been able to decorate it, match colors, and blend paper with wood."

Lavonia looked at her sister with resignation. They had had this conversation many times before, and every time it ended up with Big Mary getting angry and berating her for not going back home to England. What Big Mary didn't know was that she had left Robert's father because she knew that he couldn't follow her. His duty to King Charles wouldn't allow it.

"You saw Robert's face when he waved to us from the ship. He was happy and youthful looking. Mary, he was the one who gave Jesse the notion of establishing a company in England. He can draw on his father's name. Show him your love and give him a chance to do something on his own. Cole Manor is not his. It's yours and Mary Polly's."

"I guess you are right," Big Mary said to Lavonia, to her surprise. "Every time I walk into Mary Polly's house and see those seasoned planked floors, those horrible ceilings, and that beautifully patterned wallpaper, I ask myself, what is Robert doing living in a godforsaken place like this?" Then she let out a deep sigh. "It's so ironic. If Mary Polly hadn't come along, Jesse and I would be back in England. You and Robert would never have come out here."

Lavonia had never heard Big Mary sound so resigned. "What are you saying?" she asked.

"Jesse and I had a deal. If the crop didn't start paying its way that coming fall, he and I were going to move back. Then I got pregnant and Jesse changed. He was like a man obsessed. He bought two slaves and the three of them worked day and night. That fall, Mary Polly was born and the crop came into fold. And here I am. Here we both are."

"I'm glad that I came to America," Lavonia said. "I haven't missed having a man around the house one bit. Of course, old John Carter keeps coming by and bringing me groceries and candy. Do you think he has the notion of marrying me?"

"I told you about taking things from that old fool."

Lavonia laughed. "Do you honestly believe that I would entertain the thought of taking anything that John Carter has to offer?"

Big Mary dropped her head. "Excuse me, I'm just all pent up. A new body is sleeping in my house, and I don't take well to change."

"Maybe you should make friends with him and see what he is all about."

"I would rather make friends with the devil," she said and rose to her feet.

"Come and show me those new flowers you planted. The sun has moved over and it will be time for me to start home."

"Why didn't you have Armstrong or Shane bring you?"

"And have them report everything that we say?" Lavonia put her arm around her sister's shoulders and walked with her outside.

"Are you going to ever change?"

Big Mary laughed. "Then who would be responsible for you?" As they started towards the garden, Lavonia couldn't help but feel sorry for Big Mary. She was a jealous-hearted person who didn't know how to connect with others unless there was an aspect of that person that she could compare herself with. Big Mary even saw her as competition, and for that she was sorry. The only thing that she really wanted that Big Mary had was Jesse. The one time that she and Jesse almost got into it, she was frightened by the depth of feelings that followed between the two of them. He was a passionate, caring man who was sensitive to her plight as a single mother. He looked out for both her and Robert. The day they had arrived in Virginia, Robert was two years old. Jesse took Robert by the hand and gave him the same opportunities and rewards that he gave his only two sons. It was as if Robert had two homes.

Robert took this all for granted. He learned to please Big Mary, which was directly opposed to what Jesse wanted most of the time. He seemed to get pleasure out of siding with Big Mary, no matter the issue, especially if it had to do with discipline or punishment.

When Jesse caught Robert molesting his sister-in-law, Missouri, who was five years younger than Robert, without a word to anyone except her, he sent Missouri to live with her brother, Joel, in Kentucky.

Secretly, Lavonia was happy to see Robert go. She never quite understood why Mary Polly married him. And she often wondered if it had anything to do with the rift that she detected between him and Jesse. Lavonia knew that Mary Polly wanted control over the land more than she wanted anything in the world. She also knew that Jesse wouldn't have risked putting Mary Polly in charge if she married a stranger.

Yes, she told herself. *Jesse is aware of Robert's limitations, married or not. Robert doesn't have what it takes to come between Jesse and his precious daughter. Besides, Mary Polly and Robert might as well live with the ocean between them because their tolerance for each other and distance the ocean creates is just about equal.*

Big Mary wasn't saying much about the driver, but knowing cousin Tom the way she did, Lavonia was sure that the driver was capable. She was also sure to see them often. She thought how much easier it would have been for her own husband, Robert, to have married Big Mary. They both loved England, and they were both snobs in ways that caused others to share very little of themselves with either of them.

She recalled times when she and Mary Polly would be laughing and talking and had to turn it off when they heard Big Mary approaching. She believed Big Mary when she said that she loved Robert and Jr, because she had more patience with the boys, Robert Jr and Jesse ll. They were more like brothers than Joel and Jesse were.

"These flowers are beautiful," Big Mary said when they arrived at the garden. "But it seems to me you would have put vegetables out here and make the slaves tend them for you so you so you could do other things."

Lavonia chose to ignore her comments. She had to endure Big Mary's criticism and finally it was beginning to make sense. Robert was the last boy at home. Missouri was gone, and the only one left was Mary Polly. Who was Big Mary going to perform for now? She chuckled.

"What's so funny?" Mary asked.

"You, me, and Mary Polly," she said. "I feel sorry for Jesse. He is the only man among us."

"You act like Robert isn't coming back." Big Mary was somewhat surprised by her sister's reasoning.

"His father didn't."

Big Mary started to huff and puff. Lavonia could see that she was getting angry. "You are a fool," she said as she climbed aboard her buggy.

"I can see that you're trying to ruin my day, but I'm not going to let you."

Big Mary slapped the rump of the lead horse and yelled, "Get up here!" The horses started to move. She slapped the lead horse again, and the team took off in a manner that startled her and made it appear that she was losing control. She rounded the curve out of sight.

Henry, who had been standing on the other side of the yard, asked, "You want me to go make sure she's all right, Miss Lavonia?"

"She's alright," Lavonia said, as she smiled to herself.

Meanwhile, Big Mary settled herself and the horses for the ride home. By the time she entered the road that led to the cut off, she had her wits about her. She was still furious with Lavonia and was sorry she had taken time out of her day to visit only to be disrespected. Big Mary was clearly upset about Mary Polly and Robert's separation. If Lavonia had the good sense to worry about what could happen during such a separation, maybe she wouldn't have to worry for the both of them. She always thought Lavonia was ungrateful and resentful of all the favors she had done for her. Now she was sure of it.

The nerve of Lavonia including herself in on the day-to-day activities of her, Mary Polly, and Jesse's space without being invited. She was too nice to Lavonia. That was the problem. She tried to be a good older sister, and what did she get in return? The humiliation of a runaway buggy ride, one that knocked the wind out of her.

The least Lavonia could have done was to send Old Black Henry out to the road to see about her. Even if she didn't care enough to come herself, Big Mary didn't have to worry about her for a while because she was going to ignore Lavonia and see how she liked it. Big Mary went on thinking about what Lavonia had said about the three women being left to socialize and to be with each other. She knew that she and Mary Polly would be like oil and water but decided that it was high time they started getting to know one another. After all, Mary Polly was her daughter and not Lavonia's.

She thought about how it would be if she were more involved with Mary Polly. They certainly couldn't spend any time talking about cotton or slaves, or the heathen that she was going to be working with. But they could talk about clothes, dresses, dress patterns, and recipes. She smiled. There were things that they had in common. After all, they were both women. How she missed Missouri. She used to always hang around her, babbling about one thing or another. Mary Polly was Jesse's child, no doubt about it. The way the two of them fooled around in the barn with the animals day and night. They would always talk about the land.

Why did Jesse send Missouri away? She was only fifteen. Big Mary pulled into the yard and mentioned to Rucker, who was sitting under a tree shelling pecans, to come and put the buggy away. It had been a long day, and she was tired. As she climbed the steps to the porch, Tisha came out of the front door carrying a bag of clothespins.

"You home, Missus?"

"Are you washing again, Tisha?

"Yes Ma'am," she replied. "I couldn't find anything else to do so I thought I would rinse out Mr. Jesse's old pants." She took the wash basket from the chair where she had set it and started out to the yard.

"Where is the old man?" Big Mary asked and laughed.

"I don't know. I haven't seen him all day," she said as she made her way to the clothesline. There was a smirk on her face, and she felt the wind kiss her for the first time that day. She opened her legs a bit and stood in front of the line to let the wind blow through.

"If you do see him, tell him—"

"Tell me yourself," Jesse said as he opened the door for her. As soon as Big Mary saw him, she knew he had been drinking. The way he was looking at her confirmed it. "How was your sister today?"

"The same," she said coldly.

He recognized the coolness in Big Mary's voice but chose to ignore it. He could tell that she was in a mood, and he wasn't going to have any part of it. He watched her take off her headscarf and wrap.

"Pretty dress," he said and smiled. "That new guy, he home yet?"

"Sherrod?" Jesse said. "His name is Sherrod."

"I don't care what his name is as long as I don't have to hear him come in as soon as I get to sleep."

"Woman, it's still daylight. What happened to you out there on that road?"

"Nothing," she said and started to cry. Big Mary was usually pretty tough about things, so her tears caught him off guard. He took her in his arms, and she laid her head on his shoulder as she whimpered softly.

After a moment he asked her, "Did you and Lavonia have a fight?"

She hated it when he pried. "I'm tired," she said. "I'm going to sleep in the children's room. That way you won't have to worry about disturbing me when you go to bed." She started out and turned back. "And please make sure that that Sherrod or whatever his name is understands that he is confined to the back room. The rest of the house is off limits to him."

As she walked away from him, Jesse responded angrily without turning away from the mantle, "He knows."

"Good," she said and left the room, smugly thinking to herself, *Did he for one minute think I was going to tell him anything bad about my sister? He had to be out of his mind. No one comes between me my sister and me. No one!*

Jesse went out to the porch, sat down, and looked out across the field. "Sherrod, it's time for you to bring your black ass home," he mumbled to himself. He looked back down the road and where the path met the horizon. He saw a tall figure of a man riding a horse and a young black man running beside him.

Satisfied that Sherrod was being shown the way home, he got up, went in the house, and closed the door.

After a while he heard the back door close quietly, and then he lit the lantern in the study where he had gone to think. He reached inside the desk drawer and took out a liquor bottle. When he turned it up to his mouth, he found it empty.

"Damn you, Tisha!" he mumbled and slumped down in his chair and blew out the lantern.

He started to doze off. Then he remembered what it was like to plant okra and be ambitious about it. He had invited Sherrod and decided that it would be best to stay out of his way until it was time for the first crop report.

Once he made the decision, he dropped off to sleep. Sleep took him far away to where he could hear voices. He recognized the voices as those of his father and himself as a young man. He climbed up on the footstool that was there near the keyhole so that he could see into his father's study. He listened to himself and his father talking. It was the day after he had told his father that he had staked a claim to some land and he was planning to buy slaves. His father was lecturing him about the pitfalls of slavery.

"There is a class of colored people. Generally, the children of white men and mulatto women who pose degrees of natural intelligence, refinement, and sensitive feelings are equal to any exhibited by white people. All they need is the finishing touch, which education alone can give.

"Their minds are naturally gifted and easy to receive impressions and knowledge from without and are adorned with the various graces and beauties which learning stows, which knowledge of history and science, antiquity in poetry imparts.

"Their own inherent, unnatural impulses and perceptions of things are as viable, gifted, and elevated as the whites'. And most times, far superior to those rude savage roaches in his hands; their own fate sometimes happens to be unfortunately placed."

His father moved from his seat, and he was trying to follow his father's footsteps through the keyhole when the stool slipped and hit the floor with a loud thwack that brought both big Mary and Tisha running. He felt like a fool lying there sprawled out on the floor with his chair at his back.

"I must have dropped off to sleep."

"That's obvious Jesse," Big Mary quipped back at him. She was somewhat annoyed. "Come to bed before you wake everyone."

Who else is there? he thought to himself and then remembered that Sherrod was asleep down the hall. He rose to his feet and started towards the bed. He had been dreaming, but for the life of him, couldn't remember what the dream was about.

BRYANT ACRES CHAPTER V

If We Stick Together, We Can
Build a Human Machine

Sherrod saw Cato sitting under a tree watching a horse grazing when he approached the edge of the forest. Cato was waiting for him just as he said he would when they had parted company the night before. They had sat for a moment at the entrance to the forest on the blind side of Jesse's house and watched the activity in the slave camp.

Sherrod had asked Cato to ride with him so he could test the markers that he had laid out. He wanted a detailed layout as they traveled along the path. He wanted to determine the time and distance it took for him to walk to Mary Polly's and compare it to the time it took him to ride the distance.

Horses were primarily for survival. He had borrowed his dad's horse to get to Virginia. When Thomas left, he had sent it back to his dad in the hills. He knew his dad would need it. Since he hadn't earned the money to purchase a horse, he figured that he had better learn to use his feet. He not only needed to know how to travel to work, he needed to know how to escape if an occasion arose where an escape was required, be it planned or otherwise.

Cato was one of the three slaves he and Mary Polly planned to use as a crew captain. Mingus and Eatoe were the other two. Sherrod has chosen Cato as the person he could rely on to get him home because Mingus and Eatoe wouldn't look him in the eye when he met with them. He took their evasiveness to be a sign of mistrust and manipulation. Cato appeared to be outgoing and straightforward. He reminded Sherrod of Mamie.

There was a bit of chill in the air. He started out to meet Cato. He went back to his room and put on the flannel shirt that Nancy gave to him as a going away present, slipping it on underneath the one that he was wearing. He knew that he could take it off if the heat of the sun started to bear down on him in the middle of the day.

Daybreak had just begun when he arrived at the spot where Cato could help him onto the horse. It was Mary Polly's horse. He recognized it as the one that he brought home the night before. As soon as he saw him, Cato called the horse over and helped him into the saddle without saying a word. "Yes, Sir," Cato said. He was watching Sherrod's face for cues to communicate by.

"Mr. Bryant," Sherrod said correcting Cato.

Cato didn't understand. "How is that, Sir, Mr. Bryant?"

"Call me Mr. Bryant. Show respect if you respect me. Missus, Master Jesse, and the others will have to."

Cato didn't respond. He ran alongside Sherrod's horse as he had the night before, looking straight ahead and keeping his eye on the path.

Sherrod didn't know if Cato understood what he was trying to say. Either way, he was satisfied with his effort. In order to efficiently communicate, he knew that he would have to establish himself as a leader. He felt he had time to make the point and reinforce it as often as he needed to. He settled down on the horse and tried his best to be happy. That morning, he had a ride and he was finally going to be able to get into the work.

When they arrived at the house, the sun was up and Mary Polly was sitting on the porch waiting. "Am I late?" Sherrod asked in the way of greeting.

"If you had arrived any earlier, I would have accused you of sleeping on the road like Cato did," she said and laughed.

"Mingus and Eatoe are waiting for the two of you around back as you suggested. Are you sure you don't want me to sit in on the discussion?"

"I will come for you later when it is time to bring the crew together. You and I watch Cato, Mingus, and Eatoe to lay out details to the field hands."

"You expect Cato, Mingus, and Eatoe to explain all those details after one meeting with you?" She was loud, and he could tell that she was irritated at not being asked to be present at the meeting. He was determined not to give in to her. "I hope that I haven't misjudged you," she said and stared at him. He let his eyes meet hers without saying a word. She searched his face, and when she saw he wasn't budging, she smiled and added, "Go on, get out of here, both of you. I can't wait to see what you come up with."

Cato and Sherrod started around the side of the house. Sherrod's heart was beating fast. He had taken a risk not apologizing for his request that Mary Polly not attend his first meeting with the crew captains. She had hired him to do a job, and he couldn't stop every second to satisfy her whims. So far, she had accepted his decision. He hoped there would be no repercussions.

"Come on, Cato, we have a lot to do, so keep up. We can't be slow poking around. Do you hear?"

He knew he was being a little unfair. Cato had run all the way to Mary Polly's while Sherrod rode the horse, but that was the way it was. There was nothing he could do at the moment to fix it. His job was to not let it or any other misfortune interfere with the work.

"Yes, Sir, Mr. Bryant," Cato replied, quickening his pace. Cato was so light on his feet that Sherrod couldn't hear him moving. Sherrod looked at him thinking that if he could get Mingus and Eatoe to cooperate the same way, he would be on schedule.

Mingus and Eatoe were sitting on the back steps drawing circles in the dirt and whispering among themselves when Sherrod and Cato arrived.

"Run and get that package that you saw me tie to the horses this morning," he said to Cato.

Cato ran off towards the barn. Mingus made a strange sound in his throat, and Eatoe laughed. "You want to tell me what's so funny?" Sherrod asked.

The men continued to make circles in the dirt and act as if he had not spoken. Sherrod snatched the stick from Eatoe's hand and held out in front of Mingus.

"I want you to write the meaning of the sound you just made."

Mingus looked at Eatoe who had hunched shoulders and turned his back to both of them. Mingus yelled out in anger, a word that Sherrod had never heard. It obviously had a greater meaning to

Eatoe because he lunged at Mingus in a tirade. Speaking in his native tongue, he pounded Mingus with his fist.

"Stop it!" Sherrod said in a loud, strong voice. "On my watch, each of you will be responsible for what you say and do. Is that clear?"

BRYANT ACRES CHAPTER VI

Bring the Seeds; We Will Get it Done

The week that followed Sherrod's encounter with Big Mary helped Sherrod know how much he had to learn about being an overseer. He came to recognize that there was a balance between making demands, getting all he could out of the workers, and getting the workers to conduct themselves well.

He realized which worker was suited to which task, and he assigned jobs accordingly. Armstrong, Rucker, and Shane loved to tinker and repair things, so he put them in charge of the machinery. The others' tasks were not as technical, so their jobs remained the same.

Mingus, Cato, and Eatoe joined him on a ride to survey Mary Polly's hundred acres during the three days it took the crews to lay out the corn and thrash the wheat. The four men rode the land and chose the seventy-five acres that became the cotton field. Then, they got busy with wooden poles and lengths of rope and set the boundaries of the remaining twenty-five acres. This included the house, the slave camp, the barns, the stalls and pens, the grazing fields for the animals, the walking paths, the garden, the vegetable planting fields, and the orchard.

After the boundaries were set, Sherrod assigned twenty-five acres to each captain and his crew.

"Each of you, Cato, Eatoe, and Mingus, is to assign five acres to each member of your crew. You will then teach these men to eat, sleep, and breathe their acreage. It is now April. I promised Mary Polly cotton before I leave, and we have tillage to be concerned about."

"Let's do it," Mingus yelled. "Bring us the seeds. We will get it done."

Sherrod smiled, got down on his knees, and together they started to set the boundaries of three, twenty-five-acre plots. Each of the men had planted and chopped cotton before. They were more excited about the enormity of what they were beginning to perceive as their project than they were about the cotton. That and their need to show Sherrod what they could accomplish. He offered them a challenge, and they intended to meet that challenge.

Sherrod's mind was on the end product. There was going to be a demonstration of the gin mill in town the next afternoon, and Miss Polly had asked him to go with her. The concept of a machine separating cotton fiber from cottonseed intrigued him. He had often sat and watched his father and other neighboring men work day and night ginning the cotton by hand. If the cotton gin could gin cotton in the time Miss Polly said it could, why, this time next year who knows where Cole Manor would be.

He stood up and looked across the field. He could visualize the land as it moved from tillage to harvest to baling. He saw the ground being turned and the seeds planted. He saw three months down the road, about July, when cotton plants would have grown to where they had to be chopped and spaced accordingly. He saw growth of soft white, wool-like fibers covering the seeds of the cotton plant. He closed his eyes and saw seed hairs, which he knew consisted of single long cells, with thick cellulose cell walls that resembled a twisted, flattened tube but was actually cotton thread used for spinning yarn. He opened his eyes and smiled. He had had visions of late October and the crew picking and preparing the cotton for ginning and baling. He was on his way, and he knew it.

He lingered a while longer. When the sun hit him, he went back to work. The gin mill, he was told, also had the capacity to separate seed hairs from cotton seeds so that the fiber hairs could be baled and seeds could be crushed for cottonseed oil and cotton cakes to be used as fodder for the cattle. And, even though he had not seen this machine, he held on to what he was told, and he believed.

He liked the idea of a new discovery. It was exciting, and it made him feel like he was part of a new beginning. It also made him lonely. He felt all the passion of discovery, but there was no one to share his enthusiasm with.

There had been glimmers of possibilities during his conversations with Miss Polly, but his ordeal with Big Mary had put everything in perspective. Miss Polly was no longer inquiring on a moment-to-moment basis about the progression of the plan. He had run into her a few times, and they had stopped and discussed needs for materials, scheduling, and the like, but that was about it. She seemed down, and he knew to leave her to her thoughts and only connect with her when necessary.

In a quiet moment, from time to time, one of the slaves would provide an opening for a conversation about the Coles, but he discouraged it. He knew the dog that brought a bone would carry one, and he wasn't going to involve himself with petty he-said-she-said nonsense.

Most of the information that he did glean came from Esther or Mamie. He had never heard either of them say anything. But anytime one or the other thought Mary Polly was distracted, preoccupied, or away, they would head for the slave camp. A couple of times they had passed him, giggling and moving around as if he were sharing in their secret.

He was quite fond of both of them. They were very different, however. Mamie was a warm child, more outspoken than Esther. She was probably the only one on the whole three hundred acres of Cole Manor who wasn't afraid of Big Mary. He hadn't quite figured out why that was.

Esther, on the other hand, was a young woman, and she knew it. Her every movement was designed to draw attention to herself. It was clear when you looked at her that she didn't carry the anger or the pain that the slave women living in the camp did. Neither did she carry the arrogance of separation or superiority. She and her temperament clearly patterned after her grandma, Tisha. She and her grandmother's sense of humor were almost identical. They both stared at you and made you wonder what they were thinking. Then, they would ask you a question as if you had been having a discussion and should know the answer. Sherrod found Esther attractive, as did all the other men on the grounds. The trouble was, she knew it and that frightened him.

Experience was teaching him that his body only required five hours of sleep, and if he kept personal items for his daily use, he would experience a sense of well-being.

He made it his business to keep his schedule tight with little or no idle time. He got himself into a routine, where he left home an hour, sometimes two, before daybreak. He stopped at the creek to wake himself up. He stretched, rinsed out his mouth with some mint leaves soaked in water, bathed, changed underwear, and put on a clean shirt.

Martha, Lena, Phoebe, and the rest of the women in the camp were forever giving him packages of food and jars of apple cider and other fruit juices. These served as care packages when he didn't have time to eat during the day and needed to stop and rest on his way back to Cole Manor at night.

He would have liked to own a horse, but the walking was keeping him motivated. It was a sharp contrast to the shared traveling with Eatoe and Cato in the evenings. He spent very little time at Jesse's place, and he spent many waking hours trying to decide how his progress reports should be handled.

Master Jesse had stopped him when he came in the night before. "I am told that you are learning to be a good overseer," he said. Then he gave him a pair of boots, a greatcoat, and a whip. "Wear these when you go into town day after tomorrow," he said.

Sherrod recognized the clothes and whip to be symbols of power. He had read about them in school. Two large initials "C" and "M" were carved into the handle of the whip. They stood for Cole Manor.

"Thank you, Sir," he said, trying not to show any emotion.

He guessed he had succeeded because Jesse tapped him lightly on the shoulder and said, "Good night, Sherrod."

He had heard about how Big Mary commandeered him to humiliate Mary Polly and he thought it was time he gave Sherrod some positive stimulation, lest all the Coles made fools of themselves.

Sherrod didn't like what the boots, greatcoat, and whip stood for. He had mixed feelings about using them, so he took them to the field the next day and asked Cato, Eatoe, and Mingus what they thought.

"I think you better put your black ass in that coat, slip on the boots, and carry that whip like it is part of your hand, Mr. Bryant," Eatoe laughed sarcastically.

He never took offense at Eatoe's derogatory remarks for he realized they were tests set up for a power play with the others. He accepted what he had to say and turned to the others.

"Cato?"

"What choice do you have?"

"Mingus?"

"You solved the problem when you let us in on it. Wear the stuff. We know it doesn't mean nothing."

Sherrod was really learning to care for Mingus. "Thanks," he said, and as if he needed to reinforce his appreciation, he said it again, "Thanks, men."

"You are a strange man," Eatoe said. "One minute you are offering us the world. The next minute you need us to bail your ass out of something."

"That's all right, isn't it?"

"It's all right with me," laughed Cato. "Ain't too many times I been asked my opinion."

"If there ain't no more work here, I guess we need to stop jaw-jacking and head back," Mingus said.

It was hard for Mingus not to side with Eatoe, but he knew Eatoe was wrong. Since Sherrod didn't seem to be bothered by what Eatoe said, that helped him stay out of the conversation.

They mounted the horses and started for home. It was the first time they had been out as a group, and they were feeling satisfied with themselves.

"Ain't it nice to be able to stay on the property, not have to go to town?" Cato said. "Keeps down confusion."

"We do stay on the property, don't we?" Sherrod said, thinking about it for the first time. In his mind, he had separated Jesse's place from Mary Polly's place.

He chuckled to himself and thought about it some more. All the traveling he had done since arriving a week before had been on the Cole plantation. Whether it was Mary Polly's end of it or Jesse's, it was the same. And from what he had heard, Big Mary's sister, Lavonia, had a small corner of the land. He hadn't seen Lavonia but, in due time, he was sure he would.

He thought about October when his servitude would end. He hadn't made any plans past six months, because he wasn't sure where he wanted to go or if he would have enough money to go anywhere. He still had the hundred dollars his father had given him. He would just have to wait and see.

When they arrived back at Mary Polly's, Cato and Eatoe went off to help the others prepare the harvest for market. It had been a good crop. There would be a lot of celebrating in the camp come nightfall. The pig Miss Polly was cooking filled the air. Sherrod could smell it long before he arrived back at the camp. Ice cream freezers and large empty lard tins for apple cider, and anything they intended to spike it with, were in full view for the whole camp to see. The slaves were abuzz with merriment and laughter.

Mingus sat down for a moment on the back steps with Sherrod to discuss the work for the following day. The plan was to get the ground tilled and ready for sowing seeds by Sunday. Aware that everyone would be up until all hours of the night, Sherrod suggested they move the deadline up a day so that everyone could take a holiday.

Mingus was impressed. "You live what you believe, don't you?"

"I try to," laughed Sherrod. "Where would we be if I went back on my promises?"

"Why don't you stay for the party tonight?"

"No, I'm only here for a limited time. I have to stay sharp. Besides, Master Jesse is expecting me."

They both laughed.

"Esther's going to be disappointed;. she thought you would be her excuse to come out."

"Imagine that," Sherrod teased.

"You imagine it," Mingus said, somewhat serious, tapped Sherrod lightly on the shoulder, and ran off.

Sherrod lingered for a moment. He watched Mingus make his way to the camp. He wondered what it would feel like to hold a woman and have her look at him that certain way. He reflected on the first time he had made love.

He was fifteen and had stolen a day away from the fields, soothing his unrest in the lake. He liked the sounds the splashes made when his body moved through the water. He had grown quite a bit the past year, and he wasn't quite used to his new size. He turned over on his back for a game of watching his penis to see if he could make himself have an erection in the water. He tried without touching it, and when it didn't happen, he held it up and urinated a short distance where he could watch the stream fall in ripples at his feet.

He did it once and tried to do it again and nothing happened. He started to play with it. Making circles with his forefinger around the head, telling it how special it was, and that someday he was going to insert it in some woman and . . . Before he could finish, it started to happen. It stiffened and he released his hold on it.; It jerked and moved and just when it reached its full length—

"You're nasty," he heard a female voice call from the trees. He quickly turned over and ducked into the water, out of sight. "I saw what you did, Sherrod Bryant," old pain in the butt, Emily Jane, said as she ran along the bank looking for him. "You come out here," she demanded. "Come out right now, or I am going to tell."

Sherrod was a long way downstream by this time. He was not about to show himself to Emily without any clothes on. He swam underwater out of view, and when he was sure it was clear, he sneaked ashore, put on his pants, picked up a stick, and ran towards her.

"What are you doing down here, Emily Jane?"

Emily was the same age as he, and they had been in the same class since first grade.

"What are you going to do with that stick, hit me?" she teased.

"If you don't go home and mind your business that's exactly what I am going to do," he said.

"I liked watching you out there," she said. "I would never share that secret with anyone."

"Are you being truthful?" he asked.

She leaned over, kissed him, and gently took the stick out of his hand. "I would never hurt you, Sherrod Bryant."

He looked at her and she smiled. He felt his heart speed up and a stirring in his groin.

"Have you ever done it? I have."

"Done what?" Sherrod asked.

"You ain't that stupid; you live on a farm for God sakes."

He didn't like that she was leading him. It made him feel stupid. "Yes, I've done it. You saw how big I was, didn't you?"

She moved closer to him. She smelled like lye soap. She wasn't pretty, but he liked the smell of soap. His heart was beating loud and fast. He moved closer to her, and she leaned into him, undid the top button of his pants. His penis shot out and broke the remaining two buttons and his pants fell to the ground. He grabbed her to shield himself, and she kissed him.

He kissed her back. Her lips were warm and wet. She put her arms around his neck and let her chest rub up against his. He took her hand and pulled her to the ground. She grabbed hold of his penis and led him into her.

"I have seven brothers," she said. "I'm the only girl."

He didn't hear her. The warmth of her secretions had enveloped him and caused his insides to let go of the pressure that he was trying to contain. He gave in and a pulsating fountain opened up and claimed what was his.

He cried and she cried and then there was calm. They lay there, not knowing what to say to each other. Finally, he rolled over and looked at her. The look in her eyes frightened him. He knew he could return again and again and that frightened him even more.

"Mr. Bryant," he heard someone say, bringing him back to the present.

He turned, and there stood Esther. He remembered seeing her earlier that day, but she wasn't dressed the way she was now.

"Miss Mary Polly says it is all right for you to stay for the party tonight. She asked Master Jesse, and he said it was okay."

"I can't," he said, and rose to his feet, feeling awkward and out of place.

"What I mean is, I would like to, but there just isn't enough time for playing."

"You're afraid," she said. There was something challenging in her voice. "Afraid I will jump up around your neck and kiss you?"

He looked her in the eye and, as stern as he could say it, said, "Esther, I don't like forward women."

With that, she turned and ran around the side of the house.

He didn't want to hurt her, so he called, "Esther . . . Esther."

She heard him call, but rather than respond, she folded her arms against the side of the house and buried her face in them.

He came to where she was. "I am sorry," he said, and took her hand. She folded the tail of her dress around her fingers and wiped her eyes. He continued holding the other hand. "I am sorry, but I meant what I said."

She snatched her hand out of his. "Leave!" she shouted. "What are you waiting for? Get your black ass wherever you are taking it."

"I am leaving, but not before I tell you how beautiful you look . . . I like your dress and the color. I love the way you have combed your hair, and the way your eyes are shining."

His soft-spoken words calmed her. "I didn't want to go to that old party anyway," she said in a voice so quiet he could barely hear her.

"Come on," he said encouragingly. "Go. Have a good time. Sixteen is the age for parties."

"Seventeen," she corrected.

"I meant to say seventeen," he teased.

"I hate you," she said, feeling somewhat ridiculous.

"I know you do," he said, and ran off towards the path laughing. "See you tomorrow."

Mary Polly had watched the scene between Sherrod and Esther from the window. She was relieved when he dashed off. "I knew he was mature enough to not be seduced by a child," she said to herself. She made sure she was out of sight when Esther came inside.

Neither Cato nor Eatoe was in sight when Sherrod arrived at the end of the path. "No ride for you tonight," Sherrod said, laughing to himself.

It wasn't Esther's age that had kept him from her, he started to think as he walked. It was the position he would put her and himself in if it happened. The others loved Esther but had very defiant feelings about her relationship with the Coles as compared to their own relationship.

He thought about Esther's fake tears and chuckled. Mingus had warned him. How did he know? Had she been talking? Who else did she tell? Did Miss Polly suspect anything when Esther asked if he could stay over?

All of a sudden, he felt tired and wished he didn't have to walk the path home. The night wasn't as clear as it had been. There was hardly a star in the sky. He walked a while and suddenly he heard a horse's hoofs beating the trail. He turned to look and saw a carriage lantern approaching him. Cato and Eatoe couldn't stay away, he laughed happily. As the carriage came closer, he saw that he was wrong. The shadow was that of Miss Polly.

She pulled up to where he was walking.

"Is everything all right, Miss Polly?" he asked.

He kept walking, and she paced the horses to keep up with him.

"Somehow walking after a full day of work is not the same as starting out fresh in the morning, is it?"

"I can't truthfully say it is," he said, and laughed. Then he thought, *If she only knew how tired I am.*

"You're allowed to ride with me in the carriage."

"Okay," he said, and she stopped for him.

He climbed aboard and realized he was on the passenger side. "Do you want me to drive?"

"There is a noisy party going on back at the house. Daddy never comes in this direction at night . . . Mother, my dear mother has been in bed for an hour . . . It's okay."

He wanted to lie back and relax but the tension was too great. The tiredness he was feeling before she arrived paled compared to what he was feeling sitting next to her. He waited for her to move the horses, but she just sat there. In a quiet, calm way, she sat and made him even more nervous.

"Are these grounds really that safe?" he asked.

"I don't know what you mean," she replied.

"You, out here in the middle of the forest, alone . . . It doesn't seem to bother you."

She smiled. "I know every corner, rock, and blade of grass on these three hundred acres. Cole Manor is who I am."

"I know what it is to have a passion about a place. That's the way my folks feel about the hills where I come from," Sherrod replied.

"And you didn't?"

"I want more," he said, and turned to her forgetting whom he was talking to. "I want what you have."

As soon as he said it, he wanted to cut his tongue out and take every word back. His throat got tight and his chest hurt. He wished he had hidden when he heard her coming. The anxiety was almost unbearable.

Mary Polly smiled. She liked his feistiness.

When his chest relaxed to where he could catch his breath, he apologized. "Excuse me for being so forward," he said.

"Don't take it back, Sherrod. I'm your friend. A secret friend, but a friend." She sighed, and then added, "I came out here tonight because I knew you would be here . . . and . . ." All of a sudden, she got in touch with what she was doing and became nervous. Her nervousness made her talk fast. "And I wanted to know what it would feel like talking with you privately . . . just you and me . . . a woman and a man."

"I have to be going," he said, and started down from the carriage.

She gently laid her hand on his arm. "Get up," she said to the horses and pulled the reigns. They started off in a slow gallop causing Sherrod to fall backwards. "I am going to take you to Daddy's. No trap, just you and me riding together, no color, no positions, no barriers. Two adults who respect each other as human beings."

"Will you let me off at the beginning of the forest?"

"I will do better than that," she laughed. "I will take you to my Aunt Lavonia's, give you the carriage, and you drive to Daddy's. We are going to town in the morning. You can pick me up at Lavonia's."

"Yes, Miss Polly," he said. "I gave the crew tomorrow off. We will make up the work, okay?"

"We all have a holiday, Sherrod. You're my new driver. Daddy said he gave you the boots and things. Wear them tomorrow. I want to show you off."

"Yes, Miss Polly," he said, and was relieved when they reached Lavonia's turnoff. Talking to Miss Polly in the comfort of her home was sure better than being out in the woods under the stars with her.

"Lavonia, come out to meet Sherrod," Miss Polly called as she pulled into her yard. She then jumped from the carriage and ran up on the porch. She had on tight britches and a loose-fitting work shirt tucked in at the waist. She felt his eyes on her, and she looked back at him with a fixed gaze that cut through him, tugged on his insides, and made him feel strange and unnecessary.

He hurriedly scooted over to the driver's seat and took up the reigns. The door opened and Lavonia came out. He could tell she was related to Big Mary. They had the same shaped face and forehead. Her features weren't as sharp as Big Mary's, and she was a whole lot warmer and friendlier.

"So, you're Sherrod," she said. "Boy, what a good-looking man you are."

"Excuse Aunt Lavonia," Mary Polly teased. "She hasn't seen her husband in twenty years."

"Tell all my business," Lavonia said and put her arm through Mary Polly's.

Sherrod could tell she was really fond of Mary Polly.

"See you in the morning, Mr. Bryant," Miss Polly said, showing off.

"Mister Bryant," Lavonia said sarcastically and laughed. Mary Polly tugged on her arm. They both giggled and went inside.

Sherrod started up the horses and headed for Cole Manor. *What a day this has been*, he thought. *Master Jesse, please be in bed. I don't want to see you tonight.*

He drove quietly and fast. When he arrived at the house, he drove to the back by the barn. Luckily, one of the young field hands saw him and came to unhitch the horses and take them into the barn.

The next morning, an hour before daybreak, Sherrod slipped off to the barn and quietly hitched the horses to the carriage and walked them into the forest where he clearly couldn't be heard.

Instead of putting on clean underwear and a clean shirt, at the creek, he changed his clothes entirely. He put on clean underwear, a pale beige shirt, with clean deep tan britches that matched the coat, and the dark brown boots that Jesse gave him. When he finished dressing, he looked at his reflection in the creek. His hair was tangled so he wet a rag that he had hidden in back of a rock and brushed his hair. He then took a ribbon from behind the same rock and tied it. He placed his hat on his head, took up the whip, and drove to Miss Lavonia's house.

At daybreak, when the rooster crowed and the lights went on in Miss Lavonia's house, he was parked outside. Miss Lavonia started out in her sleepers and saw him sitting there. She dashed back inside and called Mary Polly.

Sherrod had never dealt with women the way he had in the past week. He liked to turn a head as much as any man. He could appreciate their subtlety and their individual beauty. The discovery of a woman's face, her eyes and brow, the way she held her mouth and her head, the way she laughed. The uniqueness of his situation was that most of the women he dealt with were somehow connected to Cole Manor. He was forced to interact with them. The success or failure of his work was dependent on the many relationships and an unspoken language that he was struggling to learn.

Mary Polly approved of the way he looked. "Good morning, Sherrod," she said and smiled. She climbed into the carriage and, as if her whole being had been transformed, became this woman. She was wearing a bright yellow wide-brim laced hat with white and yellow flowers, a pale-yellow dress with ruffles and bows, and beige shoes.

"Drive slow," she whispered to him as they made their way. "People in this town have to get used to seeing us ride around together." She took a deep breath and began to move her head from side to side, smiled, and waved as if she was in a parade.

"Yes, Ma'am," he said, slowed the horses, and said a prayer under his breath.

BRYANT ACRES CHAPTER VII

You Are Woman, and I Am Man

The day in town with Mary Polly came and went. It was an experience that held no surprises. The white men quietly observed him with their crude ways and manners. Their behavior towards him however was not as unsettling as the behavior of the white women, who were chatting away talking to Mary Polly but throwing him glances and giggles that he had to pretend not to see.

The black men grouped together and pretended to work as collectives whenever he was in their vicinity so they could watch and gossip about him. The black women acted as if he wasn't present but managed to bump into him at well planned times. The Indians acted as if they were oblivious to his presence. Like him, they were taking care of their business as quietly and inconspicuously as possible.

Every white person in town was curious about the gin mill. They crowded into Carter's storehouse, charging the air with excitement and merriment. Eli's apprentice was there to demonstrate and sell the machine. Production had been so successful in other parts of the country that twenty men were out on the road taking orders, the audience was told.

The gin mill itself was a crude manual contraption made of wood, rope, and wire. It had three legs, two in front and one in back. In actuality, it was a hoisting device with turning ropes and a string trap with wire teeth that snared the seeds from the cotton. The simplicity of it gave Sherrod hope. It showed what planning and studying could do for a man.

Meanwhile, back at Mary Polly's, the slaves responded to their holiday by increasing their work hours voluntarily. They appeared to have a passion about their tasks when they came back. Sherrod was running interference for them, and they felt the results. The best part was the individual attention that he gave them. He ate at their table, listened to them talk, and showed that he cared about them and for them. When there was a problem, he was there. When they were sick, he was there. He helped every man and woman in the camp feel a part of the plan.

Sherrod made two progress reports to Jesse. After that, Jesse told Sherrod he was pleased with what he was seeing and that there was no need for further reports.

Sherrod ran into Big Mary occasionally. He would give her a big smile, which she would pretend to ignore by asking him to perform one minuscule chore or the other. As time went on, she took to letting him help her in and out of the carriage. Then, once or twice, he caught her peering at him from her bedroom window. He began to understand that she was a woman who was trapped inside herself, because she didn't know who to be. He felt sorry for her, and he let the quiet unspoken relationship between them serve as a reminder of his need to never again give up his right to live as a free man.

He had seen Lavonia twice before he learned she was Mary Polly's mother-in-law as well as her aunt. He wasn't surprised by the knowledge. Families intermarrying made perfectly good sense to him, being from a colony where intermarriages often occurred.

Mary Polly stayed out of his way for the most part. Nonetheless, she was always glad to see him and she showed it by sneaking him little gifts, such as a hairbrush, a comb, and assorted colors of ties for his hair. She never gave them to him directly. He would find them in his bag or tied to the tree nearest to the spot in the forest where they stopped and talked that night.

At first, he didn't know where the items were coming from. For days, he had noticed an old newspaper tied to a tree. He came and went without inquiry. Finally, his curiosity got the best of him. He untied the paper and looked inside. He found a hairbrush, the kind he had noticed that day in town with Miss Polly. As he picked it up, Mr. Carter had yelled out, "Imported from England, got it in yesterday."

"How much?" he had asked.

"Too much for your kind," Carter replied and kept on working as if the exchange had never occurred.

He started to wrap the brush and put it back but then he noticed some writing scribbled on the inside of the paper. "For you, Sherrod," it read, "from a woman to a man. No traps. Just me. Your secret friend."

He took the brush and put it in his bag. For the first time, he was glad that he had decided to see himself home at night after that experience with Miss Polly. He wouldn't want Cato or Eatoe getting wind of her giving him presents. He didn't want anybody to know for that matter.

He took the brush and hid it under the rock with his washrag and his ties. Why shouldn't he take the brush or other personal items from Miss Polly? He was doing everything she asked of him, plus some. She liked him to look good. She said so that day in town. He would find a way to thank her, he decided. That way she would know it was okay for her to reward him.

May, June, July, and August rolled by without incident or fanfare. Sherrod had become a regular fixture on the Cole plantation. His goings and comings were all but going unnoticed, unless the Master, Mistress, or slaves needed him for one reason or the other.

Even John Carter was responding well. Sherrod had taken to going to town, running errands for Jesse and Big Mary. From time to time, a neighboring friend of Jesse's would engage him in a conversation about farming or a sick animal, and they always came away impressed by his knowledge.

One time, he was in town and John Carter was complaining about his dog, Wolf. Sherrod was familiar with Old Wolf. They had taken a liking to each other, and Sherrod always carried a piece of jerky for him when he knew he was going into the store. This particular day, Old Wolf was lying around lifeless and unresponsive.

"Something is wrong with Wolf," Carter said when he saw Sherrod. "Every now and then he will turn his head one way then the other and let out a howl that goes right through you. The howl doesn't last long, just for the time he is turning his head. Other than that, he just lays there. I have never seen anything like it."

"Do you mind if I take a look?"

"Can't hurt," Carter said, and went about his business waiting on other people.

"What's the matter, Boy?" Sherrod asked, stroking Wolf as he spoke to him.

Wolf continued lying with a fixed gaze, his tail wagging slightly. Sherrod lifted Wolf's head and gently turned it to the side. He saw some redness around the side of his inner ear. Sherrod got up and went out to the path, to the traffic area, and into the bushes. There he found a root weed that he picked and brought back to the water trough in front of Carter's store. He crushed the root weed into a jar top that he took from his bag, added four drops of water, and made a salve, which he took back inside to Wolf.

Sherrod kneeled in front of the dog, dabbed a little on the tip of his finger, and rubbed it inside the opening of Wolf's right ear. He then repeated the treatment with the left ear. When he was done, Wolf licked his hand. Sherrod responded with a smile and a pat on the head. "He has an ear infection. Put this on it once a day."

Carter took the salve and thanked him. He must have told every farmer in Virginia, because Sherrod all of a sudden became the most popular guy around, especially when there was a sick animal that his owner didn't know how to cure.

Once, Sherrod was walking past the barn and heard Jesse bragging to a neighbor. "You are right; Sherrod knows animals. He knows their weaknesses, their strengths, their faults and imperfections, the signs and causes of their diseases, and methods for curing them. He's the best darn animal man around."

Sherrod smiled and walked on by. *Husbandry in the first order,* he said to himself, and with pride thought about his dad. He had about six weeks left on the Cole plantation, and he was no closer to deciding what his next move was going to be than he was two or three months ago.

He had done well by the Coles, far better than even he had expected. The seeding and planting had gone well. There was an abundance of cotton waiting to be harvested. As time drew near, he could feel excitement in the air.

Master Robert sent word that the proper linkages from Virginia to England were in place and ready for business. Mary Polly was real sad when she told Sherrod, although she tried to sound happy when she broke the news. Things were going so well she had all but forgotten about Robert and why he was away. She was more caught up with what was happening with her venture. She was struggling to come to grips with Sherrod's leaving. She knew that once the cotton was baled and shipped, Sherrod's agreement with her would end, and she didn't like the way that felt.

Sherrod had told her that he wanted his own land and his own life. She knew the only way she could keep him involved with her was to help make his dreams materialize.

Her cotton business had been set up in a way that it could continue to grow without Sherrod, like he had promised. Mingus, Cato, and Eatoe had become well-oiled machines. Their energy was high, and they could almost predict to the day what was going to happen to the crop. She had given them permission to get married and that had helped. After the harvest, the last night of Sherrod's stay, the triple ceremony was going to take place. Sherrod had promised the men he would stand up with them and take part in the celebration.

Mary Polly had volunteered, against the wishes of her parents, to host the reception. She wanted to spend as much time as she could with Sherrod. Several times, she had tried to approach him to discuss the possibilities of extending his time.

The last time Mary Polly had that conversation with Sherrod was when Thomas Cole had visited. Thomas had come to tell Sherrod that his father had died and that his brothers, Silas Jr and William, had sent word that they were leaving the hills and wanted him to meet them in Granville.

Sherrod received the news before Mary Polly. When he came to work that morning, he was not himself. His gait was off, his clothes disheveled, and his face expressionless.

Unbeknownst to him, Mary Polly had sat in her bedroom window most of the morning worrying because he was late. She kept telling herself that he would come prancing up the path singing and swinging his bag, announcing his arrival the way he had done every morning since he had stepped his foot on her place. The morning grew later and later, and it didn't happen

She was just about to call Mingus to go look for him when she saw him walking slowly towards the house. He was so disheveled that she almost didn't recognize him. His hair was hanging loose, and he wasn't wearing a hat. Without giving thought to what she was doing, she ran out to meet him. "Sherrod . . . Sherrod, what's wrong?"

As he came closer, she could tell he had been crying.

"My father died," he said.

She started to take his arm and thought better of it.

"I am so sorry," she said. Her words felt empty and shallow against her need to take him in her arms, give him permission to scream, cry, or whatever it took for him to grieve his loss.

"Come inside. Let Esther fix us something cool to drink," she said.

"I have to work," he replied, and she flared into anger.

"Damn the work, Sherrod Bryant. Get yourself upon that porch . . . Sit. Now!" He dutifully followed her up the steps to the porch. "Esther, Mamie!" Mary Polly yelled.

Esther and Mamie heard the urgency in their Mistress' voice. "Yes, Ma'am," they said, as they came running.

"Sherrod's daddy died. Mamie, I want you to fix something cold for us to drink. Esther, you're to go to the camp, tell everyone what has happened, and tell them Mr. Bryant is not to be disturbed today, and that I hope everyone will honor his grief by continuing to work. Is that clear?"

"Yes, Ma'am," they both said and went on their way.

"Sorry about your dad," Esther called back from inside the house.

"Me too. I'm real sorry," he heard Mamie said as he leaned back and became absorbed by the pillows on Mary Polly's couch.

Mary Polly pulled up a chair and encouraged him to put his feet up and stretch out. He slipped out of his boots, closed his eyes, and put up his feet up as she instructed. His mind started to drift. He allowed himself to follow his thoughts.

"My mother died when I was born," he started. "Dad raised me. The community was my mother. I had the privilege of sleeping in any house I chose. I was always welcome. My brothers and me, we are all five years apart. They mothered me too. But nobody was like Dad. He always knew what to say to me. I would do anything to keep from hurting him, and he knew it.

"Dad was a white man. He was born in England. He could have lived anywhere in the world he wanted, but he chose the hills. I asked him about it once, and he said . . . he saw a slave cargo ship when he was a kid. He and some friends were on the dock admiring the ships and boats when a slave ship bound for America came into port. It had run into some problems, and it pulled in for repairs.

"Dad and his friends were about fourteen, and curious. They had never seen a slave ship before, so they sneaked on board. As soon as they arrived topside, they were hit with a stench of human flesh. Dad said they didn't know what the smell was, so they pulled up their shirts to cover their noses and continued on.

"They climbed below, and there lying in the bowels of the boat were hundreds of black bodies: men, women, and children, chained to each other in a space the size of this porch. Most were naked. Some were foaming at the mouth and crying. Others were praying or stared straight ahead, their eyes as white and big as saucers.

"Two white men stood over them with whips, and every time one made a sound, one of the white men would lash out and cut a blood line wherever the strap landed: on a face, an arm, a back.

"The agony of those faces, the body waste, the fear-filled eyes destroyed Dad's belief in a man's purpose for coming to the new world. It didn't stop him from coming, but he came with a mindset on something other than money.

"Dad committed himself to freedom, to an equal and just life-style. He was soft and humble and all that was good. My mother, they say, recognized Dad's gentle spirit as soon as she met him.

"I was worried when I left home. I was afraid that I would never see him alive again. He must have known when he supported my leaving."

Mary Polly searched herself for feelings and the right words to express them. She moved in her chair, and the sounds she made caused Sherrod to come out of himself, become aware of where he was.

"I am sorry for talking so much," he said.

"Sherrod, I know you are afraid of letting me know you. Let's just say our talk today is part of me helping to keep you sane. Cole Manor can't harvest its crop with an insane overseer."

He looked at her with disbelief. She held up one hand and put the other on her heart. "Purely selfish," she said, and he smiled.

"My secret friend is getting less secret," he tried to tease.

She pretended not to hear his remarks.

"Your brothers, I believe you said their names are Silas and William. Do they have any money? I mean did your father leave them enough money to, say, come to Virginia and start a little spread of their own?"

"My brothers want to go to Granville."

"Why Granville?"

"We are free men, Miss Polly. The way this cotton business is affecting men's mind is not good for half-breeds like us. Things are going to get a lot worse for people of color. We got to take what we have and make it work for us now. We don't know what's going to happen down the road."

"I hear you saying 'we'. Does that mean you are going to join your brothers?"

Sherrod knew he had told her more than he had intended to and need not take it any further. "I appreciate your interest," he said and stood up. "Dad is gone. He put a lot of good energy into raising me. I'd better start using it."

"I don't blame you for not trusting me," she said sarcastically. "I am white—"

"Stop it," he said, losing sight of the fact that she was his Mistress. "My decision has to do with the nature of my position here, not color."

"Okay," she said. "Next month you won't be my servant. Are we going to continue our relationship?"

He was surprised by her question. "I don't know."

She saw through his hesitancy. "Are you going to continue to have a relationship with Cato, Eatoe, and Mingus?" He didn't answer her. She continued. "What about Martha, Lillian, and Lena . . . Esther and Mamie?" Her voice broke and tears came to her eyes.

He saw that she was upset. "I am not trying to exclude you. I have a different relationship with the others . . . I—"

She didn't let him finish. "All this rubbish about everyone being a human being is a trick you use to get the slaves to do what you want, ain't it?"

"It's not just you that I have to consider; it's your dad, and your mom. Then there is Master Robert. You are a package, Miss Polly."

"I'm a human being, Sherrod, and I resent you trying to ignore that."

"Yes Miss Polly," he said, not quite knowing how not to fight with her.

Hesitating, she rose from her seat and started towards the door. With her hands on the latch, she said to him without turning around, "Take your dusty butt and get off my porch."

He wanted to apologize, but he knew not to. She went into the house and closed the door. He hurried down the steps across the yard to the forest where he sat and cried and cried and cried.

"Nobody said it would be easy," he heard a voice say.

He hurriedly wiped his eyes and blew his nose.

"Well, are you going to ask me to sit down?"

"Sure," Sherrod said, and made a space next to him on the grass.

Thomas sat with his back leaning against the tree.

"What are you doing here?" he asked Thomas, trying to pull himself together.

"You ran out of the house when I finished telling you about your dad, and you didn't sleep in your room last night, 'cause I checked."

"I slept in the woods. I went to work from there."

"Your dad asked me to give you this Sherrod," he said and gave him a worn weather-beaten book. "It's some notes that your dad kept for you. He said you were the most ambitious out of his three sons and that there will be many trials and many crossroads that you would come to. If you are to accomplish all that you have the capacity to accomplish, you must learn to take constructive criticism." Thomas then stood up. "I don't think I will be coming to Virgilina anymore. This is goodbye."

Sherrod stood and hugged him, fighting to hold back the tears.

"Things are also changing in the hills, Sherrod. A younger group with different views than your dad's and mine are taking over. They are for living in isolation, depending only on themselves for discovery and industry. Those who oppose and are still young enough like Silas Jr and William are moving on."

Sherrod and his dad's friend stared at each other and hugged again. For a moment, they each hung on to the past. They separated, and before starting to leave, Thomas said, "You are a half-breed who knows very little about your heritage. Make your own, Sherrod. Show these Southern white crackers what love and knowledge can do. Show them without denying yourself a relationship with them. Because, if you do that, you will cut yourself off from your father and the experiences that you need to help you accomplish your goal."

Sherrod sat in the woods long after Thomas had left him. When it was almost dark, he went back to Mary Polly's house and knocked on the door.

"Miss Polly . . . Miss Polly," he called.

"She will be right out," Mamie said, sticking her head out the door.

"Thanks for the kind words earlier; they helped," he said.

"Okay," she said, and disappeared with the sound of Mary Polly's footsteps approaching.

Mary Polly came to the hallway where he was standing.

"Would you mind giving your secret friend a ride to the beginning of Master Jesse's path?"

She stared at him for a moment. She didn't know what to say. Conflict stirred inside, a quiet ambivalence with a charge of excitement attached to it.

"Meet me down the path," she finally said. "I can ask Cato to hitch the team."

He walked half way to the creek before he heard the horses. His heart started to beat fast when he saw her. He was at a loss for words and was sorry he had asked her to come.

She was wearing a big black cotton shawl with a hood that covered her head and part of her face.

"Are you cold?" he asked and laughed.

"Get in," she said, and he did. Instead of them taking the usual path to the creek, she turned the horses and cut across the field into some tall weeds near the line that divided the orchard from the cotton. "You and I seem to always be at odds with each other," she said in the way of an explanation. "I want to see if we can't get to the root of the problem."

The moon was full, it was late August, and there appeared to be hundreds of stars in the sky. Sherrod stood up and looked as he rode. "Wow, it's something out here."

"My favorite spot," she said. "Most people don't know that the land is a triangle of some spots. This is one of those spots. I discovered it when I was fifteen."

He turned to her and without rhyme or reason asked, "Were you alone, when you discovered it?"

She giggled. "Let's just say Robert doesn't know about it." She stopped the horses, and he helped her down.

"You were right about me this morning," he said. "I never think of myself as choosing one race of people over another, but you forced me to see how I was doing that and—"

She put her finger to his lips and whispered, "What's done, is done."

He took her hand and held it. It was light and warm and little. He smiled and wondered what he would do if she were his. Then, almost as if she had read his mind, she said, "Wouldn't it be fun if we were fifteen, standing here this way?"

He turned to her, and she looked up at him with a fixed gaze that said all the things he needed to hear. He touched her hand unmindful of all that he had said to himself about being cautious. His heart started to pound. He took the hood of her shawl with the intention of laying it away from her face, but when he touched it, it fell to the ground and she stood there naked before him.

"All you have to do is say no," he said as he pulled her to him.

Heat rose from the bottom of his feet and engulfed him. At that moment, he knew he had to have this woman, no matter what. They embraced and kissed, again and again. She gently helped him out of his clothes. They came together, face to face, with the moon shining down on them, sharing their secret.

When it was done, he rolled over on his back openly naked for her to see. "I am your secret friend," he said and smiled. She started to cry, and he embraced her. "Don't be afraid, Mary Polly Cole. You are woman, and I am man. You have given me one of life's gifts; I will never abuse it. You are still Miss Polly, and I am your indentured servant with a lot of work to do tomorrow."

With that said, he rose to his feet and put on his clothes. She watched him until he was done. He then helped her to her feet, kissed her on the forehead, and wrapped her in her shawl. She hugged him. They climbed aboard the carriage and rode to the edge of her daddy's forest basking in their newfound feelings.

"I have never had an affair since I have been married," she said.

"Neither have I," he smiled teasingly, kissed her quickly, jumped from the carriage, and ran into the forest.

Mary Polly sat quietly long after Sherrod scampered off. Her thoughts were on Robert. How pathetic it was that he and she had to play the game of marriage to accomplish the things they both wanted. She made a mental note to drop him a letter letting him know that she thought he should stay in England for at least another year to make sure the business was secure before he returned.

From the beginning of the marriage, she had made it clear that she wanted no part of him physically. Unfortunately, he had taken that as a challenge to his manhood and pursued her passionately. No rejection or embarrassment dissuaded him. Finally, she decided the only way to clarify their reasons for being together was to meet his passion with passion of her own. She waited two days before she was able to set her plan into motion.

It was Thanksgiving, and she and Robert had returned home from Big Mary's feast, where he had been pampered and bragged on until Mary Polly and his mother, Lavonia, had turned their conversation out and started to chat privately with Jesse who was the only other person at the table. Robert hadn't minded having Big Mary to himself. She had cooked all of his favorite foods, and in his mind no other person at the table could equal him in knowledge or looks.

He had had an occasion to meet George Washington when he was a little boy living in the house of his father. The great General had come to confer with his dad. He had been awestruck by George Washington's appearance, and in his adult life, when Jesse saw fit to give him some responsibility and money to equal his task, he began to send to England for his clothes. His velvet pants, silk tunics, and ruffled shirts rivaled Georges'. In Robert's mind, the outfits were symbols of brilliance. He thought himself better looking than George Washington; of course, his long shiny blond hair, which he washed and brushed daily, tied back with a velvet cord, was of a much finer texture than Washington's hair or his wigs.

At night, he wore a flannel nightshirt, as did most of the men of means in Virgilina. He slept alone because Mary Polly had made it clear from the beginning, when at the insistence of Big Mary he had asked her to marry him, that they would have separate beds. The same room but separate beds. She slept in the large feathered bed, while he slept on the oversized wooden couch that he fluffed with pillows and imported linen sheets that he hid underneath her bed during the day.

After months of trying to sneak into her bed during the first year of their marriage, he took to finding other ways to gain her favor. He gave her presents, decorated her house, and made it a showplace with imported utensils and fine linens from England. He even built her a dugout wine cellar beneath the floor in the living room.

Mary Polly let him know how much she appreciated all that he was doing by making sure that Esther and Mamie kept his clothes and food in the manner that he wanted. Her attitude towards him was warm and happy, and occasionally she would give him a sisterly hug.

After the Thanksgiving meal at Big Mary's, however, he was feeling special, and he got to thinking that it was time that he exercised his rights with Mary Polly even if he had to do it by force.

He loathed the way she played and nursed the animals. And, most of all, how she insisted on bringing Niggers into his house, eating and sleeping like they were family.

He hated to admit it, but his wife was just a common farmwoman. At least Big Mary could turn a phrase and pique one's interest with thought and humor. All Mary Polly had was looks and, like any other woman, the ability to bring softness to a man when he craved it.

All the way home from Cole Manor, he had wanted to tell her to go home and put on that long white gown he had bought for her. But the ride came and went, and he said nothing. Finally, after Mary Polly checked the house and made sure everything and everyone was in its place, she retired to her room and went to bed. Robert pretended to sit up and read for a while, but his plan was to wait until he was sure she was asleep, and then he would crawl into her bed. Before she knew what was happening, he would have his way with her.

This was a holiday night. Robert had had half a bottle of wine to drink, and Mary Polly had a feeling this would be the night he would try something. She figured the pleading, begging, and bribing had stopped; therefore, another plan was in the making.

She wasn't actually tired when she went to bed. She was somewhat bored. She started thinking about her wedding. Preparing for the wedding had been fun. Friends, neighbors, and relatives were all caught up in the excitement of the event, and she liked the attention they gave her. When it was over, it left her wondering what she was going to do with the part of the farm that she had received as a wedding present.

She didn't want to duplicate what her dad was doing, and she didn't want a situation where Robert felt he had to have a say in what was happening to her family's land. What she wanted was to make lots of money. Money would give her permission to govern her own affairs. Every waking moment she spent thinking about her future and what she could do to make enough money to insure the life that she wanted.

That night, Robert mistook her stillness of thought for sleep. He quietly came into the room, took off his clothes, and slipped into his nightshirt. Mary Polly had prepared his bed as she often did when she turned in before him. He tiptoed around the room, finally arriving at her bedside. When she heard him coming, she closed her eyes.

He eased the covers back and slipped in beside her. When she was sure that he was in, she rolled over on top of him and pinned him to the bed. She kissed his face and mouth, all the while running her hands through his hair. Stunned by her aggressiveness, he pushed her aside and scrambled from the bed. He caught his foot in the sheet went tumbling to the floor.

Without a stitch of clothes on, Mary Polly bounced out of bed and frantically grabbed the front of his nightshirt and tore it from his body. He tried to push her away, but she kept coming. Finally, he grabbed both her wrists and held her, screaming, "*What is wrong with you?*"

She looked at him wide-eyed without expression. "I thought you wanted me."

He let go of her arms. "I thought I did too," he said. He grabbed hold of his torn shirt and went off to his couch, angry.

Mary Polly returned to her bed chuckling to herself. *Man want to take He don't want to give.* She chuckled some more and had to put her hand over her mouth to keep from laughing aloud.

Thinking about Robert staying in England calmed her. She smiled, said goodbye to a husband that never was, pulled the reigns gently, and started for home, the taste of Sherrod still on her lips.

Sherrod was feeling good about himself as he rushed through the forest. *Why not*, he thought. *I have worked hard, been respectful. My reward is just. She is a strong woman. She knows her own mind. Who am I to quibble with that?* He giggled gleefully, and then his mind turned to his father and sadness overwhelmed his feelings of well-being. His steps slowed as he crossed the yard to his room. The moon hid its face behind the clouds. *A fitting end to a long day*, he thought. He went inside Mary Polly's father's house and closed the door.

BRYANT ACRES CHAPTER VIII

I'm a Man . . . a Free Man

On the last night of Sherrod's servitude to the Cole Family, he met Mary Polly at the tip of the triangle in the woods. Sounds of the wedding were still ringing in his ears. The night's festivities lingered in his mind. He was sure he drank a bottle of wine, counting the numerous toasts he had been called on to make. His body swayed to the beat of the music as he danced with all the women, and the rhythm of their movements still lingered in his feet.

He chuckled when he thought about old Mrs. Shane and how she stared into his eyes as they danced. Then, as if something or someone had taken hold of her, she raised the front of her skirt above her ankles and slipped into a trance-like state with hip movements that started slow and gradually moved into a gyrating frenzy unequaled by any emulations tried by the younger women.

His thoughts touched slightly on Esther, how she and Lavonia's slave, Henry's grandson, had come and garnered all her attention to where she barely spoke to him or anyone else.

Mamie, she looked like a little doll. She was wearing the dress he had bought her as a going-away present. She pranced around the adults making sure they knew where the dress came from.

The grooms, Mingus, Cato, and Eatoe had hugged him numerous times, thanked him for restoring their faith and helping them believe in themselves enough to want a family.

Big Mary and Jesse sat on Mary Polly's porch while Mary Polly stood on the fringes of the camp and watched the goings-on. From time to time, he would catch Mary Polly out of the corner of his eye, watching him dance.

Old Tisha was also watching him. He hadn't had much contact with her, but he admired what she had been able to do with Esther and Mamie. She was clearly their grandmother. Her pride showed in the way she communicated with them and with Miss Polly about them.

When Sherrod was done processing the events of the night, he began to hum, whistle a tune.

"I am . . . I am . . .

I'm a man . . . an . . . an

A man . . ."

He chuckled with delight liking the feel of his song. He continued whistling and broke into a sharp little two-step that was energetic and timely.

"Don't worry about me . . .

Cause I'm A man . . . an . . . an."

Then, as quickly as it had started, he stopped, let out a deep sign and whispered, "A free man."

When Mary Polly Cole approached the triangle and saw Sherrod's silhouette, in all his splendor dancing and singing, she quietly stopped the horses and turned off the lantern. She watched him a moment, and then she eased from her seat to an area of the grass that lay at the beginning of a clump of trees. She quietly walked behind the trees, careful to stay out of Sherrod's view.

When she was well within his hearing distance, she called out to him.

"Don't set me above

I too am haunted . . .

By color, money,

Lust and love . . .

What ails you

Ails me."

Sherrod liked it that Mary Polly wanted to surprise him. She had immediately gotten his attention. He leaped up from where he was standing and grabbed hold of a tree branch with both hands. He gave himself a hard push and swung to where she was standing, jumped down, and landed at her feet.

"I am going to miss you, Sherrod Bryant," she said. He pulled her to him and kissed her passionately. She pushed him gently. "We need to talk."

He kissed her neck and giggled, "Tonight, we play."

She smiled. "And tomorrow night?

He kissed her. "We talk." He kissed her. "Tomorrow," he continued kissing her, "this free man talk, and talk, and talk, I promise."

She took hold of his shirt and pulled him down on top of her. His past and his future merged, never to be separated again.

BOOK TWO
1803−1814

BRYANT ACRES CHAPTER IX

Virginia isn't Big Enough for Me and Robert

Sherrod left Cole Manor and never went back. Jesse Cole gave him a hundred dollars instead of the seventy-eight dollars that was the going rate for drivers. He also gave him a glowing reference and offered him the job at a higher rate of pay.

Sherrod's plan was to add the one hundred to the hundred his dad had given him, find his brothers, and then, taking the inheritance from their father, set down roots somewhere on the border of Virginia and North Carolina.

He was satisfied that he had done all he could do for Jesse. He was satisfied with his relationships with the slaves in the camp. The teams had done everything he had asked of them. In turn, they had prospered and bonded as individuals and as a family community. Where there had been hopelessness and despair, he left hope and faith. Where there had been wastefulness and abuse, he left productivity and caring. Self-esteem and pride of self took hold. Limitations that slavery paced on those living in the camp became less of an obstacle. They knew Mary Polly would never cross Sherrod because she loved him. That was their secret and their insurance against mistreatment.

The wedding was the pinnacle for them and for him. Leaving was a natural course for all of them because they had planned for it. They had had their experience together, and it was integrated in their minds as part of their individual history. Mary Polly, however, was at a loss as to how she was going to continue the relationship

When Sherrod read the book Thomas Cole had brought from his father, he found a note from his brother, William, folded among the pages. The note asked Sherrod to meet him and Silas twenty miles northeast of Virgilina on the road to North Carolina. William wrote that they would be there camping the first two weeks of September and he hoped Sherrod would meet them there.

Sherrod was excited about meeting his brothers. He had not seen them in six months, and it was the first time ever outside of the hills, without a father to connect them, that they would meet as a family.

He had spoken to Mary Polly and asked her about the area. She had previously told him she had relatives living along the border and that she had visited her Uncle Ruben several times during her growing up years. The uncle's son, Cousin Ruben, lived in proximity to where he was to meet William and Silas.

Mary Polly was extremely sad when Sherrod told her what his plans were. Common sense told her it was dangerous for him to live near her. They had been careless the night of the wedding. What if someone had stumbled upon them at the edge of the triangle, giving in to their passion rather than waiting until they were further secluded and out of sight like that first night? Neither one of them could risk or afford being exposed.

Cousin Ruben knew of Mary Polly's success with cotton. Nearly everyone in the State of Virginia knew. Sherrod had helped Cole Manor establish itself as the fastest growing cotton plantation with Mary Polly's first crop. They were so successful Jesse went out and bought his own cotton gin. He was one of the first men in the area to own a cotton gin. Mingus, Cato, and Eatoe's productivity had yet to be equaled. Their story of beginnings was fast becoming Virginia folklore.

Mary Polly had attached a note to Sherrod's references; it was addressed to Cousin Ruben. She explained who Sherrod and his brothers were, and she told Ruben she would be visiting his area in a month or so. If he were planning on adding cotton to his crop, she would be glad to spend some time with him and his wife, Jenny, to help them get started.

Ruben was surprised and pleased to receive Mary Polly's note. He had been contemplating cotton. With the help of Mary Polly, and the three Bryant brothers, he would be able to make his dream a reality.

When Sherrod said goodbye to Mary Polly and set out to meet his brothers, he had no intentions of working for anyone. Once he met his brothers, however, they discussed their options, and it was decided that working for Ruben a year or two would increase their opportunities.

Sherrod had lived on his own, and it was hard to fall back into the routine of listening to William and Silas because they were older. But the fact that they only had six hundred dollars between them, and Ruben had offered to give them jobs, made it easier.

Ruben's farm was small compared to Cole Manor. He had two hundred acres of hard ground. He didn't own any slaves and had only two farm hands before William, Silas, and Sherrod showed up. Ruben hired William, Silas, and Sherrod for room and board plus ten dollars a month if the crop of cotton was successful and five dollars if it failed.

The way Sherrod saw it, a hundred twenty dollars a year times four came to four hundred eighty dollars, added to the two hundred he already had, would give him six hundred eighty dollars—enough to purchase a piece of land, build a house, and buy seeds and fertilizer. He never thought once that the crop would fail and his pay cut in half. His dream, he felt, would come true, and his brothers were in agreement.

That first winter was a hard one. The ground was frozen, so they could do very little. Then, spring came and they planted the first crop of cotton, as they did the year after that and the year after that. Both William and Silas knew about planting and farming, but they didn't know anything about cotton so they left the overseeing to Sherrod.

For three years, they planted and raised cotton for Ruben and his wife. Ruben worked closely with the brothers. He had six children, and he taught them to depend on the Bryant brothers the same as they did him and their mother. The added treat was Mary Polly's visits. She came every other month bringing baskets of food and news from Virginia.

Mingus, Eatoe, or Cato drove Mary Polly when she came. Their visits gave William and Silas an opportunity to get to know what Sherrod's life had been like at Cole Manor. Sherrod told them about his relationship with Mary Polly. They liked her and were close-mouthed and protective of the relationship

Many times, when Mary Polly was around, William or Silas would beckon Ruben, Mingus, Cato, and Eatoe to the field with one problem or the other so that Mary Polly and Sherrod could be together when Ruben's wife and children were out planting the garden.

Sitting on Ruben's porch talking to Mary Polly was a little strange for Sherrod at first, but Mary Polly scouted the area and found a place where they could have some private time. Once that happened, everything came together for them.

The years came and went. Before long, the brothers were celebrating harvesting time in the fall of 1805. Mary Polly came to tell Sherrod that her husband was coming home. The business had been very successful in England. His father had died, and he longed to see his mother and Cole Manor.

"Does he long to see you?" Sherrod asked. He was jealous.

"And me too," she said, not looking at him. She looked worried. He knew there was more to the story.

"Go on," he said. "Let me hear the rest. There is more, isn't there?"

She stood up, turned with her back facing him, and said, "Robert has been very successful, and Daddy is insisting that I give him a chance."

"How do you feel about it?"

"You have to understand the South, Sherrod," she said, pleading for his understanding. "Regardless of how successful I am, there is no respect or status for a woman without a man."

Sherrod tried not to show his hurt. "Then what's the problem?" he asked her. "You have a husband, and he is on his way home with tons of money and all kinds of needs."

She turned and faced him. "You don't think I am choosing him over you, do you?"

"Frankly, I don't know what to think. I have never known what to think about us. You are there and I was there and—"

She put her finger to his lips and stopped him, as was her habit. "You are my secret friend, Sherrod . . . forever and ever. I aim to be with you always."

He took her in his arms, looked into her eyes, and stroked her face. "I am going to Kentucky," he said. "I was going to wait till the end of the year. Now, I think I will leave as soon as the crop is sold."

"Why Kentucky?"

"Some more Coles," he laughed sarcastically. "Ruben said Kentucky is beautiful. He said land is cheap. William and Silas are anxious to move on."

"Are you ready to move on?"

"I am now," he replied. "Virginia isn't big enough for me and Robert."

She grabbed hold of his shirt and held on. "Daddy is a powerful persuasive redneck Southerner, Sherrod." She tightened her hold on him, buried her face in his chest. "You are my secret friend; don't ever doubt it," she whispered.

"I know," he said in a quiet voice.

In his head, he was thinking, *Take the warning, Sherrod Bryant. Daddy Jesse knows his little girl is running off the farm for a reason. Don't help him guess that you're the reason.*

"Cousin Ruben has some friends involved in building a Quaker church. They are in the logging stage and need a few extra hands. I am going to give up cotton and exchange it for raising trees and handling logs. Ruben is recommending me. He will know where I am. I plan to keep in touch with him."

"My brother, Joel, lives in Kentucky. You may see me sooner than you think, Sherrod Bryant," she said, as she turned and walked away from him.

"Send Mingus for the horses," he called after her.

He was feeling frustrated, but he knew better than to feed his discontent. Their lives were different. She had accepted that, and he had better. She was married, her husband was coming home, and that was that.

He took a deep breath and sighed. "Damn, I hate to give her up. She is part of the adventure." He took another deep breath and followed her inside.

The week that he was to leave had finally arrived. It was the night before, and he was cleaning out the room he shared with his brothers. When the cleaning was all done, he looked in his carry-all bag to make sure he had his references from Jesse and Ruben. Inside the slip where he kept them, he found an extra sheet of paper.

He unfolded the sheet and learned that it was a Bill of Sale for the three Bay horses that Mary Polly had loaned him. The bill was in his name, and it was marked paid, signed "Mary Polly/(S.F.)," which he knew to mean secret friend.

In a gesture of joy, he threw the bill up in the air and caught it as it floated towards him. He looked at it again and kissed it. How they were going to travel had been a worry to him. Now the problem of getting jobs along the route in exchange for money to replace the price of horses could be eliminated.

He called his brothers in and told them about the gift. Each in turn wished Mary Polly well. They told how they had come to trust and appreciate her and how her caring for Sherrod and for them had helped them adjust to their new surroundings. They also said they were sorry she was not going to continue to be in their lives.

Sherrod didn't tell them that her husband had returned. He felt it was none of their business, and he chose not to think or talk about it.

At times during the night, he wondered if Ruben was as oblivious to Mary Polly's involvement with him as he appeared to be. He mulled the question over in his mind and finally decided that the idea of his having the nerve to carry on with Mary Polly while living under Ruben's roof was too unthinkable for Ruben to consider. While he had never detected prejudice in Ruben, he decided that it was prejudice that kept Ruben from knowing about Mary Polly and him.

Ruben's kids knew, because once while they were all sitting on the porch watching Ruben's wife freeze ice cream, Leonadus, who was three years old, said to Mary Polly who was holding him, "Do you like me as much as you do Sherrod?"

Mary Polly laughed and Ruben turned beet red and tried to cover his feelings by saying, "Leonadus, what is getting into you?"

Ruben's wife giggled. "He has a crush on Mary Polly. He just wants to make sure she is all his."

Everyone laughed. Leonadus hugged Mary Polly and everyone except Sherrod and Mary Polly went back to the business of freezing ice cream. Sherrod watched Mary Polly from the corner of his eyes, and when he thought no one was looking, he winked his eye at her.

He smiled and realized how much he was going to miss her.

Leaving Ruben was not as hard as the brothers had expected. They had talked and planned so long they were ready to get on with it. Ruben thanked them for all they had done. His productivity had doubled in the three-and-half years they had lived with him, and he was pleased.

Before they went to Kentucky, they went over to Granville. They weren't sure if they would ever return to that part of the South. Even though they hadn't had many dealings with the town, they chose Granville to say goodbye to, rather than to go back to their home colony in the hills and risk kindling the sadness that the death of their father had created. They felt they knew Granville from the stories they had heard from the elders when they were children.

As soon as they arrived in Granville, William and Silas found a campsite outside of town and prepared it for the layover while Sherrod took the horses in to be shoed at the blacksmith.

The blacksmith was like the town newspaper. He kept up with current events as well as the goings and comings of visitors and townspeople. In a brief conversation with the blacksmith's helper, Sherrod learned that there was a new minister in town. Ordinarily, this would mean nothing to him, but the minister was black and the only blacks that Sherrod had come in contact with were the slaves at Cole Manor.

The helper had mistaken Sherrod for the noted Rev. John Chavis. When he said he wasn't, the helper assured him that the mistaken identity was a compliment. Sherrod told him he would accept it as such, paid the helper, and set out to see who this Rev. Chavis was.

There had been a fellowship church in the hills where he came from. The elders, his father, Thomas Cole, Mr. White, Mr. Johnson, had all taken turns reading the Bible and interpreting its lessons for people who attended. A formal church with an African-American preacher was something he had never experienced, and he was curious to see what this free black man had to offer.

He ran to the campsite and told his brothers what he had heard at the blacksmith's shop. They agreed that a free black preacher was different all right, but they weren't much interested in getting into town business.

Sherrod searched the town until he found the local church. It was a one-room, newly built Presbyterian church that had a large welcome sign on the door. Sherrod approached carefully so as not to make a wrong step. When he got to the door, he quietly opened it and looked inside.

Two men, one white and the other black, were sitting on a bench down in front, talking. The men turned and looked in his direction when they heard the sound of the door. He felt foolish for intruding.

"Can we help you?" the white man, whom he assumed was the head minister, said getting up from his seat and coming towards him.

"Please," Sherrod said waving him back to his seat. "I am intruding. I heard there was a Rev. John Chavis in here and I—"

"I am John Chavis," the black man said. "Do I know you?"

"Don't let me interrupt you, please," Sherrod apologized again.

"Obviously your seeing John is important," the white man said, and started towards the back of the church.

"John, I will be back here. Call me when you're finished."

Rev. Chavis studied Sherrod's face for a moment. Neither man said a word. Sherrod liked to think that intellectually he was inferior to no man, white, Indian, or black; at that moment, he wasn't sure.

When he was satisfied that he didn't know Sherrod, John said, "For a brief second, I thought we were classmates at Princeton. You have any relatives up around Delaware? There were four Indians attending the university when I was there."

Sherrod smiled. At least Rev. Chavis regarded him as a man of learning. "I am not aware of any of my relatives being up in that neck of the woods," he said, extending his hand and allowing a smile to come over his face.

Chavis took Sherrod's hand in his and gave it a hearty handshake. Sherrod felt his grip. The grip was strong and the hand soft. He liked the feel of this person, his warmth, the way he looked him in the eye when he spoke, the way he talked and dressed.

"I am not one for going to church," Sherrod said. "I saw this new church and read the welcome sign. I thought I would see what it was all about. You being a black minister and me being curious."

Chavis laughed, put his arm around Sherrod's shoulders, and steered him towards the front door. "You new in town?"

"Passing through."

"Too bad. I could use a trustworthy young fellow like you. I aim to build a school here in Granville." Chavis then leaned closer to him and said in a voice that was barely audible, "You and I are free men. Some of our people are not as fortunate. They need us to educate them. We must lead the way." Then, as if he hadn't said those words, he raised his voice so the white man who was standing at the other end of the church could hear. "Come to service on Sunday. I promise I will give you something to think about as you travel."

Sherrod promised that he would see him on Sunday and left to join his brothers, feeling somewhat awestruck by Chavis. His manner, the way he spoke and his self-assurance, was something to behold. He wondered if Chavis lived in town or if he was visiting with hopes of settling in Granville.

He walked, and he thought. When he passed the general store, he saw a newspaper, and he stopped and bought one. The paper had an article on the new church and Rev. John Chavis, just as he thought it would. He found a hitching post, leaned against it, and read.

"The esteemed Rev. John Chavis, an African-American free man will be helping good white Presbyterians and free Christians celebrate the opening of the new Granville Presbyterian Church on Sunday, October 26, 1905, at 10:00 a.m. Rev. Chavis speaks three languages—English, Greek, and Latin. He attended Princeton and Lee University. He was a private student of Dr. Whiterspoon, President of Princeton University.

"Dr. Whiterspoon is responsible for Rev. Chavis' expertise in rhetoric and the classics. He is a powerful preacher; his sermons are forceful, and free of Negroisms. Come one, and all. No slaves allowed."

Sherrod folded the newspaper and put it under his arm. He had never met a college-educated black before, and he felt obliged to at least hear what Chavis had to say. He ran and told his brothers that he wanted to stay in town a few more days. They were annoyed because it would mean extra expense that they hadn't planned on. Sherrod wanted to remind them of the gift of horses but instead agreed to pay for the extra expenses and promised he would be ready to leave right after the service on Sunday. The brothers appreciated his enthusiasm, but felt it was his thing, and they wouldn't even do as much as read the article.

Sherrod was the only person of color in the congregation that Sunday. The power of John Chavis' sermon rekindled Sherrod's urge to build and to nurture as he had done in the slave camp at Mary Polly's. The interest that Chavis displayed in the lively way he presented the public with questions on slave issues was equal to the presentations made by town leaders he had seen and heard in and about Virginia.

The proposal that the sermon supported was that importing Africans for profit be stopped. It was suggested that the influx of people being brought to this country against their will was influencing public policy and causing social ills that threatened to put a blight on the reputation of the country. The issue, as Rev. Chavis saw it, was whether or not importing slaves was going to continue or be banned.

Sherrod had heard much talk about the importation of slaves. He knew that Chavis' topic was one of the most controversial among clergies of varied denominations, as well as clergies of Presbyterian churches and their congregations throughout the South. Some denominations took stands for slavery, others against it. Church congregations and denominations at large were sometimes at odds with each other. Some denominations split and branched off.

Whatever the case, a year later, Sherrod read that the importation of slaves was abolished. Sherrod was pleased that Rev. Chavis was on the right side of the issue and worthy of his praise.

That Sunday morning, in Granville, Sherrod stayed until all of the others had left the church. Chavis seemed pleased when he saw his him waiting. He came over and Sherrod greeted him. "I want to wish you Godspeed, before I take off."

Chavis smiled. "I don't know your name, and I will probably never see you again." He moved closer to Sherrod, stared him in the eye as he had done the first time they met, and said, "But you are my brother. I want you to remember that education and faith in God are tools for building and promoting credibility. Tell your children, their children, and their children's children that there is a human thread that equalizes us all as human beings and that none of us is free until all are free."

Sherrod nodded his head in agreement and they hugged, held on to each other for a moment, and then parted, Chavis going inside and Sherrod walking away, neither of them looking back or saying a word.

Sherrod was deep in thought when he reached the path to the campsite. His brothers were at the edge of the woods waiting for him.

They had collected and packed his belongings and were ready to go. As soon as they saw him, they could tell he was deep inside himself.

"Lighten up, Little Brother," they teased. "We have men's business to take care of." He quietly climbed onto his horse. He wished he could afford to spend some time with Chavis. He envisioned a partnership and smiled. *Fathers come in different bodies, no matter the kinship*, he said to himself. And, for the first time since his dad died, he knew he was going to make it.

"Getty up," he said to his horse, dug his heels into its sides, and off they galloped. He went past his brothers and called to them as he went by, "My will is to pass and dare you two to catch up."

His brothers looked at each other, and each in turn tore after him in a cloud of Sherrod's dust.

BRYANT ACRES CHAPTER X

There Were Twelve Colored Residents in Nashville; I Made Thirteen

Most of the people who traveled from Virginia, the East, or South to Kentucky or Tennessee, traveled by water following the Ohio River into the Tennessee and then the Cumberland River.

Some came on foot following the Cumberland Gap, while others backpacked and rode horses over the mountains. Utilizing animal paths, these backpackers and hikers made their own trails.

Sherrod, William, and Silas chose backpacking and riding horses because they were used to the hills and they liked camping. They experienced their mode of travel like a refresher course reminiscent of childhood learning. They fished, hunted, and slept in the wild, careful to stay away from other settlements and camps that they came upon.

In the paper that Sherrod had picked up in Granville, there was some information about a gift of six hundred acres of land that the government had previously given to each head of household who moved from Virginia and North Carolina and settled in Tennessee.

The charitable nature of the government's land grants appealed to Sherrod and his brothers, but their reasons varied. Sherrod was suspicious. He felt that there had to have been an obligation, other than transplanting a family, connected to the land grant. He declared if he had been around at the time he would not have taken any part of free land.

His brothers, on the other hand, used the land grant issue to sway Sherrod to Tennessee rather than going to Kentucky. They asked him to look at the prospects of a place where the government had to bribe people to move to.

Sherrod thought about it and compared Tennessee to Cole Manor and the cotton gin. He could see how Cole Manor and Tennessee were at the beginning stages of new development. The opportunities were limitless. The open space, new resources, and sparse habitation would support growth and autonomy.

However, he was careful to note that the government's negative acts towards people of color did not lend itself to them believing that there would be any charity coming their way from the government or anyone else. To expose themselves to such thoughts would be an act of sabotage against any future plans they might have.

William and Silas reluctantly agreed that the only way they were going to achieve their goals was to work hard so they could buy land and anything else they desired or needed. With these thoughts in mind, they changed their minds about Kentucky and set their course for Tennessee.

Sherrod loved his brothers, but he felt that at times talking to them was as painful as an aching tooth. They thought that because they were older they should make all the decisions. He resented the way they said they were "humoring him" when he came up with an idea or a plan. If and when they accepted one of his suggestions, he had to make it seem as if it was their idea.

He thought about their many discussions along the trail and decided that once they reached Tennessee, he was going to part ways. He wasn't his brothers' keeper. They were not ambitious and had visions the size of a grape pit.

He thought as he rode, itemized his skills, and recounted the many things he could do to earn money. The sum he carried was less than he had started out with. The expense of shoeing and boarding the horses and replacing supplies the three of them had used those extra days in Granville had cost him at least ten dollars.

The closer he got to Tennessee, the more he thought about how he was going to spend his first few days.

First, he was going to take a long hot bath and get a hot meal with all his favorites: corn, fish, and spoon bread with stewed apples. Then, he was going to find lodging where he could stay at least a week. Maybe get a half pint of brandy to take to this room and help him rest. The way he had figured it, the rate of service in Tennessee would be the same as it was in Virginia and North Carolina, inasmuch as the law fixed the rates.

The night before, when they stopped to sleep on the trail, he had taken a charred piece of bark from the fire and put it to the smooth shaved piece of log he had worked on. He used the charred piece to write with and the shaved piece to write his figures on.

Dinner	.25
Breakfast	.20

Lodging	.08½
Horse with corn, oats	.33½
and fodder	
	.87 a day
EXTRAS:	
½ pint whiskey	.12½
or brandy	
Bath	.25
Haircut	.25
plus	.62½

He looked at his figures and thought about ways he could earn ten dollars and a week to get himself started. It came to him. He and his brothers had been hunting and trapping since they were children. Why not hunt and trap for skins? Wolf scalps would bring at least two dollars and fifty cents. Deerskins would bring in fifty cents and coonskins, twenty-five cents.

As he thought about it some more, he got excited. "That's it," he said out loud. "That's it," he repeated in an even louder voice. His brothers, who were sleeping nearby, stirred. "Fellows," he called.

William propped himself up to make sure everything was okay. When he was satisfied it was, he said, "It's your watch, Sherrod. Can't you be a little quieter?"

"I found a way to keep us from spending our earnings," Sherrod blurted out.

"In the morning," William mumbled and went back to his sleeping.

Sherrod looked through the trees at the sky and realized the day was starting to break. He had been up all night. He crawled over and tapped Silas on the foot. "It's time for your watch," he said.

Silas moved his foot out of the way. "Keep thinking, Brother," he said. "And make it quiet thinking, real quiet."

"Let the boy get some sleep, Silas," William mumbled. "We should reach the state line some time tomorrow."

Silas stretched, grabbed his rifle, and pulled himself to a sitting position.

Sherrod rolled over on his side, and it appeared that William and Silas woke him up as soon as he dropped off. But he knew that wasn't the case, because coffee was boiling and grits were made.

Sherrod, William, and Silas were on the last leg of their trip. A few hours after breakfast, they crossed the Smoky Mountains into Tennessee and the Chilhowie Mountains, which led them to the Little Tennessee onto the banks of the Tennessee River. The beauty of it all overwhelmed them. They pitched camp and spent the next week hunting and trapping.

Satisfied with themselves, they set out along the bank of the Tennessee River until the Cumberland Mountains came into view. There, they left the river and forged Southwest through Virgin Falls Forest and on into Readyville and Murfreesboro.

Sherrod had talked his brothers out of stopping in other small Tennessee towns that they passed. He had heard Ruben and Jenny talk about Murfreesboro. One of her brothers had moved there from Kentucky when it was still Davidson County and didn't have a general store or a county government. Listening to her speak about Murfreesboro had helped Sherrod determine that the area was organized. It was a real town. The settlers who moved to the area from Virginia and North Carolina were civic-minded and they, like Sherrod, had come to make a stable home for themselves and their families.

Later on, when Sherrod had been around a while, he learned that prior to 1780, the Choctaws, Chickasaws, and Cherokees had ruled the county. Then, in 1794, General Robertson and his expedition had defeated the Indians and that few Indian troubles had occurred after the defeat.

The general assembly passed an act that organized the county in 1803 and named it Rutherford County. It was named after General Rutherford of North Carolina who had made a reputation fighting the Choctaw, Chickasaw, and Cherokee in the area.

Civil districts determined by geographical boundary lines were organized in 1804. In 1806, the same year that Sherrod and his brothers moved to the area, the head of the family, if not over age, was enrolled into a militia company.

Of course, Sherrod, William, and Silas were not enrolled. They were unmarried free men, and they were not white. Their status had been predetermined long before anyone in the town set eyes on them.

The people of Rutherford County were used to seeing transients traveling through. There were opportunities for casual white laborers. Transient people of color, who were laborers and had no skills or money, in most cases had to indenture themselves the way Sherrod had done in Virginia.

Sherrod, William, and Silas had money, and after much discussion, each decided where he was going to settle. Silas was a barber; he decided to settle out near the ridge where Davidson and Rutherford counties met.

William was basically a farmer; he was closer in age to Silas than he was to Sherrod. Even though he was the oldest, he depended on Silas to help him make decisions. So, when it came time for him to decide, he pooled his money with Silas and together they leased half an acre of land out near Black Fox Spring near where the Cherokees camped.

Sherrod crossed the line into Davidson County and stopped at the edge of Nashville outside the view of traffic and changed into his finest clothes: tight lightweight tan pants, a matching vest and a dark brown sway back coat, clothes that had been taken from Robert Cole's wardrobe and given to him by Mary Polly. The white, high-collar cotton shirt and dark brown fedora were gifts that his father had given him as a going-away present. Silas had cut Sherrod's hair; it could no longer be seen from under his hat.

At the time there were thirteen other free people of color living in Nashville. One such person, Robert Renfro, owned the Black Bob's Tavern and the livery stable, the only inn and livery stable in Nashville. Black Bob's was located at the cross key, on the corner, across from the town square. The inn catered to the leading citizens of Davidson and was considered one of the finest hotels in the South.

Sherrod felt encouraged when he discovered Black Bob's. He had sold his skins and wolf scalps outside of Rutherford County for seventy-five dollars. He would use sixty of those dollars to live in the hotel and pay his living expenses for two months. Sherrod wanted to give himself an opportunity to study Nashville and the people in it.

When he arrived at Black Bob's and asked to register, Robert Renfro was sitting at a table, behind the registrar's desk, working in his books. He had looked up when Sherrod entered and waited for him to speak.

As soon as Sherrod spoke, Renfro stopped what he was doing and came to the front desk. "I will handle this," he said to the desk clerk.

The clerk scampered off and Renfro extended his hand to Sherrod. "Where are you from?"

"Virginia, by way of North Carolina," Sherrod said, shaking Renfro's hand. "Nice place you have here. How old is it?"

"Ten years," the proprietors gleamed. "We never had people other than white to register here."

"I guess I am about to change that," Sherrod said as he picked up the desk pen and wrote his name. When that was done, he reached in his pants pocket and took his money out so Renfro could see he meant business. "How much for two months?"

Renfro laughed. "I like your style."

Sherrod didn't reply. He had mixed feelings about Renfro. There was a subdued kind of arrogance emanating from him that touched Sherrod's competitive nature and made him feel like they were playing some kind of a game.

Renfro took a key from the wall. "I am giving you a room, on the condition that you understand you are in this hotel as an independent. Anything that happens between you and the other guests or townspeople has nothing to do with me."

"How much?"

"Eight dollars for the room. Ten, if you want room and a bath."

Sherrod paid him ten dollars, and Renfro came from behind the desk, picked up his bag, and motioned for the desk clerk to resume his duties. "This way, Sir."

Sherrod followed him upstairs, down a narrow hallway that ran into a room at the end of the hall where a common wall was shared with rooms on both sides of the hall. It was a spacious room, beautifully decorated with a large window that overlooked Main Street and far beyond the clearing of the woods ahead.

As he looked out, his mind raced back to his first night at Cole Manor. He thought about Mary Polly, Mamie, and Esther, how they had stood under the tree giggling that first night. How he had sold himself to get to Nashville. How he was every bit as smart as Black Bob and would someday be recognized in those streets below.

"Would that be all?" he heard Renfro say and realized his bed had been turned back.

"You help a man know that anything is possible," he said, and gave Renfro a dime for his service.

"This is not necessary," Renfro said and put the dime in Sherrod's vest pocket.

Sherrod pushed the dime further in. "Maybe when you get used to me, know me better, you will let me buy you dinner."

"If you are around for that long," Renfro said.

"I will be here. Nashville is my new home."

Renfro smiled, went out the door, and closed it.

Sherrod took off his clothes, folded them neatly, and laid them across the foot of the bed. He heard a knock on the door and crossed to answer it in his underwear.

"Who is it?" he called through the door.

A young female voice replied, "It's Little Doe, Sir. I have a basin of water and a towel for you."

"Set it outside the door. I will get it directly. Thank you." He stayed at the door and listened until he heard her walk away. When he was satisfied that she was gone, he opened the door slightly and stuck his head out, reached for the basin and towel, and pulled them inside. As he carried the basin of water to the table near the window, he thought about what he was doing and where he was and smiled.

"I am not a gentleman farmer yet, Daddy, but I am working on it," he said aloud and proceeded to clean himself up. When he was satisfied with his appearance, he went downstairs.

He didn't feel ready to meet the townspeople, so he crossed the street to Nash General Store for snacks to keep in his room when he got hungry. When he got to the store, it was nearly empty. He saw an elderly white man who he assumed was Mr. Nash, the proprietor, and a young slave man who was single-handedly restocking and cleaning the shelves while Mr. Nash sat and read his paper.

"You the new colored fellow at Black Bob's that everyone is talking about?" the white man spoke without looking at him or interrupting his reading.

Sherrod looked around to see whom the man was talking to. When he didn't see anyone else, he responded, "I don't know," and he proceeded to shop.

The man came and stood next to him. "What can I get you?"

Sherrod picked up a can of peaches and a jug of apple cider. "Is it always this quiet?"

The grocer laughed. "Where are you from?"

"Virginia. I was the driver for Cole Manor."

"Those Coles, any relation to the Coles in Murfreesboro?"

"I can't say if the Murfreesboro Coles are related or not. There are a lot of them. Some in Kentucky, I hear."

"I do say it's a small world. Never got as far as Virginia myself. My folks settled in Kentucky. If I had been born in Virginia or North Carolina, I am told I could have got myself one of them land grant deals that the government gave." He sighed. "Can't help where you are born or who you are born to, ain't that right?"

"That's right, Sir. But I believe a person can pick himself up and make something out of himself, regardless of his start. Like you have done."

The storeowner laughed. "You are a damn smart fellow. I bet you did a lot for them Coles."

"I tried, Sir," Sherrod said.

"Coloreds have to try real hard if they gonna get anywhere in this town. Ain't everybody as lucky as old Black Bob."

Sherrod took out his money and paid for his groceries. As he was leaving, he saw some fresh bread on the counter. "The bread looks real fresh. Your wife make it?"

"Isaac's wife made it, didn't she, Isaac?"

"Yes, Sir, she made it," the young slave man replied without looking up. "She made them ginger cakes too. Really good they is. Everybody say so."

Sherrod reached across and took a ginger cake. "I'll take this and a loaf of bread."

When he stepped out the door into the street, he noticed a group of young slave women giggling and laughing as they watched him from around the side of the livery. He tipped his hat and smiled at them as he crossed the street to the hotel.

The lobby had suddenly gotten busy. Men and women dressed in their finery were going into the dining room for dinner. *One of these days*, he said to himself, and proceeded to his room.

From what he could determine during his short stay, he figured there was a rhythm to Nashville. People moving about town in the early part of the day were basically men doing work business. In the early evening, men were preparing for family time, hassling about doing domestic tasks and any other unfinished business that the workday created. Late evening was for dinner and any form of entertainment the townspeople engaged in.

He had yet to spend a morning in town, but he was almost sure mornings were preparation time. Women came to shop, to talk to the dressmakers and shopkeepers. He thought about the slave women flirting with him outside of the livery and his mind turned to Nancy, his childhood sweetheart.

William and Silas had said she was preparing to leave the hills when they moved away. They weren't sure where she was going. He knew she had wealthy relatives in Virginia and the Carolinas, and he suspected she would end up in one of the two states.

He thought about how he had gone by to tell her goodbye the day he had left the hills. She hid from him, didn't want him to see her upset, her mother said.

Sherrod went inside and took off his clothes. It had been a long day and he was tired. He got into bed and let his thoughts return to Nancy. Her mother had known his purpose for stopping by. She told him where Nancy was and he went out back and found her sitting behind the barn.

"I came to say goodbye," he said to her after peering at her from around the corner with the hopes of surprising her.

"Why?" she asked in a voice that tried not to show concern, the same as she had done when he jumped out at her.

"'Cause I love you," he said. As soon as he did, he wanted to bite his tongue off. The words escaped his lips without forethought or plan. Tears rolled down her cheeks. She didn't move. She just sat there and let the tears flow. He got down on one knee beside her on the grass. He leaned into her. "When you are older I will find you and we will be married," he said in a voice that he hoped would comfort her. "I want my wife and children to have a fine life and a father they respect. Can you understand that?"

She crumpled onto this chest. He held her and let her sob. It was the first time they had ever talked seriously. He was careful not to give in to the passion he was feeling. When the sobbing stopped, he rose to his feet. "Don't you ever let any man steal you away from me," he said, kissed her on the top of the head, and ran into the woods.

He felt lonely thinking about it. *What makes a man make the choices he makes?* he asked himself and yawned. He heard a glass break outside his window. He was too tired and too sleepy to care. He dozed off with thoughts of Nancy fresh in his mind.

Nancy was three years younger than he. She was eighteen when she left the hills. He heard that her father was continuously pursuing young men for her to embrace in matrimony and that her mother thought it best for her to get away from his watchful eye.

The only news Sherrod was sure that Nancy had heard about him was the few tidbits she had coaxed out of Thomas Cole when he returned to the hills from his visits to Cole Manor.

Little did he know that her thoughts were often of him but not in a longing way. She felt warm and giggly when she remembered some of the silly games they played as children . . . tag and run till you drop.

Sherrod forced her to compete and oftentimes pushed her to the limits of her capacity. Like the time he told her to climb a tree. He said if she climbed it, he would climb the one next to it. She climbed to the fifth limb, and he climbed to the seventh limb so he could look down on her.

She had never climbed a tree before and she had no desire to climb one and told him so.

"I never thought you as one of those prissy girls, all helpless and not willing to do for yourself," he yelled at her. "Go home. Go back to your mama. Let her watch over you. We don't like the same things, you and I."

"Okay," she said, and started out of the woods.

"Baby," he called after her and she continued walking. "Big baby," he yelled.

She reached down and picked up a rock and threw it. It hit him in the face. Blood trickled from his forehead.

"What did you do that for?" he cried, and scared her. She ran to him tearing off the tail of her blouse as she ran.

"You shouldn't have called me Baby, Sherrod Bryant. I told you not to call me names," she scolded, as she dabbled at the cut that the rock had left. The rag became blood soaked and red.

"Get some water. I will make a mud pack," he said. She didn't move. She just stood there and watched him. "Get some water, Nancy. I'm bleeding . . . Do you hear? Do you—"

He sat up in the bed, for a moment forgetting where he was. Then he realized he was dreaming and lay back down. The sun was out. He heard people milling about outside and wondered what time it was. He started to get up, thought better of it, and turned over. The next time he opened his eyes, it was night.

BRYANT ACRES CHAPTER XI

Bring Me a Horn of Sweet Berry Brandy

S herrod spent the first week moving about and through the town taking in the sights, listening to people, finding out who was who and what some of the concerns were. He learned that Davidson County was the parent county of Rutherford, Williams, and Wilson and that this section of the state was referred to as Middle Tennessee.

Sherrod knew immediately that he wanted to live in Nashville and work the Rutherford County Line. Rutherford was located almost in the exact center of Middle Tennessee. It was green and beautiful and very appealing to the eye. The soil was either a deep black or brownish red. In some places the ground was covered with stone.

Rutherford's reputation was based on its fertile soil. He knew all that was being said about the soil was true when he put a little of the soil on his tongue and tasted it. He also knew from experience that, with careful husbandry, he could even make the stone-covered ground yield a rich harvest. Since productivity was where his key interest lay, Rutherford was where he needed to work. Besides, Rutherford was more spread out than Davidson County. It didn't have as many inhabitants. It would be to his benefit to include both counties in his plans.

When he looked out across the plains, he didn't see uncultivated land; he saw fields of rye, oats, barley, tobacco, potatoes, hay, peas, and beans. He envisioned breeding fine horses, sheep that yielded wool, and cattle that yielded meat, butter, and cheese.

There were plenty of orchards about. He made a mental note. His land was to have a large orchard that included sweet berry vines and walnut and pecan trees.

He came upon Stones River and saw several operating water-propelled mills. He saw a sign that read "The Cove Mill" and followed the course of the land's clearing until he came to a little farmhouse. Thomas Rucker heard the sound of his horse approaching and came out to the yard.

"Good morning, Sir," Sherrod said. "I am new to this area. I saw your mill back there and I wanted to know a little about it."

"Where you from, Boy?

"Virginia."

"Virginia is a big state."

"Virginia. We had plenty of cotton but no mill, grist, saw, or otherwise."

"There are great natural resources here and about for a man who works hard. That mill out there is seven years old. Louis Anthony and Henry Gilham—I'm sure you saw their pitiful little efforts back there—they built there a couple years ago. What is your interest?"

"Well, I specialize in husbandry. I know about planting, harvesting, breeding, and taking care of animals. I don't know anything 'bout logging and corn grist. I'm anxious to learn."

"You're Indian, aren't you?"

"I'm a hard worker. You know anyone looking for an apprentice?"

"Old Man Donelson might have something for you. Twenty-seven of his men were imprisoned by Indians twenty or so years ago. He forgives Indians by putting them to work. Slave labor is one of his sources, but Indian labor is his preference. Once, I asked him about all those Indians working for him and he said he was learning from them. Go figure."

"Where does this Donelson live, closer to Nashville?

"Over by Mill Creek. Ask anybody in that area; they will know. He's kind of an eccentric old cuss, has a reputation."

Sherrod rode towards Nashville. He followed the same road he had traveled earlier. When he came to the turn off, he stayed on the Davidson and Rutherford line for another two miles. Sherrod saw three Indians walking along the road. He called out, and the youngest male stopped. Sherrod asked him if he knew where the Donelson spread was. The young man pointed in the direction of the woods. Sherrod thanked him and ended the conversation by asking, "Is Donelson a friendly guy?" The young man giggled and ran off in the direction of his two companions who had continued their pace without curiosity or care that they had been stopped.

Sherrod headed across the field to the woods. The area reminded him of Cole Manor and his daily trips back and forth to Mary Polly's house. He had a hard time thinking about those times in the woods with Mary Polly, especially when he was feeling needy and wanting female company.

He rode until he saw a young white man on horseback approaching. He stopped and waited. When the man was close enough to hear him, Sherrod asked if he was on the right path to the Donelson spread.

"You sure are," the young man said and laughed. "I'm William Donelson. What can I do for you?"

"My name is Sherrod Bryant. I am looking for work. I was told to see a John Donelson."

"John is my father. What kind of work do you do?"

"Something on the river. I have never worked on the river before."

"We have room for a logger. You know anything about lumber?"

"No, but I'm a fast learner."

"Tell you what. Let's you and I ride down to the riverbank. You will see what's going on and maybe tell if it is something you want to be involved with."

Sherrod followed William down to the lumber camp where there were four one-room shacks sitting on the edge of the woods. Each was placed with its door facing the center of a circle where a fire pit and cooking pot stood.

"We have twenty men working down here. Some stay here; others live nearby. Their job is to receive logs that come downstream on the river here. My brother's camp does the cutting, chopping, and sending. Our camp hauls them in, dries them out, puts them in a pile, and cuts them."

Sherrod walked over to a pile of logs and placed his hand on top. "How long does it take a log to dry?"

"Quicker than it takes us to cut them," William said and laughed. "You see anything here that you could work with?"

"Cutting," Sherrod said. "I saw a gristmill today propelled by water. That tells me the days of a saw mill ain't too far off."

William laughed. "I like the way you think. Will seventy-five cents a day meet your needs?"

"If you promise you will give me an opportunity to grow."

"We pay our people what they're worth," a voice from behind Sherrod said.

"Hi Dad. This is Sherrod Bryant."

A round-faced, short, stocky, balding man came over to Sherrod. "I know about Sherrod Bryant, saw him signing into Black Bob's last week."

"Good morning, Sir."

"From Virginia, I hear."

"Yes, Sir, I am."

"We don't get many uppity half-breeds in this town. People like the way you carry yourself. They talk."

Sherrod laughed. "I am finding that out."

John turned to William. "How much you offer Sherrod?"

"Seventy-five cents a day."

John turned back to Sherrod. "I will make it a dollar if you over-see the camp. It will give William a chance to work inside with me."

"I don't know anything about logging, Mr. Donelson."

"You have twenty men working for you. If you were a planta-tion driver the way Nash is telling it, you will have the hang of it in no time. William seems to think you are halfway there."

"What makes you say that?"

"He was ready to give you our thinker's rate, wasn't he? Thirty-five cents a day is what we pay most of these guys."

"Thanks for believing in me, William," Sherrod said, and laughed. They all laughed. Sherrod liked the feeling he was getting being in the company of the father and son. "I will be living at the hotel in town for another two months. I am paid up till that time."

"I have no problem with you traveling out here every day, Sherrod," John said. "Two months will give William and me time to see how you're doing."

"Thank you, Sir. Thank both of you."

"Thank those no-count Indians William was trying to run down when he met you. If they had done what they were supposed to, you and I would have nothing to talk about."

Sherrod climbed onto his horse. "Who is Nash?" he asked.

"William Nash is the owner of the general store."

Sherrod tipped his hat and bid them good day. As he rode off, John turned to his son. "Let's see how much we get out of him."

"I have a feeling it will be plenty," William said to his dad. "He ain't a local. He knows his own mind."

"An Indian in fancy clothes with fancy ideas is still an Indian," John smirked.

Sherrod rode joyfully towards Nashville. He thought about crossing to the ridge to visit his brothers but decided against it. Their experiences were different and too new and separate to blend. He liked his decision to work for the Donelsons, and he didn't want anyone's opinion about it.

He realized working in that rural, makeshift log camp was a far cry from Cole Manor or where he wanted to be, but he knew he had to be patient. William Donelson was about his age and the obvious heir apparent. William had an ease about him that was likeable.

The old man, however, reminded of him of a fox. He got the feeling that he set people up to fail. The off kind of a way that he let it be known that William's workers had run out. He somehow felt that John had something to do with their leaving. That Indian kid had run away when he asked him if the Donelsons were friendly. It was John who upped his salary, and then let it be known that he was following William's lead.

He rode, and he thought some more about what he had gotten himself into. He then decided that his relationship with John could be whatever he made it. He had a job, and that's what he had set out to acquire. His success called for a celebration.

He arrived back at the hotel and decided that he was going to eat in the dining room. Hiding out hadn't helped him maintain his privacy so why not enjoy himself and help the townspeople arrive at their conclusions about him rather than leaving it to the storekeeper and other people he used for service?

He went upstairs, washed up, and put on a shirt and tie. Then, he went downstairs to the dining room and waited to be seated. Not too surprisingly, the dining room was beautifully laid out. The table and chairs were simple and plain. The colorful table cloths and matching gourds and cow horns with handles adjusted for drinking or the serving vessels had beautiful patterns that symbolized the making of the frontier, a farmer, a mother and children at play, a cook, a blacksmith. Whiskey barrels lined the wall.

Young Indian and slave maidens were taking orders, serving food and drink. Sherrod ordered turkey and deer with mashed potatoes and sweet corn. It had been a long time since he had had a home-cooked meal, and he intended to eat until he couldn't. He recognized his server as the young Cherokee that had brought him his towel that first night.

"Right this way, Mr. Bryant," she said, calling his name as if she had known him forever.

"Thank you, Little Doe," he smiled and she giggled.

Before she could recover from the shock of his knowing who she was, he said, "Little Doe, I want the first and last meal you are about to tell me about. And bring me a horn of sweet berry brandy."

"Okay," she said and scampered off.

He wondered how she came to work in Black Bob's and if she had slave status the same as the African women he saw peeping their heads out of the kitchen. If they were all slaves, how did they come to work for Robert? Was it possible that Robert owned them? A distant relative of Nancy's owned slaves. He had heard his father and the elders discussing it.

He looked around to see if he saw Robert, but he was nowhere in sight. When Little Doe came back with the food, he asked her, "Where is your Master this evening?"

"You mean Mr. Renfro?" she asked, and without waiting for his answer, replied, "He be the four African women's Master. Me, I live with family on the reservation."

"I don't mean to pry. I just want to compliment Mr. Renfro on his fine table."

"Okay . . . What you say is okay by Little Doe, but, Mrs. Renfro, she fix food. You compliment her."

"Which one is Mrs. Renfro?"

"She be the fat African standing in front. The other three be her sisters. Slave girls, all of them."

"You go and thank them for me, will you?"

"Tonight, I thank them. Now I help other people who hungry like you."

Sherrod laughed. The dining room was crowded, and Little Doe and the others were doing a good job of handling everyone. Each person was greeted by name. He listened intently, trying to find out who was who. He was tired of people knowing who he was but he having no inkling of who they were.

Halfway through his meal, he heard someone in the far corner behind him say, "That half-breed must be a man of means. He's been in the hotel over a week now."

"A fellow Virginian, I hear," he heard a second voice say.

The woman sitting at the table with the two men coughed and whispered into her handkerchief, "Jefferson says American Indians are not as racially inferior as the Africans. There are two or three of them studying up at Princeton University right now. Maybe he is one of them."

Sherrod had heard enough. He put his utensils in his half-eaten meal and motioned Little Doe over. She came over; he paid her and thanked her for the service. As he started to leave, one of the three called his name.

"Sherrod? Sherrod Bryant?"

He turned and found the conversationalists staring at him. He recognized the voice that called his name. He was the man who had responded when his friend pointed out Sherrod's presence. Sherrod made sure he looked the man directly in the eye. "Yes, Sir?" His response was more of a "what do you want" than a "may I help you."

"I am Joel Cole," the heavyset man said and stood up. "Jesse Cole's middle son."

A surprised Sherrod held out his hand and broke into a grin. "I have heard so much about you . . . Jesse . . . and Missouri . . . I feel as if I know you."

Joel shook his hand. "I kept hearing about a Sherrod Bryant being in town. It never dawned on me that you were Mary Polly's Sherrod until you got up to leave. Something about the way you responded to Little Doe. Mary Polly said you have a way with people."

"How is Mary Polly?"

"Robert is home driving her crazy. She asked me to look for you out here."

Sherrod's knees buckled. He hoped no one was aware of the panic that Joel's words about Mary Polly's request were causing inside of him. He tried to recover by continuing the conversation as if he just had a general interest. "And your father?" he said.

"Good. Still putting up with Big Mary and keeping things on track."

Now that the greetings were over, Sherrod felt he had to take his leave. "Well, it is good to finally meet you, Joel. I am working at the Donelsons' log camp. If you need wood, come by."

"I will do that," Joel said, and went back to his table.

Sherrod's legs felt like lead. The mere mention of Mary Polly weakened him, and he was afraid Joel and his guests were watching as he lumbered out of the dining room.

Nothing Joel had said endeared him to Sherrod. The word half-breed had wiped out any feelings of kinship that he might have experienced. He had seen too many hecklers in his life to rationalize or forgive him for acting like his mother Big Mary.

He started up the steps to his room when Robert Renfro called to him. "You scored some big points tonight."

"Good night, Robert," a tired Sherrod said. He was too tired and worried to care about what Renfro thought.

What if Mary Polly took it upon herself and came to Nashville or Murfreesboro or any part of Davidson or Rutherford County? Everyone was already watching him, knowing all his business. He had no real ties to her anymore . . . Or did he?

He opened the window when he got to the room. For the first time, he felt the room to be hot and musty. He pulled off his clothes and stretched out naked on the bed. Then it came to him. The last time he lay out that way was the night of the wedding, on the edge of the triangle.

He closed his eyes and remembered Mary Polly's face. The way she looked when she was in heat. And after, when she was satisfied, and quiet. He started to drift off and felt tears well up in his eyes. From a distance, he heard the sounds of his mind singing.

"I'm . . . a man

A . . . ma . . . an . . . an

A man."

A breeze blew through the window and found him asleep.

BRYANT ACRES CHAPTER XII

Sometimes I Look at Myself and I See Someone Real Special

Months of working at the camp rolled into each other, and before long it was Christmas time 1807. The fourth mill was being planned on the west fork, and even though it wasn't a Donelson mill, Sherrod and the owner, David Dickerson, had a working relationship. The actual mill wasn't to be built until 1809 but the plans were gone over again and again. All lumber was to come from the Donelsons' camp, and Sherrod was to supervise the cutting and measuring. He was also going to be part of the fitting and raising team.

People up and around Millcreek and Stones River had come to know Sherrod. They perceived him as a hard worker and a no-nonsense guy. Some even thought of him as a driven workaholic. He was not particular when it came to work. Wherever he was needed, he was there. Old John Donelson took to comparing Sherrod's work ethic to his own. He identified with Sherrod in that when he made up his mind or had a vision about something he wanted, he set his sights and timeline and worked day and night until the goal was achieved.

Sherrod came to like and respect John. He too saw similarities in their personality. The thing he liked most about John was his adventurous spirit. Both he and John were dreamers, and they believed in themselves.

His favorite *John story* was about how John during the ice storm of 1779–1780, one of the coldest winters in Tennessee history, made a river journey to Nashville with a bunch of flatboats carrying approximately thirty families. During the course of the trip, an Indian uprising occurred. One man was killed, and the Indians imprisoned twenty-seven people. Another family came down with smallpox and died. One boat sank; several others ran into a shoal and lost another thirty people. Those who survived had to leave the boat to lighten it. In spite of all the trouble, John and his group kept their sights on Nashville. They tackled the Tennessee River, the Ohio River, and the Cumberland River with a vengeance and finally landed in Nashville.

The story motivated Sherrod. It validated his belief that planned action paid dividends. When time seemed to be getting away from him, he reminded himself of the fear and anguish he had felt when he went to Cole Manor but how eventually he had designed and successfully implemented a plan. Frustration didn't come too often, but it happened when it was definite that Dickerson was going to build the mill instead of Donelson. As much as Sherrod tried to convince William and John how a mill would be in their best interest, they couldn't see it. Cotton was fast becoming the crop of the future and the Donelsons wanted in. When Sherrod arrived and realized that things weren't going to happen the way he wanted them to, he knew he had to come as far as he could with Donelson.

It was holiday time. He decided he would wait until the beginning of the year before he made any moves. The joy of the season was his knowing that he was finally going to start his life. Every deal made, every job done, would be for him come the new year. Christmas Eve he was sitting in camp trying to decide how he wanted to spend his holiday. He had visited his brothers a couple days before. They each had girlfriends, and he didn't feel comfortable staying with them even though they said they wanted him to. He had had several opportunities to ask women out but declined to do so. He hadn't been with a woman in a while. Any action on his part would be strictly a response to an animal need for physical contact. That was not the way he wanted to remember Christmas 1807. He was alone, and that made him sad. He reminded himself to do better planning as far as his personal needs were concerned. He started to rise and stretch and a familiar voice called his name. He thought his mind was playing games with himself when he heard it. And then it occurred a second time and everything in him reacted. His eyes and nose burned with possibility. His lips trembled with fear of turning around and finding more emptiness. His heart raced and beat against his chest, and his genitals stirred and made him afraid to help. Slowly, he gathered his wits and turned. Mary Polly and Joel stood looking at him.

"Aren't you glad to see us?" Mary Polly teased.

Her familiar face melted all the years into the moment. Thoughts of holding her and burying his head in her breasts drowned out the fear of her presence. He was clearly overwhelmed. "How are you Ms. Polly?" he said, trying to sound as non-committal as possible. Her eyes searched his face. He allowed them to touch his briefly, reflecting tidbits of truth in wonderment.

"I know the invitation was extended to me, but I thought for old time's sake it would be nice to bring Mary out and let the two of you talk."

"That's fine," Sherrod said struggling to take his eyes off of her. "Really it is."

"Truly, Joel has to be getting on. I begged him to bring me. I promised him that you would drop me off after I have given you all the gifts and letters Mingus and the rest sent you from the camp."

"That's fine, I mean, that will be okay. Everyone else left for the holiday. I was about to close up."

"You sure?" Joel asked. "It will be okay with Donelson and everybody? I hear he is a tough one."

"John is not like he leads everyone to believe. I was just trying to decide what to get William and Silas for Christmas."

"I know Donelson has two sons. I know one's name is William. I didn't know his other son was named Silas."

"William and Silas are Sherrod's brothers," Mary Polly spoke up. "They worked for Ruben. Remember I told you?"

Joel climbed up in his wagon, showing no real interest. "Okay then, I will be leaving if you are sure it's all right."

"Go on," Mary Polly said and laughed.

Joel brought a green sack of presents from the wagon. As he started off he mumbled, "See you later on then." He gave his horse a slap and hightailed it out of the camp. Sherrod stood by quietly, watching after Joel. When Mary Polly could no longer see her brother and the sounds of his horses could no longer be heard, she ran and leapt into Sherrod's arms. He hugged her and hugged her and hugged her. Taking in her smells, the beauty of her face and soap in her hair. Then he remembered where they were.

"Stay right here," he said moving away from her and running behind the cabins. He came back with a horse and work wagon. Mary Polly was happy. She smiled, took off the shawl she was wearing, and spread it on the wagon floor. This was her first time in Tennessee, and she liked the feel of the place. Then again, maybe what she liked was sharing space with Sherrod in the town where he lived. It had been four tedious years and not one night had gone by without some thought or incident bringing him to mind. Sherrod climbed into the driver seat of the wagon and left her standing in the camp.

"Where are you going?" she asked him.

"To the top of the ridge," he replied. "From there you can see the lights of Nashville and Murfreesboro. Lots of trees, farms, and mills, a creek and river." He opened his mouth and spurt four words that he wasn't sure where they were coming from at a pace that he wasn't used to talking in. He felt as if he didn't have a care in the world. Then he realized he had gotten in the driver seat and had left Mary Polly standing on the passenger side. He jumped down, came around, and took her hand.

"You would think I am nervous or something," he said as he helped her up.

She giggled. "That's what I miss," she laughed, "your honesty." He kissed her lightly on the forehead. "I have so many things I want to say to you," she said.

"Not yet, please, this is foreign country with big eyes and even bigger ears." She laughed and giggled some more. It reminded Sherrod of a silly schoolgirl that he had to tease into coming out to play. She talked to him about Mingus, Cato, and Eatoe as they followed the river back to the extreme height of the ridge between Millcreek and Stones River.

"Take a look at all of this land," he said to her. "It's all going to be mine one day." He let the wagon roll to a stop and helped her to the ground so she could get a better view.

Knowing what he had done for Cole Manor, she believed him. She slipped her hand in his, and together they stood for a long while looking out across the rivers and streams, the woods and the fields and trails. The wind stirred and brushed against her cheek. She shivered and he took off his jacket and slipped it around her shoulders. "I love you, Sherrod Bryant," she said.

He swept her up in his arms and walked with her to an elm tree that was divided at the route. In the center where the route split and each trunk took its own direction, nature provided a hammock broad and wide enough for them to nestle together. He laid her there. The tree trunk, the tall grass, the stones and rocks provided a space that was private and hilly enough to warn them if weight of any sort disturbed the framework of heaven around them. They lay comfortably in the base of their resting place, Sherrod's body providing a cushion for hers. They held onto each other for a long while trying to get used to being in the same space.

He started to think about their relationship at Cole Manor, how it had evolved at Ruben's and how it had grown to include his brothers. He wanted to rush her out to visit at their place but thought about the women who were now their wives and knew he couldn't. He looked at her face, touched her hair, and became enthralled with her eyes that were fixed on him. Deep and feeling and as clear as the color they projected. Her stare brought an unsolicited sigh up from a place that was unfamiliar to him. Without forethought or care, he gave in to the gravity of his inner force, pulled her to him, engaged her in a kiss that sent messages he had no control over.

She ran her fingers through his hair, positioned herself in the contours of his body, and returned his kisses with her eyes open so that she could watch him as he took her in. After a moment, he opened his eyes and when he saw her watching him, the point of desire pushed hard against the buttons of his fly. She put her hands inside and relished in the pleasure of his response and the heat of her own.

"I'm angry about all the time we have missed," he said, and she kissed him. "I'm angry at you for coming back into my life and disrupting my thoughts," he mumbled as her tongue danced with his. "I'm angry," he screamed as she let him inside her.

He turned over, rolled off the tree, and pulled her to the ground. He got on top of her and pinned her beneath him with his hands holding her arms above her head. Oblivious to her struggle, he entered her with an unyielding command. Summoning her to be sure that she understood he was no longer her boy. That he was a free man and that she was to give him what he asked of her. She submitted and confirmed his due, and he showered her with the gifts that he had saved for her. She moaned her gratitude, and he felt validated.

They lay quietly in the hammock and held each other. Finally, she turned to him, "Robert hasn't received anything from me that belongs to you Sherrod," she whispered. "He made demands and I rejected him. He went to Mamie, settled it with her; wanted to make me jealous."

"Mamie!" Sherrod exclaimed. "*Little Mamie?*"

"She is sixteen, Sherrod."

He climbed down off of her and from the hammock. "She wasn't sixteen five years ago when you decided to make a go of that marriage."

"Three years ago," she corrected him angrily.

"Don't mince words with me," he said raising his voice.

"Sherrod, she asked me, and I was okay with it. She had a crush on you and Robert is the next most important man. He is rich, he treats her special now that Esther has gone off and gotten married, and she has become real special to everyone." Sherrod stared at her. She tried to touch him and he pushed her away. He started to pace.

"You make me ill with your puritanical ways. You are not naïve; you know the way it is. Yes, you bury your head and you pretend not to hear or notice because it is easier, but you know."

"When I was a kid, I used to wonder how Daddy could have left his people to live with us in the hills the way he did. He gave up worldly things for something decent and good. I don't understand white men treating blacks like cattle, and then going to them in one of man's most personal acts. No, I don't want to know about it. If you can't understand that, I'm sorry."

"Don't, Sherrod, don't you . . ." She realized how hurt he was. She folded her arms and sat quietly.

After a moment, he said, "Sometimes, I look at myself, and I see someone really special. Someone who cares about life and love. I think I understand God's creation and what he meant for us to do on this earth. I hear and see slavery, the buying and selling of people. I hear and see Indians bothering and fighting each other to satisfy the white man. I say to myself, 'Somewhere, somehow, someone in these people's lives made some bad decisions.'

"I go out, and I meet the enemy. I look him in the face, and no matter what he calls me or how he tries to engage me in negative behavior, I wear him down. Help him understand that I am not about distraction. It is not my problem, not my battle. Then I hear about Mamie and I know that somewhere along the way, the decision I made wasn't wholesome enough to help her ward off predatory wishes of a racist bastard like Robert."

He started to cry, and she put her arms around him. Her heart was not accustomed to giving in to a man's need. When he quieted, she asked him if he would rather she play lover to Robert and have him steal favors from Mamie behind her back? "What were Mamie's words when you spoke?" she asked. "She knows I love you, and she wanted to keep Robert happy so I could come find you."

"You lie!"

"She asked me to forgive her, and I hugged her. I told her she was my daughter and then I told her what to do so she wouldn't get pregnant like her mother did." Mary Polly then got down on her knees in front of the hammock where Sherrod had come to rest.

"Southern white men are hard-hearted, callous, and greedy. They preach humanity and talk about the common good while they butcher and slaughter people who go against their wishes. Daddy fathered Mamie and Esther. He thinks I don't know it.

"I was there the day Tisha told her daughter, Emmie, the girls' mother, she was going to be sold. And he yelled and screamed. It brought chills to my heart. She talked about how Daddy had raped her at ten years of age, and she talked about killing Daddy. Tisha slapped Emmie when she said it. She slapped her again and again and made me understand that her leaving was a matter of life or death for all of them, Mamie and Esther included.

"Finally, when it was all said and done, Tisha looked up and got me listening. She held her fingers to her lips and trusted me not to tell anyone what I had heard. I have never mentioned it to anyone until now."

Sherrod helped her up to where he sat. They were both somber and quiet for a long while. Finally, he said, "Let's not talk anymore." She started to tremble, so he hugged her and hugged her until they both tumbled off the hammock onto the ground. She rolled on top of him. He grabbed her arms and brought her to rest between his legs.

"Play nice," she said. He laughed, and she flipped over onto her back and lay beside him. "I have been a good girl, Mr. Bryant. There is no need for you to be angry with me."

"I know," he said as he took hold of her dress and eased her out of it. She helped him undress her. When it was done, she put her arms around his waist and squeezed him with all her strength.

"I will always be yours."

He buried his face in her breasts and proceeded to kiss her neck, down to her breasts, and the rest of her. "You are quite a secret," he said, and they both laughed playfully. She turned to him, and they passionately rekindled their lovemaking with hopes that it would bury the aftermath of her story. When they were done, it was almost dark. Sherrod became concerned. "What is Joel going to say?" he asked her.

"Joel has his own game to play," she replied. "We will meet him at Martha's house; they are a distant neighbor of sorts."

Sherrod smiled knowingly. "Do you Coles ever think of anything else?"

Mary Polly laughed. "You are not going to make me feel guilty for being involved with you, Sherrod Bryant!"

He squeezed her. "I don't aim to try, Mary Polly Cole." He took her hand and walked with her back to the wagon. When they arrived at Martha's house, Joel was asleep.

"He had a little too much brandy," Martha said and giggled. Sherrod recognized her as the woman with Joel at Black Bob's tavern, but she gave no indication of recognizing him. "He can stay all night. It won't be the first time," Martha bragged.

"It's Christmas Eve and I am visiting," Mary Polly said. She took hold of her brother's arm and tried to shake him awake. A drunken Joel thinking it was Martha tried to grab Mary Polly around the waist. "Come to Daddy, baby."

"Cut it out Joel," an embarrassed Mary Polly scolded. "Sherrod, help me put him in his wagon." Sherrod took hold of Joel's arm and helped him to his feet and walked him out to the wagon. Once they were outside and away from Martha's house, Sherrod suggested they stop and build a fire to sober Joel up. Mary Polly was against it.

"I don't want you traveling these trails this time of night with him asleep," Sherrod explained.

"Then you will just have to follow us," she said.

"What would that look like?"

"It would look like the three of us had an enjoyable evening and you helped me bring Joel home after he drank too much." Sherrod complied, and gracefully, Sally Cole invited him in for coffee and

Christmas cookies. With her encouragement, they left Joel asleep in the wagon. Their home wasn't much of a farm, but it was fixed to perfection and Sally was proud of it. She clearly loved Joel and treated him like a child when he came in out of the cold.

"Hey Sherrod," he said surprised to see him. "You sure know how to spin a good yarn," he laughed. "I see you have met the little woman." He tried to hug Sally, but she gently pushed him away.

"Quiet before you wake the kids." Sherrod felt he had seen what he intended to see. "I better be going," he said and stood up.

"Why not wait until morning? You don't know these woods the way my horses do," Joel said. "Sally will find you a bed to sleep in. If not, we will throw your ass on the floor."

"I will sleep in my wagon till morning, if you don't mind."

"We do mind," Mary Polly said. "It's Christmas Eve; let's be a little joyful around here." She grabbed the plate of cookies from the table. "Joel get that ham and some bread. Sally, get some glasses and a jug of cider. Bring it out to the barn. You Coles have guests. Show us some of that Southern hospitality."

Sally laughed. "Maybe we will decorate the tree. I think something colorful to surprise the children."

"Now you talking," still drunk Joel laughed.

"Do you have a tree already cut?" Sherrod asked.

"I don't think so."

"With your permission, I will go cut one."

"Do you have an axe?" Sally asked.

"That's what the man does for a living, Sally. I imagine he has a wagon full of cutting tools," Joel laughed.

"Maybe one or two," Sherrod said and went out the back door. He hadn't seen the barn. It was a new barn that towered over the house and took up most of the clearing in the back. He proceeded past the garden and the chicken coop to the woods. He forgot to go to the wagon for the axe and had to go back. He was feeling somewhat awkward but was pleased to be having a family-style Christmas, and Mary Polly.

Mary Polly held a special place in his heart, and as much as he wanted to deny it, he was aware of her sacrifice and the risk she took. He liked Sally, and he decided it would be in his best interest to make friends with Joel.

The Coles were a large family, and as in all families, there were weak links. Joel was one such link, and if he supported him, he would not only be helping Mary Polly but himself as well. Sherrod found a small tree with evenly distributed branches. Sally and Mary Polly cleaned up Joel's worktable and put the food and drink on it, while Joel brought out cranberries and pieces of tally and popping corn to be prepared and used for decorations.

When all the supplies had been gathered, the four of them sat down to eat and work. "Before we begin, I'd like to ask God to bless us and our families," Sally said. All heads bowed and the talking stopped. Sally began, "Dear Lord, I wanted a special celebration this year, and you have seen fit to provide it. First, Mary Polly, and now Sherrod. You know the struggles Joel and I have gone through, worrying about John and Missouri. You saw fit to spare them when they had Whooping Cough. You knew I could handle two sick babies if I stayed healthy and strong. So you blessed me and kept me disease free. I am grateful, Lord. Joel is a loving man. He sometimes feels overwhelmed with all of us depending on him, but you and I both know the love and joy that this family experiences during the good moments. It is times like these that take us through the hard times, Lord.

"Bless us as we end the year 1807 and embark upon 1808. We promise to do our best. And we always remember that you are God and that all things rest in your hands. Bless our new friend, Sherrod Bryant, our sister Mary Polly, and our children, John and Missouri. These things we ask, amen."

BRYANT ACRES CHAPTER XIII

It's a Proud Kind of a Big Mistake
That I Have Got to Make Work

Mary Polly stayed in Tennessee until the day after New Year's. Sally and Joel talked Sherrod into staying with them until she left. He agreed on the condition that they let him help Joel add another room onto their house. They had two children, and he felt the boy should have a room of his own.

Joel was pleased with his suggestion and was more than willing to accommodate Sherrod on the trips back and forth to the Donelsons' log camp. As they came to know each other, Sherrod learned that Joel was the middle child of Jesse and Big Mary. He felt neglected and pushed out by his older brother, Jesse Jr, and his cousin, Robert. But he loved his sisters, Mary Polly and Missouri.

"I am in Tennessee because I have a host of cousins here," he told Sherrod. "They are older and more established. They have patience with me and don't care if I don't become a big business or involved with what is going on here in the county.

"I am a little guy, and that suits me fine. I will never be famous, and I don't want to be. Sally loves me, and my kids are depending on me to make everything okay. I can do that. Sally's folks live in Kentucky so I know she would rather live there, but I don't need that influence. Both families are out of the immediate vicinity, and that suits me fine."

"Where does Martha fit?" Sherrod asked him.

"The same way you and Mary Polly fit," he said to Sherrod's surprise.

"A friendship that comes about through hard work. The joy of achievement is very satisfying."

Sherrod replied with a straight face, "I am pleased that you and Martha have forged such a relationship."

"Martha befriended me when I came to the county last year and was looking for a place to buy for my family. She and her brother owned the property where we lived. Martha has never been married, and she really didn't want to sell. I had to talk her into it." He laughed. "Maybe 1808 will bring the end of the conversation."

"Either that or buy fifty more acres from her," Sherrod laughed.

"Don't stop visiting because Mary Polly leaves," Joel said. "Sally likes you and so do the children. We could use a family friend, especially one that Big Mary didn't irritate. We can't choose our families, but we can choose our friends."

"I am grateful that you asked me to be yours."

The two men didn't always talk when they were together. Most of Sherrod's interaction was with Sally and the children. Joel was always off somewhere in the yard working or preparing ice for the ice cream and getting meat from the smokehouse. If Sherrod left Sally to join him, he would send him back to the house with an errand or something to discuss with Sally.

Sherrod discussed the situation with Mary Polly before she left, and she assured him that the way Joel was interacting was a sign of trust. She told him about the relationship he had with Emmy, Mamie and Esther's mother, and how he had withdrawn once she was sent away, how much he loved Mingus and Old Tisha. *Should I become comfortable with the role I am playing in Joel's family?* he thought to himself. He was sensitive to both Sally and Joel's needs to have an outsider to talk to.

Three months into the new year, Joel came to Sherrod and told him that Martha was out of his life. He also told him that Mary Polly was coming to spend the better part of the year with them and that he needed him to help build another room.

Sherrod was surprised to hear that Mary Polly was returning to Tennessee so soon. He knew she had gone to Kentucky to visit Jesse Jr, but she had not spoken of a return trip to Tennessee. For her to stay the better part of the year had many implications, most of which frightened him.

He wondered if she had returned to Virginia and found the situation with Robert and Mamie intolerable, if Robert was off to England again, if the crops had failed and she was being blamed for it, or if she had the silly notion that they could become a couple.

The better part of a year was not forever, so it was definitely some sort of plan of hers. He didn't want to ask Joel or Sally too many questions out of fear that he would appear guilty of something.

When Joel mentioned it, Sherrod said, "That's a long time for her to be away from home."

Joel's response was that traveling back and forth was a hard journey. "She wants to help Sally with the babies. Two babies in two years is a lot. I can't tell you the problems we had moving here from Kentucky. When the babies got sick, Sally blamed herself, but deep inside I couldn't help but think she was blaming me. I was the one who wanted to move to Tennessee." Sherrod couldn't help thinking there was more to it. He went to Sally hoping to get some clarification.

"I hear you and Joel will be building a room for Mary Polly. Isn't it nice of her to come and help with the babies?" Sally said all excited. "Sherrod, I have five brothers. It hasn't been easy being the only girl in the house, especially when your dad is dead and your mother expects you to take care of your brothers. I was the oldest." She paused and took a deep breath. "Thank God for Mary Polly. She is like a sister to me."

Sherrod knew he would just have to wait and see what was on Mary Polly's mind. The job with the Donelsons had reached its peak as far as he was concerned. He had planned to leave at the beginning of 1808 but his involvement with Joel had served as a diversion. Now he was glad that he had waited.

He had enough money to buy a few acres of land but that wasn't the way he wanted to do it. So, instead of making a hasty purchase, he added to his stash by continuing to work for the Donelsons and taking side jobs from Dickerson and from Joel and any other man in Rutherford who needed him on a short-term basis.

Joel, however, wasn't exactly paying him for his work. Occasionally, he gave Sherrod a dollar or two for helping out. Sherrod always took the money; it kept him from feeling sidetracked. He had no home to speak of. He spent two days a week with his brothers, two days in the log camp, one day with Sally and Joel, and two days at Black Bob's Tavern. His days at Black Bob's kept him focused on the goal. Even though the townsmen knew what his jobs entailed, he never spoke about his work when he was in town.

Renfro got to a place where he looked forward to Sherrod's coming in late on Friday nights. He would have his room waiting and most of the time he would wait for Sherrod to arrive before he left for the night. Renfro's usual greeting was a tease. As soon as Sherrod entered, Renfro would say, "Is this the week?"

Sherrod would look at him and say, 'Not yet." They would both laugh, and Sherrod would go up to his room and Renfro would leave for home. The last Sunday night in March on his return to the log camp he stopped by Joel and Sally's as they had asked him to do when he had left them last Friday afternoon. Mary Polly and the family were waiting for him on the porch when he arrived. He rolled up on his horse and a cheer went up. John and Missouri ran out to greet him.

He gave each of them a hug and walked with them back to the porch where the adults sat. "Hi," he said to Mary Polly. "I wasn't expecting you this soon. The room isn't finished. You are a real surprise." He turned and looked at Joel and Sally. They were staring at him with strange expressions on their faces. "What?" he asked, wondering if there was something he had said or done or if there was something he had not seen.

Sally grabbed Missouri. "Come on in the house kids. I need to give you baths. Joel, you grab John for me and bring him in." Joel dropped his head to avoid Sherrod's eyes. He grabbed John and they went inside leaving Mary Polly and Sherrod alone.

"What's going on?" Sherrod asked. "Joel and Sally are sure acting strange."

"You are about to become a father," Mary Polly said. "I guess I thought I should tell you in private."

"What? What are you saying?" She tried to take his hand, but he moved out of her reach. "Joel and Sally have agreed to help me and let me stay here until the child is born."

"Hold on," he demanded. "You are telling me I have fathered a child with you? You and I, that there is a baby?" He plopped into a seat, put his head in his hands, and sat silently looking at the floor. His children were to be a part of his future, not his present.

Mary Polly tried to reassure him. "Look, I know it's a shock to you. I have had three months to sweat over it. It is really quite simple." Her tone and everything about her irritated him.

"There is nothing simple about it, Miss."

She stood up and walked away from him, feeling bewildered and angry. "Don't say it. Don't you ever call me Miss again!"

He looked at her through eyes that burned with anger and shock. "I take fatherhood seriously and I resent you trying to hurry me through whatever it is I am trying to feel about what is happening here."

For the first time, she became frightened. She didn't know what she had expected, but it certainly wasn't his anger. "What has happened—" he said and realized he was raising his voice. He lowered it immediately almost to a whisper.

"Sherrod Bryant and Mary Polly Cole are going to have a baby, not just Mary Polly. I was trying to keep you from worrying," Mary Polly said. She had to defend herself.

"I'm a man, Mary Polly. I don't need you to keep me from doing anything. Finding out I'm about to be the father is a stunner. Do you understand? A stunner." He thought about what he had just said about being a father and he felt his chest swell. "It's a proud kind of mistake that I have got to make work."

"Ok," Mary Polly said. "If it's the truth you want, well here it is: I didn't trust you enough to think you would want to be a part of it."

"Then why did you come back here?" When she didn't respond, he knew. "When that baby is born, he is going to stay with me. Is that clear?"

"Where will he live with you? Wherever you choose to live for the night? At Black Bob's, maybe?" The accusatory nature of her words cut into his anger. He knew she was right. He studied her face. Her eyes looked tired, and his tone softened.

"That's a fair question," he said. "Let me think. Okay, I've got it. We will ask Sally and Joel if I can rent the room we are preparing for you. That way, I can pay Sally to help me care for the baby."

"Then you don't mind that Joe and Sally know?" Mary Polly asked.

"There are plenty of mixed couples living together in this country. I'm not afraid of publicly declaring what is mine." For the first time, his grandiosity irritated her. She wondered how she was going to talk to him about her plans without insulting him.

"My baby is going to have the best of everything. The best education, the best clothes, the best parents," she said. "Right now, you and I are in no position to be the best parents. You live here, and I live in Virginia. As long as I stay in Virginia, I will have plenty of money to do what we have to do to take care of our baby." She talked and he listened. "I want you to help Sally and Joel take care of our baby, Sherrod. I want to give you money to buy what is needed for the baby and for you. I want to buy you land, lots of land, so that you can build. In three years, I want our child to have one of the finest homes in this country."

Sherrod took her in his arms. "You really have thought this out, haven't you?"

Mary Polly smiled. "You've spent years telling me about your dream. I am prepared to help you make those dreams a reality. I want to do it for you and for our child."

Sherrod dropped his head. "I don't feel included. I don't feel like I am contributing."

Mary Polly took his hand and placed it on her stomach. There was movement. He smiled. "This is no time for pride, Sherrod Bryant. We have to do what is best for the child."

Her stomach growled and they both laughed. Joel and Sally came out. He was sure they had been listening from the other side of the door, but he was too overwhelmed to do anything but celebrate with his child's family.

"Joel, Sally, kids, come over here. A celebration is in order. Joel, bring out the ice cream freezer. Mary Polly has a craving." Joel and Sally hugged them both.

"You have nothing to fear," Sally said watching his eyes. "The details surrounding your child are secret for the four of us alone to share. Joel and I have talked about it, and it's our promise to you and Mary Polly."

Sherrod hugged her and Joel. "Thank you," he said, and felt his eyes get misty.

"Why? We are practically brothers now," Joel said, and Mary Polly's eyes began to tear.

"Let's get on with this celebration before I start crying and can't stop," she said. Life as she knew it would never be the same again. She knew this to be true. Sherrod shared Mary Polly's sentiment. His heart was happy, but heavy. He had to protect himself and Joel from suspicion. It was well known that he and Joel were close. Nash even took credit for getting them together.

Sherrod and Joel both let it be known that Sally was going to be caring for a new baby soon. Sally rarely stepped foot off the farm, so there were no questions one way or the other. Mary Polly simply didn't get involved. None of the neighbors knew about her, and she kept it that way. It was not as difficult as Sherrod thought it was going to be having Mary Polly around. She was aware of her gossipy family's nature and she didn't want any of them to know her whereabouts, so she stayed close to home. Big Mary and Jesse were pleased that she had decided to go and help Sally. They knew the children had been sick. They felt less obligated with Mary Polly in attendance.

Besides, they weren't much for traveling. And Sally was still a stranger to them. Before the babies were born, they had begged Joel to bring her home, but he never got around to it. Before they knew it, they were grandparents.

The mail was slow. They were still basking in the details of the birth when the new child had been sick but were now welcome. Robert didn't care that Mary Polly left. The cotton continued to prosper, money was plentiful, and that was all he cared about.

The succeeding six months were worrisome for Sherrod. He told William and Silas about the baby and carried Mary Polly out to see them once or twice. Her condition prevented her from doing too much traveling, but she wanted to see them so they went. Neither William nor Silas's women cared that Mary Polly was white. Both of their mothers were white, so her color had no bearing on their interaction with her.

Sally and Joel spoiled Mary Polly. Sherrod continued to keep his regular schedule as planned. He had a hard time staying at Black Bob's. The impending baby replaced the tavern as Sherrod's symbol of the future. The superficiality of hotel living became a mark of loneliness.

Rather than be occupied with being successful for the sake of being successful, he wanted an easier life for his child. However, he continued to go back and forth as he had done. He was a regular in town, and he didn't want to draw attention to himself. On Thursday nights when it was time for him to stay with the family, Mary Polly would put Missouri in bed with her and Sherrod would sleep with John.

Not leaving the Donelsons had served him well. He was able to continue helping others with raising a barn, building a church, or adding an extra room to a house. It allowed him to keep up with the new style of building that was happening in and about the counties. It also provided him with information about new kinds of trimmings, weatherproofing, and cooling aids. When the new settlers came, Sherrod quickly learned their names and interests. Times were changing, and Sherrod wanted to stay prepared.

There was a lot of unrest in and about Nashville. White people were blaming Africans and free men for any type of failure that occurred, whether it was a crime, an illness, or the failure of crops. They were even talking about free men having to be certified, which meant he would have to carry a certificate attesting to his character and his morality.

Even though Sherrod was highly esteemed as an individual and expectant father, he was in touch with his ethnicity and the fact that he belonged to an unwanted group of people. For the first time, he was sensitive to what his father had said when he had discussed the significance of skin color in America.

His status as a free man was in constant jeopardy and so would the status of his mulatto child. The challenge of it all was no longer a welcome motivation, but it was motivation nevertheless. He thought about the camaraderie between himself and the slaves at Cole Manor. He remembered the night he had introduced the structure of reorganization and teamwork. He remembered the discussions, disagreements, and most of all he remembered the cooperation and willingness to try.

He thought about Mary Polly and her relationship with her father and her husband and knew in his heart he would never have the same kind of camaraderie with Mary Polly that he could have with a wife of color.

Their sharing a child, in whatever way it developed, would be as together of a couple as they could ever be. She was from a different world that lived by different rules and laws. He and his child would never totally be a part of that world, even if he and Mary Polly decided to be a couple. He felt sad sorting it all out.

Living and visiting Joel and Sally's house was like having a home, but it wasn't his home. It reminded him of the time he spent at Ruben's. It was comfortable and loving, but a look of entitlement from either member of the couple reminded him that he was living on the fringe, unsafe and unsure about what would happen if Ruben or Joel were called out and forced to choose between him and the larger world.

He compared their friendship to Mingus, and he knew if forced to choose when the smoke cleared he and Mingus would be standing together or lying dead together. He couldn't say the same about himself and Joel. Mary Polly's life was hers to share with him when she felt the need. His life was about building. He needed her resources so he could build a town where free men could live, be educated, work, worship, and thrive, the dream of a town that promoted character and sense of well-being for people of color and the family that now included Mary Polly. The prospects of the impending child made it so.

The more he thought about it, the less of a burden it became. Mary Polly said she would finance a life for their child; it was up to him to lay out and implement a plan. He would read the newspaper, attend public meetings, and passively participate in civic activities so the townspeople would get used to seeing him be active. When an opportunity presented itself, he would be ready. He vowed to have it done inside Mary Polly's three-year timeline.

I Have Delivered Many Creatures; None Can Compare

Mary Polly went into labor on Saturday. Sherrod was staying in town at Black Bob's. The night he ran into John Buchanan in the lobby, John invited him to sit and talk for a spell. Buchanan wanted to voice some concerns he had about the water rights on McCreary Creek and some of the solutions that had been proposed at the meeting they had attended earlier.

Buchanan, Hogart, Realy, and Donelson all knew that while Sherrod wasn't a property owner, he was a great proponent of the town and many of the solutions that were being proposed came to them in private conversations with Sherrod.

The fact that Sherrod had been an overseer on a large plantation in Virginia was highly respected. He was perceived as an educated Indian but an Indian nonetheless, therefore, not in any way an economic competitor.

Sherrod had a habit of studying problems that came up in the meetings. He would arrive at a solution and privately go to the person who would gain the most benefit from that solution. At first, he was only problem solving for the Donelsons. Then the others got wind of Sherrod's extraordinary ability, and they began to seek him out and interact with him on their own.

Buchanan was a kind of standoffish type of man. When he approached Sherrod for a talk, it became official that Sherrod was an accepted part of Nashville's political network. As long as he stayed low key and didn't publicly try to benefit from his relationships, he could move about the town uninhibited.

When Renfro saw Buchanan sitting with Sherrod, he was ecstatic. He tried to find ways to let Sherrod know that he was considering the fact that Sherrod finally become an important member of the town. Sherrod saw Renfro fluttering in and about, rolling his eyes, and making faces to show his approval. Sherrod was amused. He never talked to Renfro about business. He figured that Renfro got where he was with help from a lot of people who weren't visible, and that frightened him. He was sad that he couldn't quite trust Renfro, because he would have liked to.

He gained a lot of strength from Renfro's pioneering and his ability to please the townspeople. In a funny sort of way, even the body language Renfro was displaying during his conversation with Buchanan was encouraging. It helped him control the anxiety he was feeling and stay in the conversation. Then Joel entered the hotel. As soon as Sherrod saw him, he knew it was time. Joel was stone-faced and wearing a work shirt that he never wore. He waved at Sherrod from the doorway and tipped his hat to the side. Sherrod told Mr. Buchanan that he and Mr. Cole had been tending to a sick heifer and that he was being summoned. He hoped that they would be able to continue their conversation soon. Mr. Buchanan promised that they would talk and he expressed a wish that everything would work out well with the heifer.

Sherrod followed Joel out to his horse. "Mary Polly went into labor early this morning," Joel said. "She asked me not to come for you until it was almost time. I couldn't hold out any longer. The children are asleep. Sally is alone with Mary. I don't know anything about delivering babies, and neither does Sally."

Sherrod realized what a burden he had placed on Joel. "Everything is going to be fine," Sherrod assured Joel.

When they arrived at the house, Sally was standing at Mary Polly's side with a cloth lying across the foot of the bed and a pail of boiling water at Sally's feet. Mary Polly lay flat on her back with her legs apart, her knees up and feet planted firmly out in front of her. She had a sheet draped over the bottom part of her body. It covered her thighs and fell like a tent against her knees.

Mary Polly lay there quietly. She looked overwhelmed and tired.

Sherrod gently moved Sally aside. "I have brought many creatures into this world," he said trying to calm Mary Polly and the fear that he was holding inside. "Helping you, Mary Polly, bringing our child to life is God's gift to the both of us."

"I'll get some more rags and water," Sally said and ran from the room.

In Sally's mind, Sherrod was the man that every woman dreamed about. She certainly had felt safer and more secure since he came into her and Joel's life. Even though Sherrod and Mary Polly would never marry, he was family as far as she was concerned. The child about to be born made it even more so.

Sally went into the other room and saw Joel sitting by the fire. He was tending the fire and boiling water. She went to him and hugged him. "Everything is going to be fine," she said. "You are about to become an uncle."

Joel put his arm around her waist and buried his face in a skirt. "We are lucky to have Sherrod in our lives. Do you think he and Mary Polly are going to be able to pull it off?"

"You should hear the way Sherrod is talking to her in there," Sally replied.

"I know the baby will be all right," Joel said. "What about after the baby comes? John and Missouri, what do we tell them? We tell them that God sent us a baby to take care of until he has a home of his own. That's what we tell them. That is what we tell everybody. We are taking care of my brother's child until he comes for him. It's not a lie, is it?"

"No, it's not a lie."

"I love you Sally; you are smart and good." Sally hugged him and wiped the tears from his eyes.

"I have to get back." As she neared the birthing room, she could hear Sherrod talking to Mary Polly. How refreshing it must be, she thought, to have your man talking you through some of the worries. Mary Polly was in a lot of pain. She vacillated between listening to Sherrod and giving up.

"Breathe Mary Polly, breathe," Mary Polly heard Sherrod say, and it irritated her.

"I'm trying, damn you!" she screamed. He continued talking to her in a gentle voice. Missouri cried out and Sally went to her. Sherrod wiped Mary Polly's brow.

"This is your moment Mary, your time to bring life into the world. Bear down now, breathe. I know it hurts, but you can do this." He saw the head of the child and he felt his heart speed up. "That's it, that's it, you're doing it, Mary, you're doing it!" The baby pushed his way through. Sherrod grabbed it and Joel heard the cry.

"Isn't there anything that man won't try?" Joel mumbled and started towards Mary Polly and the baby. "Sis, sis!" Joel said.

"I'm all right, Joel. I'm all right; we're all right." Mary smiled as she hugged her brother and watched Sherrod hold the baby.

"It's a boy," Sherrod said. "It's a boy. I have a son." Sherrod wrapped the baby in the part of the bed sheet that Sally had prepared for that purpose. "He has ten fingers, ten toes, and voice that is as loud as the dickens," Sherrod said to no one in particular.

"You have done well, Daddy," Sally said. She took the baby and placed it in Mary Polly's arms. She then hugged Sherrod, and he hugged her back, crossed the room, and hugged Joel.

"You have both done well," Joel said and Sally hugged him. She then went to Mary Polly.

"I love you sister," she said. "And I love this baby." She took the baby from Mary Polly. "What will you call him?"

"Henderson," Sherrod spoke up. "Taken from the word hinder, which means to counteract, resist, strain, or prohibit. This country has next-to-no tolerance for people of color, and I don't see the situation improving. This child represents his family resisting the constraints that society has placed and continues to place on people of color."

Joel took his nephew and held him. "This person of color will be a person of means, Sherrod Bryant. He will never know what slavery is, indentured or otherwise; I promise you that."

Sally took the baby from Joel and gave him back to Mary Polly. "Let's leave the new parents to their family. It has been a long night for them and for us." She hugged Mary Polly and Sherrod. "Good night," she said. Joel smiled at them as they went out.

"Joel refused to take any of Daddy and big Mary's money," Mary Polly said. "I was surprised when he said that Henderson would be a person of means."

"Still water runs deep, Mary Polly. Joel has a lot of heart. He is afraid to share his feelings sometimes, but he's right there. I am truly grateful for him and Sally."

Mary Polly took his hand. "Thank you."

"I should be thanking you." Sherrod smiled and hugged her and the baby and said, "It's hard to believe. Wait until William and Silas hear." He turned off the lantern, put the baby in the middle between them, and lay down to rest with his family. "The road ahead is not going to be easy for you," he said. "Do you know how you are going to handle leaving?"

"I have until the end of the holidays," she said. "I better get on back after the holidays." She reached under the pillow and gave him a wad of money. "I've been meaning to give you this. Take it and put it in a safe place until you are ready to use it." He took the money from her.

"I wish there was a way that you didn't have to go back, or that I could stay here with you until you left."

"Things have changed between us, but our lifestyles must remain the same. We cannot draw attention to ourselves. As hard as it is, I will handle it. The worst part is that I will never be able to properly acknowledge that Henderson is my son." He hugged her and the tears came. He cried and she cried. They hugged the baby together and quietly in their own thoughts admonished the world for being such a sorry place.

*****Henderson started to go over the sequence of events. Daddy Bryant left and everyone started fixing and doing things around the house. He started to get worried. Then he remembered the night he went to sleep and dreamed that Sherrod and Mary Polly were married and living in Bryant Town. All the children at school were teasing him. His mama was different than theirs. Mulatto kid, mulatto kid, child of a white woman, they called after him, and he threw rocks at them. When he woke up, he was angry and full of questions. If Sherrod was with Mary Polly, why wasn't he off visiting her instead of some half-breed Indian woman that he hadn't seen since he was a child? Why did Sherrod let Mary Polly get on that boat? Why did he live with Papa Joel and Mama Sally in the first place? To his surprise, the answers to these questions came to him when he was quiet. As he answered his own questions, he became more and more sad. Some anger was there as well, but Daddy Bryant had instilled in him that anger for anger's sake was wasted energy. He tempered the anger and rationalized it. Yes, Mary Polly was his mother and it was sad that she had to visit rather than live with him and his daddy. But that's the way it was, and as hard as it was for him to deal with, it had to be harder for Mary Polly and for Daddy Bryant. He wondered what had caused her to stop visiting. The memory of that day on the trail when Tom and Filbert accosted them came to mind. Uncle—he remembered Mary Polly calling the man "uncle." It all started to make sense. Somewhere there might be other uncles, aunts, and grandparents on Mama Mary's side of the family.

"What's keeping you up so late tonight, Renfro?" Sherrod asked him. Renfro pushed him gently inside the door and then crossed to the window and lowered the shade.

"Some of them other Coles were in the dining room tonight. Little Doe heard one of them say that Joel hasn't been around as much since 'that half-bread Sherrod' has been going over there. Old Tom, he's meaner than the devil asked if you had a woman. His brother said nobody has ever seen you with one. Then there was some talk that maybe you were after Joel's wife."

"That's crazy talk," Sherrod said angrily.

"I know it and you know it, but you know how white folks are once they get a bug up their butt," Renfro whispered. His voice was so low that Sherrod could barely make out what he was saying. "Them Coles are a clannish group. They even did some talking about suspecting Joel's wife was part Indian. Suspecting that's why Big Mary ain't been out here to see her grandchildren. Who's Big Mary?"

"Thanks for telling me," Sherrod said while taking Renfro gently by the arm and leading him to the door. "It's been a long day. People are going to talk no matter what."

"Long as you're satisfied with it," Renfro said. "You are one of my best customers and one of my favorites. I am to look out for you."

That's a switch from what you said last time, Sherrod thought but smiled at Renfro and said, "Thanks." He then opened the door and closed it after him.

What a day, he thought, and stretched out on the bed. Before he could reach for the covers he was asleep. Sometime near dawn, Sherrod woke up with a fright. The power behind Renfro's words stirred in his mind and woke him up. He went to the window and looked out at the moon. The street was quiet. Two cats could be heard fighting in the distance.

He went back and sat on the edge of the bed. Joel had to get himself a slave woman. No, he needed two slave women and a man. Yes, three people would do it: one to help Sally cook, one to wait on the children, and another to work with Joel. He knew that Joel and Sally were against slavery. Maybe if he had Mary Polly buy them and they actually belonged to him and Henderson, Joel and Sally could treat them as family. He thought about it some more as he lay back in bed, tossing and turning, his mind fluctuating between selling Joel on the idea of letting slaves live in his house and him being a father to Henderson.

It was hard for him to tell who Henderson looked like. He was light-skinned and red like most babies. He had big, light-brown eyes and a full head of hair.

The next thing Sherrod knew, the sun was shining in his room making a large reflection on the wall. He realized he had fallen asleep. Sometimes he liked losing track of time. Other times he hated it. When he looked at the height of the sun in the sky, he determined that it was nearly noon and he had missed breakfast. He dressed and went down the road to Mr. Nash's house. Sherrod asked his daughter, who had stayed home from church, if there were any more of those yellow sundresses that he saw in the store window. The Nash girl went inside and came back with one. "A Christmas present for my brother's wife," he volunteered. He paid her and rode off. He was anxious to see Mary Polly and the baby, but he took the long way around and stopped to tell his brothers the news. When they heard the news, they picked up Sherrod; William took his arms and Silas took his feet and they tossed him back-and-forth, swinging out against Sherrod's efforts to get down. After a couple swings, they still had him on his feet.

"You two are a couple of kids," Sherrod said. He was quite annoyed.

"Get used to it, Daddy," William laughed.

Silas slapped him hard on the back. "Can't you just enjoy how happy we are for you and the baby?"

Sherrod knew that Silas was right. He yelled, grabbed Silas by the legs, and wrestled him to the ground.

"Watch out Silas," William laughed. "Little brother is a daddy now. No more pushing him around." Silas started to get angry. He struggled for top position and Sherrod pinned him to the ground. He struggled some more and Sherrod let him up.

"If I was pumped up the way you are today, I could probably hold a bear to the ground," he said. Sherrod knew his older brother needed to save face.

"You're probably right," he said and helped Silas to his feet. In his mind, he was thinking of how it felt to be a dad. *This day I am a daddy*, he said to himself. *No matter what happens after this, I know what being a daddy feels like.* It was a feeling that his brothers had yet to experience. William and Silas were doing well as tenant farmers. Their lease was up and they were looking forward to renewing it. Their women were away at church so William cooked breakfast.

Sherrod wanted to tell them what Renfro had said, but he decided against it. They didn't understand or trust people like Renfro, and they wouldn't have been much help to him. By the time he got to Joel's house, it was late afternoon and the slave plan was ready to be presented. To Sherrod's surprise, Joel liked the idea.

Before he went to Joel, he told Mary Polly what Renfro had said. She confirmed that her family suspected Sally's father was Indian and they felt he died when Sally and her brothers were young, long before Joel met Sally. They had no way of proving their suspicions as their feelings were based only on the appearance of some of Sally's brothers. Sally's mother had come to town as a widow with small children. She was a domestic and hired her sons out as farmhands, while Sally stayed in the house to do chores. Joel had befriended one of the brothers in Kentucky, and the brother took him home to meet Sally. Mary Polly admitted the Cole family had never discussed Sally's family history with her. She said that Joel had made a point of not taking Sally to Virginia to meet the family as was the Cole custom. This told Mary Polly that Joel knew what the suspicions were.

As far as Joel buying slaves for Sherrod, Mary Polly was all for it. She told Sherrod how to present it to Joel and said to take fifteen hundred from the money given for the purchase. It was understood that the slaves would belong to Sherrod and live with Joel in trade for the care of Henderson and Sherrod's weekly sleepover.

Sally was pleased about the extra help. She agreed that he should ask his uncles and cousins to help him purchase the slaves so that they would feel their importance, and Joel did as everyone suggested. He went to his Uncle Tom with the problem of needing slaves to help him manage the farm. Uncle Tom took Joel to a neighboring friend's house.

There they purchased three slaves: Lewis, Nance, and Helen. After the purchase, they went back to Tom's house to celebrate. Tom's brothers, Filbert and John, and their sons all turned out to welcome Joel into what they considered manhood.

"You are a Cole," he kept hearing. "Slavery is a fact of life. You either control them black bucks, or they will take what's yours." Joel listened, half-heartedly. He was reminded of the time he hid under the table in his father's study and listened to him talk to his friends about farming and the cost of labor and how the Africans had been taken out of their country to free up the plantation owner and provide him time to plan and to play.

Joel vowed that he would treat Lewis, Nance, and Helen like he did all of his friends. They were Sherrod's slaves and he was only doing it for his sister, his nephew, and his friend Sherrod. When the party was done and he and the slaves got into the wagon to head home, he wondered if he was living his life or someone else's. All he ever wanted was to be grown so that he could make his own choices and do what he wanted to do. Now, he thought himself settled with all kinds of obligations and chores that he wasn't sure he wanted any part of.

Lewis, Nance, and Helen saw the move as a possible chance to improve their lot. They hated it where they were. The people were nasty and poor and blamed them for not producing enough grain to make them rich. Lewis was in his 40s, Nance was a year or two older, and Helen was in her late 30s. The three of them didn't know very much about each other. They had been together less than six months. Their Master had inherited Lewis from a dead uncle. Nance had been a nurse for the wife's children, and Helen had been won in a crap game in some shanty along the river.

Christmas came and went. The slaves in Joel's household were settling into their roles. Sherrod met with them the night they arrived, showed them the bunks that he had made for them in the barn, and promised that they could improve their housing as the relationship grew. He appointed himself overseer and told them that Mr. Cole was not to be disturbed with petty problems. Lewis was to help with the heavy outside chores feeding the cattle and plowing the land. Helen was to help him seed, make a vegetable garden, and cook. Nance was to do whatever Sally needed her to do in the house.

Sally had never had help before. She had problems delegating tasks to the women. Sherrod let them know that he would hold them accountable if anything went undone, whether Sally asked them to do it or not.

The mood was sad around the house the week that Mary Polly was to return to Virginia. She suffered with thoughts of leaving Henderson, and everyone felt her pain. They spent hours on end helping Mary Polly shop for the baby for clothes and toys and whatever she couldn't find. Sherrod stayed the week at Joel and Sally's and tried to assure Mary Polly. Joel withdrew like he always did when problems arose. He was afraid to let Mary Polly go home alone. He had nightmares about Jesse and Big Mary finding out about Henderson, and rather than alarm the others with his thoughts, he kept them to himself. Outwardly, he appeared to have no interest in what was going on around the farm, but Sherrod spent hours trying various ways to involve with the slaves.

Soon after Mary Polly's departure, Joel told Sherrod that he needed to get away. He needed to go to Virginia to visit his parents and make sure that everything was okay with Mary Polly. He asked Sherrod to take care of his family until he returned. Sherrod agreed and Joel left. He stayed in Virginia for a month. Sally went about her routine showing no discomfort at Joel not being there.

She busied herself helping to plan the spring crop and doing chores for the children. Sherrod knew that she was trying to be accepting of Joel being away, but regardless of what she was trying to portray, she was having a hard time with it. She moved a little slower and was not as quick to smile as she usually was. Sherrod went out of his way to tell her how well she was handling things and how well she was doing while Joel was away. She appreciated him noticing, because she was lonely.

She had never been separated from Joel before and was surprised at how much she missed him. She felt that sometimes she took him for granted and made up in her mind that she was going to appreciate him more when he returned. Sherrod chose that time to teach Henderson how to sit alone. His efforts were met with mild success. Henderson was a big, six-week-old baby, and it took an additional two weeks of trying before he would sit up for his daddy.

Managing chores was easier with help. Sherrod assigned Lewis the job of adding larger slave quarters to the barn, building a pigpen, and reordering hay and grain for the animals. When Joel returned, he was happy to see his family and what had been accomplished while he was away. He could see growth taking place, and he told his wife he was glad they had made the decision to expand while he was away.

He had a long talk with Sherrod. He told Sherrod that he had been uneasy about Mary Polly leaving her child. He said that he knew she was depressed and he had taken it upon himself to join her in Virginia to give Sherrod an opportunity to prove to Mary Polly and himself that everything would work out without her being present. Sherrod knew Joel went because of his own need to walk Mary Polly through her separation from Henderson, but whatever the reason, he was grateful. He was glad that Joel had an opportunity to see his folks. Joel told Jesse that Sherrod was helping him set up a decent farm and Jesse sent greetings. Joel also reported that Big Mary had missed Mary Polly and appeared glad to see her. They all missed her and were glad that she was home.

They wished that he and Sally lived closer with the children. Robert was trying to decide if he wanted to move back to England, and everyone was encouraging him to go back before he lost Mary Polly's fortune drinking and chasing after the young girls in town. Joel's brother, Jesse Jr, had come up and so did his sister, Missouri. It was a homecoming for the family, and Joel said that he had gained insight into what he had to do to suit his needs and those of Sally and the children. He couldn't say enough about Mary Polly's accomplishments at Cole Manor. Seeing a real plantation helped him realize that the Tom Cole branch of the family was by no means a representation of what Coles could do once they set their minds in the right place.

He also realized that Mary Polly was not a housewife but a high-powered, driven Southern white woman that would die if she tried to relocate. Rutherford County could not give her the status that she needed. It was a great hideaway that added to her sense of self. She sent Sherrod the message that she would come to Murfreesboro every June and December, and he was to send her notes reporting on Henderson's progress every month that she was away. The messages were to be loaded with sayings and behaviors of Henderson but attributed to John and Missouri and it was to be signed by Joel. Sherrod complied with the request for notes.

He mourned Mary Polly's departure by stepping up his pace. He continued to work for the Donelsons, helped Joel build his farm, supervised his slaves Lewis, Nance, and Helen, and interacted with Henderson on a daily basis.

Even though Henderson was the youngest in the family, he identified with John who was four years older. He let Missouri help Sally feed him when he was with the three of them alone. If John or Sherrod were present, he struggled to feed himself, most of the time ending up with food all over his face and eyes. Henderson and Missouri were fifteen months apart, but he was placed on the same routine. Sally nursed him the same as she had John and Missouri, and no matter where Sherrod slept or how late or long he worked, every morning first thing he came and got his son, the same as Joel used to do when she needed a break.

Sally came to wonder how she had managed before Nance, Helen, and Sherrod had come into her life. As she thought about it enough, she had to laugh to herself and be reminded that along with all the help came an extra child. She loved Henderson the same as she did her own.

When people said to Joel, "I thought you had two children." Joel would laugh and say, "Sally is not going to be happy until she has ten." He knew Mary Polly was a little envious of Sally with nursing Henderson but she was also very grateful to both Joe and Sally for loving her and her child enough to do so. Mary Polly's life was not at all like she had planned. If she had to have children, having Henderson the way she did was just perfect, except for the distance that is. She liked being the Madame of Cole Manor, being the talk of Virginia and receiving all the attention that was showered upon her.

At social events, town fathers would sneak her in. When decisions were made governing the town, people of means would call on her and ask for her opinion. Many of the young women emulated her fashion and worked at being in her company.

Her choice of lifestyle was just as she wanted it. Yes, her family was secret. Yes, it was hard to deny the pleasure of watching her son develop, but along with that came family and social obligations she was glad she didn't have to deal with.

On her good days, she was proud of her secret. On her lonely days, she reminded herself that as much of a secret as her family was, it was her family forever and ever.

With that in mind, she dug into building Cole Manor up even more. She bought a gin mill and moved it onto the property. She bought ten additional slaves and asked Mingus, Cato, and Eatoe to use them to increase production. Money had never been of interest to her, but the birth of Henderson had changed that.

She took the books away from Robert. She told Jesse that she didn't like the way Robert was conducting himself and his personal business in town and that his behavior was affecting her and Cole Manor's credibility.

Big Mary was disappointed in Robert. When he returned to Virginia, he spent very little time with her. He had changed. He was opinionated and arrogant and no longer looked to her for guidance. He thought her to be a silly old woman not worthy of his time and treated her as such.

Big Mary pretended not to notice until Mary Polly suggested the money be put in her charge. With that, Big Mary responded with a vengeance. "Give the little boy an allowance," she said. "If he can't live without that, send him back to England with his bad manners and wayward ways."

Mary Polly had never felt so supported. She almost felt vindicated. Her son's future depended on how she handled the financial end of the family business, and her aim was to secure the position as a financial manager. That way, her son and Sherrod could live without the racial constraints ordinary people of color would have to experience.

BOOK THREE
1815—1854

BRYANT ACRES CHAPTER XV

Nashville is Not the World, But Sometimes it Feels Like It

Robert was outraged when Jesse suggested giving him an allowance. He accused Mary Polly of not serving his efforts and asking that he be sent back to England for a year. Jesse gave him a large sum of money and informed him of Mary Polly's plans to oversee the England office. Robert felt trapped and didn't like it that Mary Polly was taking over the business in England, but he was smart enough to go along with what Jesse wanted. He grabbed the money and started his vacation with a secret promise that he would seek employment elsewhere once he returned to the States.

The traveling helped Mary Polly's enterprising skills grow. Once she got Robert out of the financial picture, she and Lavonia took to traveling back and forth to England. Big Mary wanted to join them, but Jesse was against it, and no good Southern wife went against her husband's wishes.

Twice a year, the women traveled, with Lavonia first returning to Cole Manor and then Mary Polly going to Rutherford County. Once or twice Lavonia asked to join her in her side trip to Rutherford, but Mary Polly discouraged it saying she needed some quiet time away from the people she lived with, away from the demands of her parents and the plantation and Virginia. Lavonia had never seen Mary Polly look so soft and beautiful. She suspected that Mary Polly had a man in Rutherford County. When she asked Mary Polly if there was someone new in her life, Mary Polly said there wasn't, just as she should have. Lavonia was her mother-in-law, and as much as she trusted her, Sherrod and Henderson were not secrets to share.

Lavonia didn't take the rejection lightly. Mary Polly's decision angered her. She made a mental note to contact her brother, Tom, to see if he knew anything. She told herself if her finances were not limited, she would go to Rutherford with Mary Polly whether she liked it or not. She knew she wouldn't be able to go to England as she was doing if Mary Polly wasn't paying, but so what. She was Mary Polly's mother-in-law after all. Her son, Robert, had made a contribution to Mary Polly's riches. She didn't want to push her luck as a mother-in-law, but as an aunt, she had a right to know. Yes, she was going to contact Tom. Mary Polly had left her little choice. She hadn't seen Tom or Filbert in years. They didn't get along with Big Mary because she looked down on them. They would never come to visit her in Virginia, and Robert was such a disappointment. His choosing to go back to England was a good idea. It offered her an opportunity to go visit.

The visit took her outside of herself. Traveling with Mary Polly helped. Mary Polly was sure smart. She knew how to attract people. Yes, indeed, Mary Polly was teaching her a thing or two, and she hadn't had so much fun since she was a schoolgirl.

What she wouldn't give to know what was beckoning Mary Polly to Rutherford and Nashville as often as it did. And why couldn't Mary Polly let her in on it?

Mary Polly would become excited and overwhelmed near the end of every European trip. She would turn her mind towards Rutherford and Henderson. Mindfully, she would tune Lavonia out and let her thoughts wander with anticipatory thoughts of her son. What was he doing? How much had he grown? Did he remember her? During these times, Lavonia would find Mary Polly non-communicable. Lavonia dreaded leaving England, but mostly she dreaded the changes in Mary Polly, the not knowing. Mary Polly was oblivious to the change in her behavior. She had her fun with Lavonia, but she wished Lavonia could say goodbye gracefully rather than clinging on at the end the way she did. When the boat docked, she and Lavonia separated and that was their saving grace as far as she was concerned.

Trying to have private thoughts and being with Lavonia was like mixing oil and water. Lavonia needed constant attention, and the only way to get away from her was just not to be with her. When Mary Polly saw Henderson that first trip back, she realized how fast Henderson was growing. It made Mary Polly sad. He was extremely attached to Sally. He called her Mama, the same as John and Missouri. Mary Polly was jealous, but she worked at Henderson knowing her. By the end of the month when it was time for her to return home, Henderson was so attached to her he didn't want her out of his sight.

Mary Polly made plans for Henderson's schooling and religious instruction. She didn't care that he was only six months old. Sally was a Quaker. That was acceptable to her, but books were hard to find locally. She searched the stores in England until she found learning toys and stories for the children to read. She encouraged Sally to work on their hand-eye coordination and memory. Henderson was a fast learner, and she spent time thinking of ways to teach him about his environment.

She and Sherrod had become very comfortable with each other that visit. Henderson was the topic of conversation. Cole Manor and her activities outside of Rutherford County seldom entered their minds when they were together. Racial issues were beginning to impact Sherrod, however. The State of Tennessee had enacted a law requiring free people of color to carry passes. The position of this emancipation certificate was a coveted prize for most people of color living in the state in 1811. For Sherrod, it was an insult. Freedom had never been an issue with him except in 1800 when he had assigned himself for six months into Jesse Cole's charge as an indentured servant. Even then, it was his choice. Now, after five years of living in Tennessee as an upstanding citizen without the threat of danger or harm to himself or others, he was being categorized as someone other than who he was. And now that he was able to make a living and lived as a credible free citizen, he was being asked to carry a pass.

Everyone in town knew Sherrod, except for the occasional stranger. At no time during that period before the Civil War was a free man's right to own property ever questioned. He was able to own land, property, personal belongings, and slaves. The past gave the whites managing rights, and he resented it. He tried to talk to Mary Polly about it and found that he couldn't. She knew about the past and how he felt about it but said it was the law and he shouldn't take it so personal.

Her remarks cut into him and forced him to realize that she had no concept of what was being asked of him. She saw the strong reaction he had to what she said and tried to smooth it over. "You and I know you are better than them. Let them play their silly games.

They have been doing it for centuries, long before you and I were born. Look at my situation. If I don't stay married regardless of where my husband is or how much we don't get along, everything I accomplish will be wiped out. White men are small minded. You have to be bigger than them, like you have always been."

Sherrod didn't argue with her the way he would have done in days past. Instead, he accepted that it was what she believed; she was a product of her world, and he was a product of his. What he needed here was a female that understood his experience as a man of color, a woman who wasn't connected to his daily life in any way. It was the first time he admitted Mary Polly was incapable of filling all of his needs, and it made him sad. He pushed the thought of another woman from his mind and forgot about it until the next time he was at Black Bob's.

Little Doe was coming down the steps as he was going up. "I need to bring you a clean towel," she said as she passed him. He smiled and let her know that it would be ok for her to come up, and kept walking.

Sherrod had not mentioned the pass again to Mary Polly. She had left for home, and this was his first day back at the hotel after her departure. He had just learned that the land he wanted was finally for sale and was feeling better than he had since the free man's pass law had been implemented.

He was starting to relax from the ride into town when Little Doe knocked on the door. He opened it for her, and she gave him the towel. He thanked her, but she stood there peeping around him to see what was going on in his room.

"Would you like to come in?" he asked.

She looked back over her shoulder to see if anyone heard his invitation. When she was satisfied they were alone, she said, "I get off work now."

"Come in for a minute, and we will leave the door open."

"Close the door," she said and quickly stepped inside. He closed the door behind her.

"Tonight, we talk, just talk," he said. "I know how your tribe is about courting people without marriage."

"I'm already spoken for. I can't marry you. Little Doe trusts you," she said and smiled.

He and Little Doe saw each other alone every time he was at the hotel after that. She was really easy to be with, and he liked their relationship. On three scheduled Sunday evenings when Mary Polly wasn't around, he made his way to the Choctaw Nation. He visited first with the tribal chief and then with the men in the village. They sat and talked about the workings of the US government while Little Doe sat in her tent with her mother and sisters. When the discussions ended, Little Doe's father would call her out. "Mr. Bryant would like you to visit with him on the trail to Nashville," he would say, and Little Doe would come out and greet Sherrod as if she was surprised that he had come.

Often, the two of them would go to an abandoned cave or to a bluff of Little Doe's choosing. Once there, they would make love. Sherrod would take her by the hand and walk her back to her camp. The chief liked Sherrod. He was a powerful man, and they recognized him as one of them. For four months he went to visit Little Doe's camp. That last Sunday, the chief stopped him at the entrance to the camp and asked him to leave and not return.

Without a word, Little Doe quit her job at Black Bob's. Sherrod was disappointed she had not thought enough of him to give him a reason for ending their relationship. He swore off outside women, increased his workload, and prepared for Mary Polly's spring visit.

By the time Mary Polly arrived in June 1811, Little Doe was all but forgotten. Sherrod turned his attention to the land he wanted to purchase, and it was the first thing he discussed with Mary Polly when they were alone. Sherrod showed her two hundred acres of prime land on McCreary Creek at Stones River that was for sale. It was prime property and part of the parcel of land he had shown her from the ridge her first day in Tennessee.

Mary Polly knew of Sherrod's love for the river. She knew he had been around it long enough to appreciate its function and the possibilities it offered. Land adjacent to McCreary Creek was property he had coveted since the first time he rode into Tennessee, and she wanted him to have it. She encouraged Sherrod to approach Matthew Brooks Sr. and make him an offer.

Sherrod had tried to stay out of the race war, and he had managed to some extent. Now, he had to come to grips with the fact that his birth put him in it. Before he did as Mary Polly suggested, he went to Mr. Brooks' neighbors, John Buchanan, John Carter, and Adam Coolidge, to ask them if they had any problem with him buying the East end of the tract of two hundred seventy-four acres Brooks had for sale. Each intern welcomed him to the area.

With a new heightened sensitivity to what white people were not saying when they talked, he accepted their welcome speeches with the knowledge that his step forward made him indebted to them. When they came and asked to be repaid, he knew he had better be in a position to give them answers based on decisions that were in his own best interest.

In November 1811, Sherrod approached Mr. Brooks and for three hundred sixteen dollars, he purchased the two hundred seventy-four acres on the McCreary Creek side of Stones River. The deed described the property as "*****The beginning of which starts at the Thorn beam on the West Bank and the Ching of Ross bush on the East bank of said creek, at John Buchanan's North boundary line the same being John Carter's Southeast corner. The boundaries being Buchanan's line East on 141 Pole's to three White Oaks going North 153 poles to two dogwoods and a small black walnut on the South boundary line of Thomas Coolidge's property. Going along that line North 80 more degrees West, 166 poles to the center of McCreary's Creek then up said creek with its measurements 202 poles to the beginning, the purchase to include all water rights."

Sherrod named his property "Bryant Town." He hoped would the name motivate growth and prosperity.

Sherrod purchased the land more than one hundred eighty-five years ago. With the exception of small remnants of Sherrod's family cemetery on the Eastern left corner of McCrary Street, the Nashville International Airport occupies the land Sherrod had purchased. John Buchanan and Sherrod Bryant are buried in their family plots and therefore are still neighbors. When one considers Highway 55 and the limousine rental agency that separates these family cemeteries—one segregationist and the other integrationist—the scope of that purchase is magnified and still stands.

Sherrod's caution caused him not to tell Joel or Sally about the land until after Mary Polly came back in December. It was with her financial help and support that he was able to buy the land, so he thought it would be more acceptable to her brother and sister-in-law if she told them herself. It wasn't as if he was hiding the purchase from them, because he didn't officially own the title of the land until after the holidays in January 1812.

1812 marked a good beginning for all of them. Sally was pregnant, Henderson was three years old, and Sherrod was meeting his timeline. He couldn't have been prouder. Mary Polly was also proud. She sent Sherrod out to buy four young African male slaves to help him build a house. Even though Lewis, Nance, and Helen belonged to him, they had become an integral part of Joel and Sally's life. He and Mary Polly thought it best to let them be.

Joel had become quite the farmer. Mary Polly had talked him into planting cotton. She had helped him with sales, which brought him a fair amount of money and prestige in town. Sally had the baby and named her Mary Ann. She and Nance started a little toddler school, where three-, four-, and five-year-olds would learn games and songs from books Mary Polly picked up during her travels. Helen managed the house and kept the baby, Mary Ann. She served the toddlers' mothers tea and cookies while they sat around in Sally's kitchen sewing and waiting for their children.

Henderson was very much a part of the Cole family. He even looked like his cousins. He was a light-skinned child. However, his ears and genitals were darker than the rest of them. That told Sherrod Henderson's color would change. He will either be Sherrod's shade of brown or a little lighter like his Uncle Silas. Being the baby in the family, everyone spoiled him. Then Mary Ann came along. From birth, Mary Ann was an even-tempered baby.

Henderson delighted in every move she made. He would make faces and funny noises, and she would giggle. Every time she giggled, he giggled. Wherever she was, he wanted to be. Henderson called Joel "Papa," the same as Joel's own children. Sherrod, he called "Daddy Bryant." Sally, he called "Mama," and Mary Polly he called "Mama Mary."

He was a stocky little boy, very physical. He loved horses, partly because Mary Polly bought him a rocking horse when he was a year old. From the beginning, Sherrod put him in the saddle with him, and together they rode around the farm talking and laughing. When he was too young to sit alone, Sherrod held him in one hand and slowly walked the other horse while he told Henderson about the land and what it was used for.

Henderson loved his time with his father so much so that when Sherrod arrived in the mornings, Henderson met him with riding pants and a hat in hand. For this third birthday, Sherrod bought Henderson a spotted pony that he named Paint. When Sherrod took the title of the land, the second thing he moved onto the property behind his own Bay horse was Paint.

When Mary Polly asked him why, he said it was because he wanted his son to identify his Daddy's home with the fun they had together. Paint cemented the bond they had forged.

Buying slaves for his own personal use was harder for Sherrod than it had been when he purchased them for Joel. Somehow, he saw the recent purchase as a gesture made for the safety of Henderson. Buying them because he needed cheap labor was a different kind of mindset. He sat with it and thought about it for a long while. Finally, he concluded the four young men he was about to purchase did not have to be slaves. They would only be slaves legally. He would be responsible for them as such, but practically, they would be his workers and, if warranted, part of his family.

He explained this to George, Samuel, and Zink when he brought them home from the auction block. The young men weren't sure when they were born and appeared to be in their early 20s. They had just arrived from New Orleans and had spent the better part of their lives for the overseer who had hired them out to several large plantations before he came upon hard times.

Sherrod paid the overseer one thousand dollars apiece for them. The overseer presented the best four strong, healthy, and well-fed men who were not self-starters but were more than willing to work. The slaves thought Sherrod was annoying when he talked to them about loyalty and trust. Because of this, they did not like him. When he talked to them about farming and what he had done, they liked him better because they understood what he wanted. Sherrod didn't want a fancy house his first time on his own. He and the men built a two-room cabin with back and front porches. One room was used for sleeping and other was used for sitting and planning as well as for eating.

He bought several bushels of feathers from the chicken farmer on the road to Nashville. He asked Helen to make him a mattress from a half dozen open-sided grain sacks sewed together front to back and stuffed with feathers. The mattress cover wasn't as hard so he had Samuel make it for him. Samuel also made a batch and "A" tables from several boards he nailed together.

Next, he had the men help him raise a barn with a large loft and crawl space. There was enough room for the slaves to sleep until they had the means to make better sleeping places. Zink, Samuel, George, and Henry were not used to working with their Master. At first, they were uneasy, but after a while they learned that working hard and honestly went a long way. Then they were able to relax.

At times, one or the other of the men wanted to tell their story, but Sherrod discouraged it unless the man was really disturbed by the memory and was having trouble functioning.

One night, Henry started screaming in his sleep and Sherrod went to see about him. The other men were irritated by the disturbance and said that Henry was giving them away, no matter what they said to him. Sherrod woke Henry and invited him up to the house. Sherrod fixed some coffee and the two men sat at the table. Henry was afraid that Sherrod was mad and he was about to be punished.

"I tried to stay awake so I wouldn't have a dream. I'm not doing it willfully." he babbled. "I don't want you to cut my tongue out so—"

Sherrod stopped him. "I want to help you Henry. Tell me what's wrong."

"Nothing is wrong."

"Your dreams. Tell me about your dreams. What is frightening you?"

"My mother, she knew ole Master was hungry. She boiled oil to make fish. She floured the fish, she . . ." He started to cry. "Ole Master kicked her. I yelled at him 'Don't hurt Mama.' He threw a rock at me. Mama moved to protect me and the boiling pot of oil splashed all over. Ole Master, he wanted his dinner, so he kicked the pot and spilled the rest of the oil on Mama. She fell to the ground. Master laughed and stepped on Mama and crushed her broken body with his foot. 'Look what you got your mom into, boy,' he said. I was afraid to cry, afraid to help Mama. I was struck with fear and I couldn't move. I tried to move, honest! Honest!

"Mama had warned me not to say anything. From the time I was born to that day ten years later, she warned me. No matter what happens to me, you say nothing. I spoke, Mr. Bryant. I spoke when I knew I shouldn't have. It cost me mama's life. Every inch of her body was burned. She looked at me with her eyes sunken in, the charred face that smiled. I cringed and she died. I leaned closer to make sure she was dead. When I knew for sure that the Master couldn't hurt Mama anymore, I turned to him and said, 'You want me to start you a fresh kettle of fish?' Ole Master was so startled he turned and ran from the camp. Mr. Bryant, he saw the devil and the devil looked back."

Sherrod put his arm around Henry. "You did what you could, Son. Your mother knew that. That's why she smiled. She knew that you were going to be all right, and you are. God chose me for you to be here with, and I aim to see that you and I learn how to be good Christians together."

"Thanks Mr. Bryant."

"We aren't going to be good for much else in this white man's world if we don't believe in each other," Sherrod said and smiled.

"I think I will be all right now," Henry said and stood up.

Sherrod bid him a good night. "We have a lot of fencing to tackle tomorrow. Get some sleep because I want you to be ready."

Henry was ready. He was always ready after that. Whatever Sherrod needed, he was there to get for him or help him with it. Zink, George, and Samuel came to understand that Henry had a way of relating to Sherrod, and they looked to him for guidance. Meanwhile, Sherrod quit his job at the Donelsons. He still visited them once a week, however. If either of the Donelsons needed to consult with him about something, he was readily available. When he bought his place, William Thompson gave him the run of the lumber camp. He let him use the tools, cut wood, and order materials from various places throughout the county and abroad. Sherrod wasn't in a hurry to start his crop. He wanted to fence off his land, assess his resources, the creek, screen, ponds, fruit trees, bushes, and vines. He wanted to get used to his house. He wanted to make it so that Henderson could come and go. He knew that it was best to leave him with Joel and Sally's until he was older, but in his heart, a house with his son was his home—his real home.

"This is the week," Sherrod yelled and ran behind the counter and slapped Black Bob on the back.

Renfro couldn't believe his ears. Sherrod told him about the purchase and Renfro said, "I knew you was a businessman the minute I laid eyes on you. Man, I don't know what to say. You said it. I can't tell you how much this place has motivated me. You have been an inspiration. There were ten of us free men of color. Now, I believe there are twenty-five of us," Renfro said in a boastful way.

"This is a night of celebration. Are you ready for that dinner I promised you?"

Renfro took off his apron and threw it on the desk. He called his man from the back and asked him to mind the desk. "I'm in the dining room, eating with my friend Sherrod if anyone is interested," he told the man as they headed for the dining room.

Sherrod chuckled to himself. *Now I'm his friend?* He walked behind Renfro. It was his place, so he would show him the courtesy. The lights in the hotel burned a little brighter than usual and in spite of the fact that free men were now being required to carry passes, he was very much a part of what was happening in Nashville that night.

"Good evening," he said to the other guests in the dining room as if he expected to be greeted.

"Congratulations Sherrod," one said. Then another and another. Sherrod thanked them and smiled to himself. Then he said, "Now let us be. We are here to dine, not to get involved with you. Leave us to our privacy. Leave us to eat and talk and enjoy our success. We don't give a damn about what you are thinking." Sherrod felt that he had to work with them, but he didn't have to play with them. That certificate they made him carry took care of any socializing he might have done. If he wasn't a part of them, then he wouldn't pretend he was. They needed symbols of differences.

Up until then, Sherrod had been committed to living his life as if each and every person was a logical human being and capable of reason and capacity to listen and understand the difference between reality and wishful thinking. He knew that there was an emotional component that individuals brought to situations and events. He prided himself on his ability to distinguish between what was real and what wasn't. He usually knew when a person was caught up in fantasy and when he wasn't. He had a knack for cutting through the irrational and the rational. While he didn't always like government decisions, for the most part he thought his fellow countrymen were learned, experienced, and good human beings of intelligence who communicated and processed feelings into the equation the same way he did.

But their certificate proved him wrong. It taught him that he could no longer receive white folks as he used to. He now knew that no matter what he and Renfro accomplished, they would never be townsmen in the same way that Buchanan, Donelson, and other white men were. The requirement that he carry a free man pass told the story, and he was coming to grips with it. He thought about it while he and Renfro chatted. He asked Renfro, "Are you lonely in this town?"

Renfro smiled. "You know Bryant," he said, "I haven't given you enough credit."

"Maybe, just maybe, I am beginning to understand the world," Sherrod said. "This certificate thing has really shed light on the issue. It opened up the stage. Nashville is not the world, but sometimes feels like it is when you live and fraternize with some of the people we live and do business with."

Renfro decided it was not a good idea to let the discussion go any further. He pretended that he thought Sherrod was referring to his land purchases and responded accordingly. "Both Buchanan and Gilman will make right fine neighbors," he said.

He knew that Renfro was afraid to go any deeper into the issue, and that was fine. There was no way he was going to talk to anyone about anything serious again, with the exception of his brothers, whom he could trust.

Renfro knew that Sherrod was aware he had evaded the issue and still acted as if nothing had happened. That was what he liked about Sherrod. He was smooth and smart.

They were very different people, and they both knew it. They had always known it. Renfro admired Sherrod's spirit and knew that

Sherrod admired his. There was a tad bit of competition between them. Even when Sherrod had nothing, he carried himself like he did. He made any observer unsure and unable to figure out if he had something going on or not.

"I always knew that you were someone to be reckoned with. At first, I made excuses why I shouldn't like you. But you kept coming, like a bad berry. You lingered in my thoughts for days. The way you came in here and made the white folks respect you is something to behold. Your presence even demanded attention."

"You have done all right yourself," Sherrod said. He could see that Renfro wished it could be different.

"Yes, but I was born here. I'm a fixture in these parts."

"I am going to be a fixture too. You watch me," Sherrod said and winked.

Renfro held up his glass. "The room is on me tonight. You pay for dinner, and I will pay for the room. Deal?"

"Deal," Sherrod laughed, and they settled down to their meals. The conversation was light, and Sherrod knew that he had come to the end of a chapter. He wished that Mary Polly were sitting across from him and celebrating. She had been somewhat distant when he left her. He knew it had to do with her preparing her mind for the return home.

When he left Black Bob's that night, he thought himself lucky he had two brothers. He went out to where they lived. On his way out to their place, he got to thinking about how his brothers lived. They were sharecroppers on a place that barely made ends meet. He thought about asking them to come live with him on his land and helping him build. He had his differences with them, but times had changed. And he thought it would be good for Henderson to be around his own people and get to know his uncles.

The impact of what was happening to people of color around the country was sending a message. It was time for all people of color, free or slaves, to reevaluate their feelings. Then and there, he decided that Bryant Town meant his brothers too. It was to be a town of colored people, Indians, blacks, and people of mixed blood, descendants of his brothers, their wives, children, and slaves. By the time he arrived at his brother's house, he had worked out a plan. He discussed the town with William and Silas and encouraged them to participate in his dream. He asked Silas to go back to the hills of North Carolina and bring back a wife. He told him that Martha, his childhood sweetheart, was better for him than the woman he was seeing. He told William that the woman he was seeing wasn't in his best interest and he shouldn't marry her. Then he added, "My two hundred seventy-four acres is a good start for all of us."

William and Silas looked at each other. They were speechless. Sherrod's plan for the town didn't come as a surprise to them. They had endured hours of arguing against what they considered his misplaced ideas, but all of that had changed when he bought the land. William and Silas had a discussion when they discovered the land he acquired included McCreary Creek. "Why does that boy think he is moving into them rich folks his territory?" Silas said to William soon after Sherrod came to spread the news.

"He's Sherrod Bryant," William said and laughed. "I would be dumbfounded if he wasn't my little brother. It's time you and I owned up to his accomplishments; the man has a way about him, admit it. Daddy always said he was special. I always thought he was just saying that because he never had a mother the way we did. You know, an excuse for Daddy to spoil him."

"You have more feelings about that than I do," Silas said. "You two are closer in age. All I have to say is downplay this discovery or his head will get too big, and he'll start thinking that he's as old as us. We won't be able to tell him anything."

"Faith brother, faith." William laughed. What he wanted to do was remind Silas that the life they had carved for themselves wasn't where he wanted to be five years up the road. In due time, Silas came to the conclusion on his own. The plan for Bryant Town and the suggestion that he return tomorrow convinced him that Sherrod was special. Like the townspeople of Nashville, he began to see his brother through new eyes and he listened to what he had to say.

Sherrod had already built his house. He promised to help William build his and suggested that they have a house ready for Silas and Martha when they returned. The more the Bryant brothers heard, the more they began to embrace the idea of a town.

"I think it will work," William said. He was the oldest, and he figured it was his place to give Silas permission to accept Sherrod's plan and his leadership. Once William spoke, Sherrod knew that his brothers would support him no matter what.

"Given the climate for free people of color," Silas said, "we need to be careful about discussing these plans with anyone. That includes Mary Polly, Sherrod."

"Not a problem," Sherrod said and thought, "*If not telling Mary Polly is what it takes to bring you in, then so be it.* He smiled and found himself laughing about the fact that despite having an idea of his intentions, Mary Polly was content not to be an important part of it. There were meetings between the brothers the following months, networking meetings. They discussed and agreed they would stay away from cotton. Joel and Sally were doing quite well with it, but the viciousness of the trade and the way it promoted slave labor was a problem they wanted to stay away from.

They wanted no parts of tobacco either. It was big business. So big that the government was regulating it and becoming more and more involved in its production. Chickens, butter, eggs, and vegetables were stable products left to simple farmers. Beef, pigs, and wild game were not all that exciting either, so that wasn't a threat.

Silas was a barber. William was a stonemason and rock smith. Sherrod was a logger. He knew how to build the gristmill and a sawmill, and he had the resources and power to run both. The women would weave and be in charge of making linen, cotton, and wool for fabric of all kinds. They would do the dying as well as the baking. Bryant Town would be self-reliant, and there would be no visible means of any of its people attempting to earn money. Education and religious instruction would be private as well. There would be no defined trails or pathways through the property. The main road would be the path from the front gate leading to Sherrod's house and to his barn. The other houses would be built in the brush away from the eyes of passersby. This was Sherrod, William, and Silas's plan. They discussed it, shaped it, and rehashed it.

Silas finally decided it was time to say goodbye to the life he had been living and set out on his journey to where Martha was waiting. He wanted to start his new life. He wanted Martha to meet Henderson and give him a cousin to play with at some future date. She had moved in with her mother when he left. She had done so willingly because she had faith that she would someday follow Silas.

Six years was a long time, and he was somewhat afraid but excited to see her.

BRYANT ACRES CHAPTER XVI

Indian Secrets, Old and New

When Silas returned to Bryant Town, William was married to Mandy. Their cabin was located in the center of twenty-five acres of land that Sherrod had put in William's charge. In the center of the neighboring twenty-five acres was a two-room cabin with a barn and an outhouse. This was Silas's new home awaiting his arrival.

The land where they built their town was in the Southeasterly corner of Davidson County in what is now known as the fourth civil district of the first precinct of Davidson. The boundaries included Rutherford and Wilson County, where the lines of acreage cross for several miles and where Stones River and McCreary Creek makes their way through the land that makes up most of the acreage. In the beginning, Sherrod bought cattle, horses, and hogs. He made William and Mandy responsible for the production and selling of dairy products. He assigned the hogging and stud service to Silas and Martha.

He bought eleven additional slaves: Willie, Isham, and Harris, who were sent to work with William; Oscar and Moses, whom he assigned to Silas; Mallia and Henry, who were assigned to do the daily chores in his household; and Walter, Vitch, Jamie, and Jonny, whom he assigned to Henry. Their job was to help establish new businesses as the need arose.

Sherrod primarily purchased young males because he knew they would find wives and have children, thereby increasing the population of Bryant Town.

In 1814, John Tilford built a grist and sawmill on the West fork. Samuel Tilford built a mill on the East fork. Sherrod built a sawmill and distillery somewhere in the middle between the two. He added trapping, selling furs, tanning skins, fishing, and logging to his list of businesses. Oscar was an excellent trapper. He built traps for himself and others. Jonny and Jamie finished and ran the fish, poultry, and meat market. Sherrod, Walter, and Vitch set up a lumberyard. They cut trees, logged them to the mill, and cut them into lumber.

Vitch also managed the blacksmith shop. George forged copper, and Samuel cut stone and did stone masonry. Helen came and helped India and Henrietta plant and harvest the crops. By 1815, Bryant Town was up and functioning. Sherrod was so proud of his first crop that he shared it with their neighbors. The chickens were producing. The lumberyard was filled to capacity, and the weaving had been successful. The residents were Silas's family, William's family, and the fifteen slaves, and Sherrod had an abundance of everything. So much so that waste began to mount.

After much discussion with William and Silas, Sherrod decided to feel his way about town to see if any of the merchants would be interested in dealing with him. He went into Nash's grocery store and looked at the fruit and vegetables. He didn't purchase any but settled on two cookies instead.

"I hear you have the best supply of vegetables and fruit in these parts," Nash said.

Sherrod laughed. He had learned that white men loved getting things from you that they think you don't want them to have. "I am a small farmer," he said.

"I hear that you have the largest melons, tomatoes, and squash in Tennessee," Nash smiled. He loved surprising his customers with his knowledge of their business.

"Where would you hear that? Never mind. Donelson and Buchanan, they appreciate what you are doing out there. You have to learn to let some of us town people appreciate you. Let us taste some of those tomatoes they say you planted by the light of the moon."

"Old Indian secret. Maybe I can spare a bushel or two of tomatoes and squash, perhaps some melons. How much you paying?"

"Ten cents a bushel, if you let your boys bring in some of the skins I hear they are tanning out there." Nash searched Sherrod's face to see if he was connecting. When he was satisfied that Sherrod was interested, he continued. "Hogat said he heard you were trapping and tanning. I told him to speak to you about it. You hear from him?"

Sherrod went to the far end of the store and looked back across the room.

"What are you doing? I am talking to you and you're jumping around like a jack rabbit."

"I am measuring your room for a sample or two of furniture," Sherrod said. "The cabinets I have make the stuff you're selling here look shabby."

"Buying from you would sure cut costs; shipping and waiting could be cut down if I bought from you."

"I will bring you a couple of cabinets and you can see if you like them," Sherrod said and went out the door. He sure hoped he was doing the right thing dealing with white men again. Supplying Nash with goods was not part of the original plan, but he figured it would be advantageous if he could get Nash and some of the others, like Hogat, to depend on him. Sherrod felt he and his town would be safer if white people voluntarily came to them rather than them actively pursuing customers for trade.

With some trepidation, he began supplying Nash with goods, and by June 1815, his decision to sell outside proved to be a wise one. Businesses were booming. Sherrod built trails and paths to the various shops and opened up Bryant Town.

Many changes took place in 1815. Oscar and Helen got married. She moved to Bryant Town, took over the fabric weaving, and became a midwife for the town. Joel and Sally were generous in their support of her. At the insistence of Sherrod, Oscar went to them and asked for Helen's hand. They spoke to Sherrod about it.

"The children are growing up," Sammy said. "Helen deserves a life. She belongs to you, Sherrod."

"It's okay for her to go with Oscar." Henderson liked it that Helen went to live at Daddy Bryant's. In his mind, it meant he would be spending the night with Sherrod more often. Sherrod took him to Bryant Town when he wasn't busy cutting a deal or trying to make one. The morning ritual of him and Henderson riding together continued. Sherrod wanted it, but in his mind, he was usually far away on business and what he could do to improve Bryant Town. He wanted to make it more autonomous.

Henderson spent most of the ride babbling, going from one conversation to the next. He was so happy to be with his father. The occasional 'That's right Henderson," or "I can't answer that. Let me get back to you" didn't bother Henderson a bit. Most mornings after the ride, Sherrod would admonish himself for not paying more attention to his son. He would promise to do better the next day. The next day would come and the hours that followed, there would be more self-admonishment.

Nance had a crush on Henry. She was still living with Joel and Sally, so the way she satisfied her urge to see Henry was to take John, Missouri, Mary Ann, and Henderson to Bryant Town once a week.

Counting the weekly visits, Henderson, who was turning seven, saw Sherrod an average of fifteen hours a week. In June and December when Mary Polly came, she insisted on picnicking and family time during the weekends. So, the number of hours increased. That year, in 1815, just before Mary Polly made her June visit, Little Doe came to see Sherrod. She had a four-year-old child with her. She said the boy was Sherrod's son and asked him to help support his needs.

Mary Polly was due in town soon, so Sherrod busied himself trying to figure out how to best present it. Finally, he concluded that the only way was to just come out and tell her. Mary Polly was in Europe when Little Doe and the boy, Silas the third, moved in.

She always had her visits to Rutherford County dovetail with her trips to Europe. The trips abroad were taken as a cover for her trips to Tennessee. She and Lavonia took spring and Christmas cruises to England. They spent a month and then went on to Paris for an additional week of shopping. Lavonia then headed home, while Mary Polly went to Rutherford County. The night before the 1815 European trip was to end, Mary Polly and Lavonia were in their cabin, the waters were smooth, and both women were readying themselves for bed. They had thoroughly enjoyed themselves and each was content in their own thoughts.

After a while, Lavonia said, "Tomorrow I will go home and you will go off to wherever it is you go off to."

Mary Polly was surprised by Lavonia's tone. She knew that Lavonia always started gleaning when it came time to separate, but this was the first time she said anything. Mary Polly didn't know how to respond. She hoped if she said nothing, Lavonia would let it drop, but Lavonia had no such intention.

"I sometimes feel cheated," she said and took a deep breath. She had given the situation a lot of thought and wanted Mary Polly to know what she was saying was painful to her. "Not that I think I am entitled to follow you, Mary Polly. You are very generous, and I appreciate your inviting me like you do." She rose from her bunk and started to pace. "It's just that it's difficult to separate from you. We arrive stateside, and poof, you are gone, and I am left with strangers."

Mary Polly covered her face with her pillow. She was so angry. She was afraid she would say something she would be sorry for. The two of them had a close relationship for as long as she could remember.

What she liked about Lavonia was her ability to play and tease without a lot of heavy emotional family issues coming between them. They had always found a way to respect each other's boundaries.

They had never discussed Mary Polly's marriage to Robert or the fact that Lavonia was primarily dependent on Jesse and Big Mary for financial support.

Now, all of a sudden, Lavonia was talking to her as if she had a right to know where she was going, and she didn't like it. Yes, Lavonia was her mother-in-law and aunt, but it didn't give her the right to be in her business. Furthermore, what concern was it to Lavonia when she was openly flirting and carousing with men on the ship and when they were in England? Neither of them discussed what happened when one or the other disappeared with a man for the night.

The unspoken secrets they shared were a part of the joy of them being together. It bonded them, or so she thought. "What is it about my time alone with Joel and Sally that you don't understand, Lavonia?" she finally said it. "Joel is my nephew. I have never seen his children or met his wife. Not to mention that I have two brothers in Rutherford County."

"Everything you said is correct."

"What do your concerns have to do with my private time with my family?" Mary Polly was angry and raised her voice when she spoke.

Her anger frightened Lavonia. "I don't mean to probe," she said sarcastically, and it angered Mary Polly even more.

"Probe! What or wherever it is that I go," she exclaimed sarcastically, "I can see how sorry you are." Mary Polly turned over and with her back facing Lavonia and said, "As far as I am concerned, this conversation never happened." She blew out the lamp and settled herself for the night. She thought to herself, *All these years she took my money and pretended she understood me.*

Her anger warmed her cheeks and kept her from resting. She tried to push the incident out of her mind, but it continued to linger. *My God, why did I ever invite her?* she asked herself. Then almost as if answering her own question, she thought, because she was afraid that big Mary would tell Jesse not to trust her traveling back and forth across the ocean alone. She resigned herself to the situation and decided the best thing for her to do was to forget the usual breakfast with Lavonia and leave the ship. She wanted to make very little contact with her until both of them were back home safe in Virginia.

Lavonia lay in the dark seething. She wasn't expecting Mary Polly's anger. True, they had never discussed their private business, but she always thought it was because they didn't know how to approach the other given their age difference. Not because they didn't trust each other. What would be the big deal if she were seeing another man? Common sense told everyone that she and Robert weren't exactly making it. And the way Mary Polly carried on with men when they were traveling, well . . . Lavonia went over it again and again. Finally, she said to herself that it must be somebody married, somebody the family knows.

She thought about it some more and discussed it with herself long into the night. She went over all the men she had seen Mary Polly with over the years. When she couldn't come up with a clue, she decided the best thing to do was to get off the ship before Mary Polly did. She would avoid her at all costs. She wanted to get wire service and fire off a letter to Tom and Filbert as she said she was going to do back in December. She wanted to tell them Mary Polly was in Rutherford County two months out of the year and had been for the past six or seven years. She would ask them if they had seen her. She would show Mary Polly how to be angry. She would show her how not to treat a friend. She knew that Tom and Filbert didn't care much for Robert but they were men, and no decent man was going to stand by and let an unfaithful wife do her business under their noses.

It was almost comical to see the two women, mother-in-law and daughter-in-law, try to avoid each other. Mary Polly started to get up and saw Lavonia squirming so she hurriedly put the covers over her head and pretended to be asleep. They were both already packed, so it was easy for Lavonia to dress and quietly slip out of the cabin while Mary Polly lay and watched her through her covers.

As Lavonia closed the door, Mary Polly called to her. "I will see you in July, Lavonia." Lavonia pretended not to hear her. A man she had met at dinner the night before caught her eye so she hurried off to catch up to him, hoping that he would carry her bags.

BRYANT ACRES CHAPTER XVII

How Come I Get to be Brown

Mary Polly didn't realize how tired she was until she reached Joel and Sally's house. Her fight with Lavonia had taken its toll. Their relationship was the one thing in her life that had remained constant. Since the day she was born, Lavonia had claimed her as a daughter she never had. Once Mary Polly's anger subsided, she realized how troubled she was over what had happened. The first thing Mary Polly did when she arrived at the house was to play with the children and catch up on all of the things involving Henderson: how tall he had grown, the size of his feet, how he could write his name, and climb up on Paint without any help.

Joel picked her up in town. He immediately saw how unsettled she was. After some initial horseplay and everyone tending to her arrival, Joel invited her to walk with him to the barn. Once they were outside, he asked her what was wrong. She told him what happened between her and Lavonia.

"She was always jealous of you," Joel said to Mary Polly's surprise.

"What makes you say that?"

"The way she copies your dressing style, matches your colors. The woman is a different generation than you. One would expect her to be trying to keep up with Big Mary, not you."

Mary Polly thought about what he was saying. She went over it in her mind and tried to remember how supportive Lavonia had always seemed. For some unknown reason, the night she took Sherrod to meet her came to mind. Lavonia was outrageous that night. The innuendo and insinuations were extremely provocative. She remembered thinking how silly Lavonia was acting. The night on the boat when the man from Alexandria stopped to talk with her, Lavonia broke in and picked up the conversation. She acted as if she weren't even there. She thought about other incidents and situations and began to get a better perspective.

"I'm deeply disturbed by all of this," she said.

"Don't be," he laughed. "Big Mary, Lavonia, Tom, and Filbert, they are controlling people, petty and selfish. They love to control others.

"Lewis went with me to Tom's last week to see the new style of hoe he kept bragging about. When we got there, Tom was more interested in harassing Lewis than talking to me or showing me the hoe.

"'Who's the coon with you?' was what he said as soon as we stepped down from the wagon. I know he sold me Lewis, but that didn't give him the right to keep picking at him the way he did. It was one problem after another. 'Get me a drink of water, boy. Joel may cater to you like he does good white men, but you're still a Nigger walking with your head up your butt.'

"I didn't say anything to Tom, but I apologized to Lewis after we left. Oddly enough, Lewis said he was worried about how what was going on was offending me. He said that I had this strange look on my face; it was stone-like. Mary Polly, he was right. I felt like killing Tom, and that's not Christian. I think he has seen the last of me. If I can't sell my cotton on my own, it won't be sold. Tom is kin, but as far as I'm concerned, he is not family. Big Mary is family. Lavonia . . . well, she is getting old and hasn't had much luck with anything. Her husband left her, and her son is a failure. Maybe, just maybe, she considered herself more of a mother-in-law than an aunt after you and Robert got married."

Mary Polly hugged him. "How did I get a brother that's so smart?" He grinned and she added. "You have this way of speaking. You make everything seem all right." Joel took her hand and walked her back to the house. Sherrod was there when they arrived.

"Hey," he said and hugged her.

Sally told Sherrod Mary Polly had arrived upset. He could see she still looked a little frazzled. She clung to him for a long time when they hugged, and he held on to her. Finally, she looked up at him. "You are either getting bigger or I am shrinking." Everyone laughed, and Henderson came running, followed by Missouri and John.

"Mama Mary," he called.

"Mama Mary!" they all called.

She knelt down and hugged each of them one by one. "Mary is Santa Claus to these children," Sally said and laughed. "They think she is as old as they are and won't let her rest for a minute."

"I promised Henderson that I was going to take him out for a ride. Do you want Missouri and Mary Ann to go with us?" Mary Polly asked in the way of a response.

"Missouri and Mary Ann can stay here. You and Henderson enjoy your time together; it's precious time."

"Thanks, sis," Mary Polly said to Sally and smiled. Then she and Sherrod walked outside with Henderson.

"Why don't you to come for dinner? I will hurry home and ask Henrietta to cook one of those chickens she's been feeding around the yard."

"Who is Henrietta?"

"The new girl I bought off of the auction block. She reminded me of Esther when I first met her."

"I know Esther liked you. Were you taken by her as well?"

Sherrod laughed. "Are you jealous?"

"Keep talking, Sherrod, and you will be eating chicken with Henrietta instead of Henderson and me."

Sherrod slapped his horse and rode off laughing. "See you in a couple of hours," he said.

No sooner had he said it, Little Doe and Little Silas came to mind. If Mary Polly was already feeling jealous, how was he ever going to explain Little Doe and Silas to her? That stupid brother of his had built their house just up the path from his, right at the entryway. There was no way Mary Polly was going to miss it. It was the first thing a person saw when they entered Bryant Town. What could he have been thinking when he allowed the house to be put there?

Mary Polly had never thought about Sherrod being with another woman. She didn't know why; she just hadn't thought about it. Now that she was thinking about it, she didn't like the feeling. For thirteen years they had been together, and now she thought about it some more and asked herself what she thought he was doing for affection during those long stretches when she was away. Until that moment, she hadn't asked him. They had never discussed what they expected from one another. It certainly hadn't been part of her thinking, and she was sure it hadn't been part of his. Otherwise, it would have come up.

She assumed he knew she wasn't a one-man woman. How could she be? She was married. She rode quietly beside Henderson thinking about the new wrinkle that Henrietta was presenting. It had come so soon on the heels of her discontent with Lavonia. She really wished Sherrod hadn't introduced Henrietta the way he did. Henderson tried several times to talk with his mother, but she had either not heard him or chose to ignore him. He was feeling ignored and didn't like the quiet, so he rode off. He hit Old Paint with the heels of his boots the way Sherrod had shown him, and the horse took off in a trot.

"Wait for me," a surprised Mary Polly called after him when he was out of her sight. She brought her horse to a gallop in pursuit. When she had gone up the trail a little further, she saw two white men holding each side of Old Paint's reins and Henderson sitting between them. At first, she didn't recognize the men and was frightened. Then the older one got down off his horse and called out to her. She recognized him as her Uncle Tom. He was standing there smiling as she can closer.

"Afternoon, Niece," he said and tilted his hat. "You the woman with this mulatto kid? You who he calls Mama Mary?"

"I haven't seen you in a while," Mary Polly said determined not to let either of them see how annoyed she was.

"I heard Joel had a mulatto kid out there trying to pass him off as Sally's," Filbert said.

"What do you want?" Mary Polly asked them.

"We thought this kid was the bastard child of Nance or Helen's, but we never suspected you had any claim to him."

Mary Polly pushed her way past Tom and took Henderson's reins. They began to ride back towards Joel's house. "Good manners are not something the Coles are known for. Good evening, gentlemen."

Tom and Filbert laughed and called after her. "Tell Big Mary and Jesse we'll be dropping in on them come late summer." As she rode away from them, she heard one of them yell. "We'll be sure to tell them about their new grandchild!"

Mary Polly lashed into her horse and scared Old Paint. Her horse took off and Old Paint reared up. Henderson tried to calm him. "It's okay," he said. "It's okay." Mary Polly rushed back to where they were. She was in awe of Henderson's control over his horse. So much so that she almost forgot about what had just happened. Her uncles had frightened and angered her, and she had reacted irresponsibly.

"You are really an excellent rider, Henderson. Mama Mary is proud of you," she said, feeling terribly guilty.

"Who were those men, Mama Mary?" he asked completely oblivious to what had happened with the horse.

"Some mean old strangers we will never talk to again," Mary Polly replied.

"What's a mulatto kid?"

"Something you don't have to worry about," Mary Polly said trying to block out the ramifications of what had just happened.

"Will Missouri, Mary Ann, and John have to worry?"

"No, they won't have to worry either. Now stop asking questions and watch where you're going. Old Paint has already acted up. Let us not have him doing anything else."

"Daddy Bryant said we could come and eat chicken with him and Henrietta."

"Henderson, I asked you to watch where you are going and stop talking so much."

"You said to stop asking questions; you didn't say anything about talking." Mary Polly let her irritation get the best of her.

"Stop all of it," she yelled raising her voice and frightening him. He started to cry. She pulled alongside him, took the reins from his hand, and pulled Old Paint to a stop. She got off of her horse and took him off of his. She was sorry for yelling at him. She couldn't take him home without letting him know how much she cared about him. "Those were some mean, bad men back there, Henderson," she said taking her finger and wiping his tears. "I'm mad at them, not you. I didn't mean to yell. I just wanted to get you back to Papa Joel, okay?"

"Okay," he whimpered. She tied Old Paint's reins to her horse and set Henderson in the saddle in front of her.

"Mama Mary loves Henderson," she said. "I don't want anybody to hurt you ever. I love you and when people say mean things to you or about you, I get upset. Okay?"

"Okay," he said and leaned back in the saddle to where he could feel the strength of her body against his.

"Giddy up," she said and brought the horse to a gallop. She knew she had to get back to Virginia before Tom and Filbert did. As best she could, she would orchestrate whatever happened between

Big Mary and her brothers. Hopefully, Sherrod would come looking for her and Henderson after he realized they were not coming as planned. If he didn't, she would have to leave everything in a note, hoping he would understand the urgency of her situation.

She arrived back at the farm and told Joel and Sally what happened. They insisted she wait until the plan was formulated before she left. They knew the consequences of Mary Polly's actions as well as his and Sally's actions of shielding her. If Jesse and Big Mary found out, both of them would be disowned and disinherited.

At Sally's suggestion, Joel went to get Sherrod. They needed his input and decided they shouldn't act without it. Mary Polly agreed to Sherrod being a part of the plan. It had been years since she had included him in on her comings and goings. For the first time, she was sensitive to how far apart they had to come since Henderson was born.

While she waited for him, she wondered if the pressure of being responsible for Henderson had contaminated their relationship in any way. Both of them primarily focused on Henderson's future, even more than his present. She acknowledged the fact that the climate of the country was not colored-folks-friendly. More and more segregation legislations were being introduced and made into law.

Men appeared to be obsessed with the oppression of blacks and Indian, and that hadn't helped the situation any. She recognized even though Sherrod was politically connected, his power was based on his mastery of organization, task orientation, and the ability to maximize production. The gift of money to the establishment of Bryant Town was almost a non-issue as far as she was concerned.

It was interest paid on work he had performed when other Virginia farmers were floundering.

She knew in her heart things could never have been any different between her and Sherrod. She liked the way he made love to her. He made her feel alive and appreciated, but there were other qualities such as their love for the land and their adventurous spirit, and the forbidden aspect of their lives. Mary Polly conceded that it helped each of them experience an expression of self that was rooted in emotional interdependence. Dependency was too telling. Henderson was the bond that held them together. No matter the distance between them, she knew she had to hold on to that. It would probably be all she had of them for a long time, if not forever.

Late that afternoon, Sherrod was sitting on the porch smoking his pipe and wondering where Mary Polly and Henderson were. It had been several hours since he had separated from them and he was wondering if she had truly gotten angry about Henrietta. He thought maybe she was trying to punish him. He thought to himself how it was amazing how women pick up on things. He couldn't for the life of him figure out what he said to give her the notion that he was sleeping with Henrietta.

Hell, he tried going to the reservation pretending to speak with Little Doe so they could slip off to some cave or some other godforsaken place. Look what it got him, playing with Little Doe in the woods, peeping, and hiding like a schoolboy brought about a child. If that wasn't enough to own up to, he was being asked to explain his relationship with nine-year-old Henrietta.

Henrietta was a pretty little girl. She knew how to cook, but she was a child. One thing white folks didn't understand about slaves, given the opportunity, they master their job. If cooking was the order of the day, then cooking was the thing to be the best at. Luckily for him, Henrietta's previous Master owned a poultry farm, and cooking chicken was her specialty.

"Good chicken, good fried chicken," he said out loud. He reminded himself he was thirty-four-years old. If he wanted to take a woman to bed, he damn sure was going to do so. He laughed. *Henrietta is pretty, but she's a child. My commitment to a woman, as far as I'm concerned, is based on what she and I decide between us. That includes you, Mary Polly.* He smiled and took a moment to enjoy his change of heart. Then he thought, *When Mary Polly sees Henrietta, the joke is going to be on her. Especially when she finds out how much Henrietta likes her because she was once my Master and is now my friend.*

Sherrod hadn't bothered to tell Henderson he had indentured himself to Mary Polly. He felt some things needed to be left unsaid, and this was one of them. The longer he sat there and waited, the more he became uneasy. He finally decided he better go and see what was keeping them. He got up from his chair and put out his pipe. Something way out in the distance caught his attention, and he recognized it was Joel riding frantically towards him.

Sherrod grabbed his hat and ran towards the barn. "Samuel, Oscar, saddle up my horse," he called.

Samuel immediately appeared with the horse. "She is already saddled, Sir."

Sherrod jumped on the horse and rushed off to meet Joel. As soon as their paths met, Joel turned his horse and motioned him to follow. Sherrod caught up to him, and Joel called out, "Tom and Filbert accosted Mary Polly on the trail."

"Let's go," Sherrod said and they headed for Joel's place.

As he rode, he thought about his relationship and how what just happened would affect it. He knew he cared deeply about Mary Polly. He had never allowed his fantasies to include her as a mate in any of his dreams. The closest he had come to settling on her was at the time she announced Henderson's impending birth.

In his joy, he had all but proposed marriage. Since then, he had been forever grateful she had the good sense to be realistic about the situation and the position an open union would put them and their child in. There was no doubt in his mind that Mary Polly was definitely his salvation. Not that he felt he wouldn't have been able to carry out his life plans without her; she had facilitated the process. She moved along faster and even he could imagine.

In his mind at that point in time, June 1815, Mary Polly was more Henderson's mother than his lover. Yes, they occasionally slept together. The passion between them remained intense and usually flowed rapidly after a strong argument or disagreement. Other than that, they behaved towards each other like an old married couple.

The thought of it amused him. The enormity of what happened flooded his mind, and he kicked out all other thoughts. He pulled on the reins of this horse and rode past Joel. Whatever Mary Polly needed him to do, he would do it. His job was to help her understand that.

Sally took the children and left for a visit with friends as soon as Joel left the house. "We are going to make this work for everybody, Mary Polly," Sally said, trying to reassure her sister-in-law.

Mary Polly hugged her. She really wished she lived closer to Sally and Joel. They loved her unconditionally, that she was finding out. She realized this was a practice that for most people was particularly nonexistent.

After Sally left, she started to cry. Tom and Filbert's actions marked the end of her June and December trips, and she was really sad about that. Not seeing Henderson was an unbearable thought. Her trips to Europe wouldn't be missed. She cried and cried and allowed herself to feel the anger that tore at her insides. Finally, her mind slipped into survival mode, and she started to make plans.

I will send Joel whatever money I have in my possession at home and ask him to give it to Sherrod. I'll tell him he is to help Henderson purchase land when he turns sixteen. This will allow him to build his own dream, she said to herself and then added, I will take five of the six thousand dollars I am now carrying and give it to Sherrod to use for his own needs. Sherrod will take Henderson to live with him in Bryant Town. Henderson's color is changing and obviously there has been talk among the families in Sally's school. *Henderson belongs with Sherrod. It is time.*

Mary Polly's mind then shifted to the six years she had spent away from Sherrod and remembered how she had anguished over it. Being away from Henderson, she felt as if something was dying inside of her. She knew what she was about to face had no equal.

If she and Henderson had only gone with Sherrod, she thought, they would have missed Tom and Filbert. She and Henderson would have been sitting at Sherrod's this very minute eating chicken and fighting about Henrietta. Joel and Sherrod arrived. She had never seen Sherrod so angry and fired up. He was hopping mad, with his jaw tight and nostrils flared.

"I could kill Tom and Filbert," he said. "I could do it and no one would ever know how it happened."

"If you did, a lot of good black African slaves in these parts would pay for it," Joel said. "It would start a slave massacre the likes of which none of us could live with."

"I don't want murder of any sort on my conscience," Mary Polly said and hugged Sherrod.

"Do you think that you can beat Tom and Filbert to Virginia?" Joel asked.

"If they are even going to Virginia," she said.

"Tom and Filbert are white trash," Sherrod said. "They pick at you and Mary Polly because they are jealous of Cole success. They were bluffing back there in the woods. They don't know where Henderson came from. He could be Helen's, or you could have purchased him."

"We can't take any chances, Sherrod," Mary Polly said. "I hope you are right, but sooner or later our secret is bound to come out."

"We have to act in the best interest of our child."

"Well, don't worry about Henderson. Joel and I have talked. I am taking him to live with Oscar and Helen."

"What will you tell John, Missouri, and Mary Ann?"

"Henderson and Mary Ann are so fond of each other. She is too young to understand he is leaving her."

"We are going to get out too, Mary Polly. Sally has wanted to get back to Kentucky. I can't stay here knowing what Tom and Filbert have done without reacting to them. Like Sherrod, I don't want to do anything and have someone else blamed for it. Sometimes inaction has a price to it; moving is our price, and we will pay." He thought about what he had said and attempted to smile. "Besides, if we are in Kentucky, you can visit Mary Polly. Henderson can visit, and you too Sherrod." They all knew that it wouldn't be safe for Sherrod to visit, but they chose not to think about it. Instead, they moved to practical matters.

"What will you do with the farm?" Mary Polly asked him.

"It's a working property. Martha McFarland will be glad to buy back. She'll also be happy with all of the improvements. It's a steal."

"Okay, then, as soon as I can book passage, I will leave."

Sherrod took her hand. "That chicken is still sitting there waiting."

"Why didn't Henrietta eat it?"

Sherrod squeezed her hand. "There is no time for nonsense," he said in an authoritative manner. This man Sherrod, that she had been with for almost thirteen years, was not a kid she kept hidden secretly in her mind. He was a man, and he knew it. And bigger than that, he was letting her know it.

The difference she could see was that he was acting on his own behalf. Sherrod had never been so aware of that before. He had a quiet new kind of self-assurance that she liked. Sherrod had come into his own, and no matter what happened, he and Henderson were going to be all right. She told herself she needed to take solace in that. She walked with Sherrod to the carriage. They were both quietly contemplating the separation. When he came around to help her up, she stopped him. "I can't go this time," she said. "I have a lot to sort out. I don't know when I will see you again, but you will hear from me. Henderson is our love child, secret friend. I have an open heart, and I will be loving him and you. I trust you to settle our child and make him his own man."

Sherrod kissed her long and hard. They clung to each other for a while. "Let's go pack Henderson's things," he said. He was finding it hard not to cry. He was aware she was also struggling with her tears. He thought busying themselves with activity would be the best way to say goodbye. They walked back to the house. Their life together as they knew it was coming to an end, and they both know it. He felt sorry for Mary Polly. As much as Mary Polly loved Henderson, she could never own her relationship with him. Sherrod was glad he recognized her failing; it kept him from having to discuss it with her. As sad as it was, he was pleased Joel had decided to move back to Kentucky. It would cut his ties with Tom and Filbert, and he could continue to build without interference or distraction.

"I think it's best you say goodbye to Henderson on your own," he said to Mary Polly when they arrived back at his house. "Ask Joel to take him to the boat with you. Let him see where you are going. It will give him something to hold on to."

"You are my friend forever, Sherrod Bryant," she smiled through tears that threatened to choke her at any second.

"Is this a permanent goodbye?"

"Joel will be our only contact."

"Are you sure?"

"You don't understand Southern white folks," she started to explain, and he stopped her.

"I love you," he said.

"Now you tell me," she said with a voice filled with pain. He kissed her on top of the head, climbed onto his horse, and rode away.

As he reached the thicket, he heard a guttural scream that he knew to be Mary Polly. He stopped for a moment and turned in the saddle. He looked back as tears flooded his cheeks. "Damn you, Tom! Damn you, Filbert!" he said. He dug his heels into his horse and brought them to a fast trot. "That mulatto child you used today to railroad Mary Polly is going to bury your ass one day. His daddy and mama are going to see to it," he swore under his breath. By the time Sally returned with the children, Mary Polly was packed and ready to leave. She took Henderson by the hand and let him outside.

"Have I been bad?" he asked.

Mary Polly hugged him. "Of course not, sweetheart. What makes you say that?"

"Missouri said those men stopped Old Paint because I was bad. She said I ran off and left you."

"Henderson, those men stopped Old Paint because they were mad at me."

"But they said I was a mulatto."

"Mulatto is a color," she said and took his hand and held it up next to hers. "Do you see these hands?" He nodded yes. "Are they the same?"

"No," he said. "I'm brown like Daddy Bryant. You and everybody else are white. John is white, Missouri is white, and Mary Ann is white."

Mary Polly interrupted him. "That's right. God made some of us brown and some of us white."

"The kids at school say I am a tar baby. What's a Nigger?"

"There is no such word!" Mary Polly snapped. "Those children are mean and need to be spanked."

"How come I get to be brown?"

"Because you are luckier than the rest of us. You have two families. A white family and a brown family."

"You don't know what happens to me at school."

"The next time something happens to you at school, you tell those children they are just mad because they only have one color in their family. You have two colors like beautiful flowers. All beautiful flowers have more than one color."

"Can I go now?"

"In a minute," Mary Polly said and coaxed him upon her lap. "After today, you are going to be living with Daddy Bryant."

"Goody," he smiled. "Are John, Missouri, and Mary Ann coming?"

"No, they are going to stay in this house. They will visit you, and you will visit them. You know how much fun we have when I visit. That's the kind of fun you will have when you John, Missouri, and Mary Ann visit."

"I don't want to visit. I want to stay with everybody."

"But Daddy Bryant is lonely over there by himself. Do you want Daddy Bryant to be lonely?" Henderson folded his arms, pursed his lips, and said nothing. "Henderson, Mama Mary and Daddy Bryant are your mother and father. Sally and Joel are Missouri, Mary Ann, and John's mother and father."

"No, no, no!" Henderson started to cry. He then jumped from her lap and ran towards the barn. Mary Polly lifted her traveling skirt and took off after him. When she caught up to him, she grabbed hold of his shirt and held him. He struggled to get away.

"I don't want to live with Daddy Bryant. I want to stay here with Missouri and Mary Ann."

"Henderson, I am going away on a boat this evening. I need you to be a big boy so you can come and say goodbye to me." He stopped struggling. "Have you ever seen a boat up close?" He didn't respond. "I bet if you are really good, your Uncle Joel will take you on a boat."

"Does Papa Joel love me?" he whimpered.

"Of course Papa Joel loves you," Mary Polly said and hugged him. "Papa Joel and Mama Sally love you with all of their heart. They always will."

"Is Old Paint going to Daddy Bryant's too?

"Old Paint and you are going to live with Helen and Daddy Bryant. Remember how Helen was when she went to live at Daddy Bryant's? Well you are going to be just as happy."

"Can Missouri and Mary Ann see the boat too?"

"If you want them to."

"I don't care if I am brown," he said. "Daddy Bryant is brown. Old Paint is brown. Helen is brown and Oscar is brown."

"That's right," Mary Polly said and continued to hold him. He pushed her away.

"I don't want white people hugging me," he said. "I will hug Missouri. I will hug Mary Ann and I will hug John. Not old white people like you, Mama Sally, and Papa Joel."

Mary Polly's knees buckled beneath her. Her chest tightened and she struggled to hold back her tears. "I love you Henderson," she said, but he didn't hear her.

He was on his way to the house calling, "John, Missouri, Mary Ann. We are going to see the boat!" Mary Polly leaned against the barn door and sobbed uncontrollably.

Joel walked up behind her. "Are you going to be okay, sis?"

"I have just been rejected by the brown side of the family," she said and a weak smile passed through her tears. "Lord, please keep him safe," she whispered.

BRYANT ACRES CHAPTER XVIII

A Dream Come True

Mary Polly went back to Virginia as she planned. Joel and Sally moved to Kentucky. As far as Sherrod knew, Tom and Filbert stayed in Tennessee.

Henderson was upset and standoffish his first month living in Bryant Town.

The adults thought it best that Henderson not leave home until he was used to it so most of the visiting was done by Sally and the children.

John, Missouri, and Mary Ann visited every day until they left for Kentucky. The children missed Henderson, and so did Sally. She was concerned about the separation and the impact it was going to have on him and her family.

In the beginning, whenever Sally and the children came, Henderson would beg to go home with them and the girls would cry. Finally, Oscar got the notion that by distracting Henderson with activities he liked, before Sally announced it was time to go, their laboring the point of separation would be minimized. While Henderson learned new tasks, Sally could slip away with the girls. A great distraction for Henderson was shoeing the horses. Oscar let him help shoe the horses, and Helen persuaded him to feed the chickens in the yard while she weaved.

Henrietta idolized Henderson from the moment she saw him. There was two years' difference in their ages; he was seven and she was nine. When she wasn't busy cooking and working in the kitchen, she would sit and listen to Henderson talk.

She had been cooking since she was seven. Her previous Master forced the chore on her. She loved to eat, and in her way of thinking, cooking put her near food she knew she would not otherwise have privy to.

Whenever she sat with Henderson, she brought cookies or cake. They would sit and eat while he talked. He talked about Sally, Joel, Missouri, May Ann, John, Old Paint, the things he had learned in school, and the new things he was being taught in Bryant Town.

Not once did he speak of Mary Polly. If Sherrod, Joel, or Sally mentioned her name or tried to talk to him about her, he would say, "I don't like her. She left me, and I don't like people who leave."

After several tries, it became clear Henderson wasn't ready to talk about his mother. The adults talked to him about her less and less.

When he received gifts, a toy, or a book from her, he would hold on to it for weeks. He even slept with it, carried it to do his chores, and sat with it at the eating table. If anyone asked where he got the item, he would say, "My Mama Mary sent it to me from the boat." Anything more than that was not forthcoming.

Sherrod treated Henderson like royalty. He made it clear to everyone in Bryant Town that Henderson was his son and therefore commanded the same respect shown him. He let Henderson know he had to address adults as Mister or Sir and Miss or Mistress, that he was to rise promptly when a woman entered the room, and that he was to give her his seat if need be.

He was taught to rise at daybreak, dress, do his chores, have breakfast, and go to Nance's for his lessons.

Nance had come to live in Bryant Town when Joel and his family moved away. Her job was to school the children of Bryant Town, particularly Henderson.

Nance was the daughter of a free based born Negro from North Carolina; free based in that she was of African descent, born to self-supporting free parents that were established members of the community. When the Colonial Assembly Act of 1712 was passed, she was declared a slave.

Under the laws and regulations of the Colonial Assembly Act, all free based born children were bounded out to white Masters and Mistresses until they reached the age of twenty-one. The Master and Mistress of these children were responsible for their overall well-being. The law also stated that they must be taught to read and write.

Nance's mother got involved with her Master and carried on with him long after her servitude ended. When the mother was twenty-three, Nance was born. With the support of her white father, Nance's mother took care of her. She taught Nance to read and write, worship God, and help her fellow man, be he free or a slave.

Nance had been a happy child until she was twelve years old. Then her mother became very ill and couldn't care for her. Her white father, who was preparing to relocate to Missouri, offered to buy Nance from her mother. When the mother said no, the man became angry and said he would no longer support the mother or the child.

Nance's mother, anguished with fear of what a loss of income would mean, worried and as the days went on, she became weaker and weaker. When Nance asked her mother what was wrong, she told her about the offer.

Nance didn't want her mother to starve and be without medical care so she went to the man. He had a dry goods' store in town, and most of the time he was in the back room counting stock or napping while his clerk or slaves ran the store.

Nance was careful to go around to the back of the store where she would be undetected when she approached her mother's lover. She eased up to the door and knocked. She had never visited the store or the back room before. The times she had seen him were early mornings when he left the house after spending the night with her mother.

The door was open, so she rapped lightly on the doorframe. She could see his head above a stack of empty feed bags piled high on the floor.

"Who's there?" he called, and frightened her.

"It's me, Nance Mae," she managed to reply. She seldom made contact with him. Once or twice he had tried to talk with her before he left the house, but she didn't know him, didn't like him, and was only standing there being polite because her mother said if she wasn't, they would starve to death.

"Nance who?" he said and stood up, trying to see her.

"Nance Mae," she repeated, "from over on Cherry Street."

"Why didn't you say so? Come on in, Gal. Your Mama with you?"

"No, Sir. I came on my own," she said as she stepped inside.

The stench of dirty feet and dirty grain bags permeated the room. The odor was so strong it brought tears to her eyes. She wanted to gag but knew if she did, her purpose for coming would be ruined.

He stared at her for what seemed like an eternity. The look in his eyes frightened her but not as much as her mother's dying.

"Did your mother tell you that my wife will need help with the children when we move?"

"Yes, Sir, she told me."

"What else did she tell you about me?"

"Nothing else."

He smiled. "That's one thing about you coloreds. You can make things any way you want them to be."

Nance didn't know what he was talking about, but she decided she'd better tell him what she came to tell him. Even though she didn't know, she didn't like the sound of what he was alluding to.

"My mother is sick, Mr. Dillard. She needs a doctor, and some food. She said you promised to take care of her when I moved with you to Missouri."

He reached out and touched her head.

"Did she also tell you how good I am at making girls feel?"

Nance moved away from him, and he laughed. "Tell your Mama we will be leaving day after tomorrow, and you be ready, Gal. My Missus don't like to be kept waiting."

"Yes, Sir," she said and ran out of the store, promising never to acknowledge or feel anything he said or did to her as long as she lived.

From that day until the day the Dillards fell on hard times and had to sell Nance to Tom Cole, she acted as if she were living a dream whenever she was in his presence, no matter what the occasion was.

Nance's life with Tome Cole was different in that he ignored her as long as she did the work. She managed to do that for fifteen years, and then she came to live with Joel. Now, here she was living in Bryant Town with Sherrod and Henderson and all the free men and slaves that made up the Bryant clan.

Her reading and writing skills had kept her in good stead with Mrs. Dillard and Mrs. Tom Cole, and at last she was able to share it with people of color. Sharing with her people made her feel her mother's sacrifice had not gone unchecked.

When Sally and Joel were preparing to move, Nance was asked to stay at the school that she and Sally had founded. Sally declined the offer on Nance's behalf. Her mission, as it was explained to her, was to primarily educate Henderson and the other children of Bryant Town, including Henrietta and the other slave children.

Henderson was a smart little boy and a quick learner. He asked the questions and applied them to the task. By the time he was twelve years old, he knew every business in Bryant Town and what their functions were. He knew the names of the rivers and the creeks, and he knew where they were located. He knew that Davidson and Rutherford counties had once been a part of North Carolina and in 1796 had become part of the State of Tennessee. He knew that James Monroe was the President of the United States. He also knew that slavery existed; it was a part of his existence, outside and inside his community.

He learned fast the difference between free men and slaves. He understood that Daddy Bryant was a man of privilege and that he was also a person of privilege because he was Daddy Bryant's son.

When Sherrod started to openly go about finding himself a woman, Henderson did not know how to act. It didn't have to do with Sherrod and Mary Polly. He wasn't used to seeing his father with a woman and didn't know where it fit.

He knew Mama Mary was his mother and Daddy Bryant was his father, but he had never put the two together as husband and wife, or as parents. They were both connected to him and, as far as he was concerned, their only connection had to do with him.

He had learned Sherrod was his father, and even though John, Missouri, and Mary Ann called him Daddy Bryant, for them it was just a title, the way it was when he called Joel, Papa Joel. No matter what anyone said about Sally, however, as far as Henderson was concerned, Sally was his mother. He had early memories of her nursing him, bathing him, and dressing him. In every sense, that made her his mother.

He understood that Mary Polly was his mother also. He liked Mama Mary and knew she loved and cared for him. But having a mother who wasn't there just didn't sit right. Sally wasn't there either, after she moved away. He only saw her once a year when Joel came and picked him up for his annual visit to their house in Kentucky.

It was not the same with Mama Mary. It had been five years since he had seen her, and he was now twelve years old. He was still having trouble forgiving her for telling him the truth about his family. He understood that she had to let him know Joel, Sally, John, Missouri, and Mary Ann were a family separate from him. Yes, they were also a family together with him, but not in the same way. He didn't like it at age seven, and he still didn't like it, even if it was the truth.

After Mary Polly left Rutherford County that last time, Henderson tried to convince himself he didn't care about her. Then one dark night not too long after she left town, he found himself awakened from a deep sleep in tears and feeling very alone. He went over what was happening and realized he had been dreaming about Mary Polly. He left his bed and went in with Sherrod. Without waking up, Sherrod put his arm around him and drew him close. After that, dreams about Mary Polly were of happier times.

Sherrod didn't court much, but then something happened. He came to Henderson and told him his childhood sweetheart, Nancy Johnson, had contacted him and he was going to Ohio to be with her for a few days.

Henderson tried not to think about it. Then he overheard his teachers Nance and Helen talking. He was out sitting on the porch, and they were inside fixing and doing their work.

"I hear this Nancy person is a real looker," he heard Nance say. "She sent for him, you know. She must be real sure of herself to think that he remembers her after all these years."

"Child, I heard the message came over the wire. Oscar was in town and the telegraph man, Whitler, called him over. Of course, Oscar can't read. He didn't know what it said, but Old Man Whitler practically told Oscar, gave him the message. You know, white folks ain't used to black folks getting no messages in the first place.

"Whitler scribbled on a piece of paper and started to give it to Oscar, then tore it up, and said, 'No wonder none of these pretty

Nigger gals can catch hold of Sherrod. He got one in Ohio laid claim to him.' Of course, Oscar didn't know what Whitler was talking about."

Helen giggled, and then Nance giggled. Henderson failed to see what they were so tickled about. This Nancy they were so busy talking about, it wasn't like they were ever going to meet her or get to know her. He thought about it for a minute and asked himself, *Or, are they?*

He started to go over the sequence of events. *Daddy Bryant leaves and everyone starts fixing and doing work around the house.* He started to get worried. He remembered the night he went to sleep and dreamed Mary Polly and Sherrod were married and living in Bryant Town. All of the children at school were teasing him because his mama was different than theirs. "Mulatto kid. Mulatto kid. Child of a white woman," they called after him, and he threw rocks at them.

When he woke up, he was angry and full of questions. If Sherrod was with Mary Polly, why wasn't he off visiting her instead of some half-breed Indian woman that he hadn't seen since he was a child? Why did Sherrod let Mary Polly get on that boat? Why did he live with Papa Joel and Mama Sally in the first place?

To his surprise, the answers to these questions came to him when he was quiet. As he answered his own questions, he became sadder and sadder. Some anger was there too, but Daddy Bryant had instilled in him that anger for anger's sake was wasted energy. He tempered the anger, rationalized it.

Yes, Mary Polly was his mother and it was sad she had to visit rather than live with him and his Daddy, but that's the way it was. As hard as it was for him to deal with, it had to be harder for Mary Polly and Daddy Bryant.

He wondered what had caused her to stop visiting. The memory of the day on the trail when Tom and Filbert accosted them came to mind. "Uncle," he remembered Mary Polly calling the man. It all started to come together. Somewhere there might be other uncles, aunts, and grandparents on Mama Mary's side of the family.

Sherrod had told him wonderful stories about Grandpa Silas and how he never knew his mother, who died during his birth. Henderson knew his uncles William and Silas and their children, Flex, Edward, and James. They were his family on his father's side. He knew that Joel, Sally, John, Missouri, and Mary Ann were family on Mama Mary's side. Who were her parents? He wished he could meet his Grandma and Grandpa Cole. It would help him know what being a grandchild felt like.

He asked his father about them once and was told their names were Big Mary and Jesse and when Daddy Bryant was young he was a slave on their plantation. He explained they were okay people but had problems understanding people who were different than themselves and they would never accept a colored grandchild.

Henderson almost had it straight in his mind when Sherrod returned to Bryant Town that early fall afternoon in 1820. Sherrod had rented a carriage when he arrived in Nashville. He hadn't wired home because he didn't want white folks in his business. Before anyone in Bryant Town knew it, he was driving up the trail with his new bride sitting beside him. Henry was the first to see him approaching the main thoroughfare of Bryant Town.

"Mister Bryant is home! Mister Bryant is home!" Henry cried, and everyone in Bryant Town heard his cry. They poured into the street for a look-see.

Nancy Johnson had grown into a beautiful, shapely woman with sharp features and olive toned skin. Her long brown hair was pinned at the back and fell beneath a white straw hat with a navy-blue band and white flowers decorating the brim. She had large brown eyes that were deep set. Her linen suit was ankle length with a coat that had a bushel and a belt that tied in the front. Her white lace, high collar Victorian blouse had a female profiled cameo pinned in the center. She had style, and when she walked, everyone knew that she knew who she was.

Sherrod pulled the carriage to a stop. She sat looking straight ahead until he came around and helped her down. Henry took the reins of the horses and stood at attention until his Master told him to take the horses to the barn. Henderson watched from the window.

"Gone out and meet your Daddy," Henderson heard Nance say from the doorway where she stood watching the goings on. "That is your new mama. You want her to feel welcome, don't you?"

"I have a mama," he said. "I have two mamas, Mama Mary and Mama Sally."

"Now you have three, so gone out there and act like a man," Nance scolded. "As nice as your Daddy is, you ain't gonna hide in here and make him look bad if I can help it."

Henderson knew she meant what she said, so he reluctantly went out. With his hat in hand, he greeted his dad on the porch. "Hi Daddy Bryant," he said shyly.

"There you are," Sherrod said and smiled. "Nancy, this is my boy."

The sweet-smelling lady beside Sherrod walked over to Henderson and extended her hand with all of Bryant Town watching. "I am glad to make your acquaintance, Henderson," she said.

He looked up and she winked her eye at him. She was the most beautiful woman he had ever seen. She exuded warmth, and he basked in her glow. The feelings brought a smile to his face, and he found himself saying, "I am glad to meet you, too." He reached out and put his hand in hers.

Sherrod hugged him. He put one arm around his shoulder and the other arm around Nancy's shoulder, gave a hearty laugh, and called out, "Helen, get those pots to rattling. Me and Mrs. Bryant have been traveling for twenty days. We are hungry for a home-cooked meal."

Nance gingerly approached Nancy. "I can run you some water, show you where things are if you like."

"That will be great," Nancy said, and followed her out of the room.

"Sorry I didn't give you any warning," Sherrod said. "Nancy caught me by surprise. After traveling to Paris and England, I didn't think Nancy would be interested in this kind of living. Davidson and Rutherford counties certainly would put her out of touch, but she said it was me she wanted to be with."

"I was wondering when you were coming home," Henderson said, trying to talk grown up. He was all smiles and somewhat excited. Sherrod took that to mean Henderson was as taken by Nancy as he hoped he would be.

"How is Old Paint doing?" Sherrod asked, testing him.

"Not well," Henderson said. "I think it's time you start letting me take care of the Bay out there."

Henderson was used to asking Sherrod for what he wanted, but asking to ride the Bay caught him off guard. He turned to Oscar, who was waiting by the door.

"Can he handle the Bay?"

Oscar laughed. "He is your son, Master. He learns quick."

"Okay then," Sherrod said. "At dawn, you show me how well you can do and the Bay is yours."

"Thanks," Henderson said and ran out to the barn to tell the others.

When he was out of earshot, Sherrod turned to Oscar. "What is with the Master stuff?" he asked.

"Beg your pardon, Sir, but your wife . . . she looks like she want everything to be like they is with white folks."

"My wife follows my lead, Oscar," Sherrod said angrily. "And you can tell Henry and the others what I said. I don't want to hear any more of this nonsense."

"Yes, Sir," Oscar said, and scampered out to the barn where Henderson and the others were.

Sherrod crossed to the door and watched him go. He looked out across the front plain as far as he could see. *A dream come true*, he thought to himself. Nancy wasn't exactly sitting in the hills waiting for him to come and get her, but she still wanted him and that was good. From this day forward, it was going to be his and her life together, he thought and smiled happily.

Mary Polly came to mind and a flash of anger crossed his face. The last time he heard from her was the day she got on the boat. Yes, for a while she continued to acknowledge Henderson, but there was never a word for him. After Joel moved off to Kentucky, he refused to discuss his sister. When Sherrod broached the subject, Joel acted as if he didn't hear. He changed the subject and steered the conversation in another direction.

Every year on Henderson's birthday, however, Joel showed up and took Henderson for a month's stay in Kentucky with his family. Henderson looked forward to it. Sherrod could tell, because two months before, he would start to talk about Missouri, John, and Mary Ann. It was becoming more and more apparent how much he cared for Mary Ann. She was four years younger, but that didn't seem to matter.

Sherrod thought about how well Henderson was growing and how he, without the benefit of Mary Polly, had been able to provide for their son's needs. "We raised Henderson together as long as you could," he mumbled to himself and allowed his feelings of anger towards Mary Polly to subside. "He's all mine now. We're part of another family now."

"Who are you talking to?" Nancy asked, walking up to where he stood.

He turned to her and pulled her gently into his arms. "Life," he said, hugging her. "I have never been married before. Is it always going to feel this way?"

"You don't mind that I have been married?"

"You are mine now," he said and tightened his hold on her. She pretended to squirm, and he laughed. "Henderson needs brothers and sisters; what do you say?"

She playfully pinched his back and moved away from him. He could see she had changed her clothes.

"Let's get this party on the road," he called in to Helen. He started away from the door and saw Little Silas standing across the path watching him. When Silas saw Sherrod, he looked at him and ran up the road.

"Who is that?" Nancy asked.

"They say he's my son," Sherrod replied. "I used to fool around with his mother when I was lonely and unattached."

"Are there any more loose children I should know about?" she asked.

"None of them are loose," he said, irritation clear in his voice. "Silas is home in Bryant Town with me."

Nancy pinched him again, and they both laughed. Nance came to the door and Sherrod asked her, "Have you seen Henrietta?"

Unbeknownst to any of them, Henrietta was out in the barn talking to Henderson. "I am afraid of your Daddy's new wife," she said to Henderson.

"She is nice, pretty and nice," Little Silas spoke up as he came through the door.

"How do you know?" Henrietta asked. There was an edge to her voice. It was Henderson she wanted to reassure her, not Little Silas.

"He's right," Henderson said. "You go in there and help her out and everything will be okay. Everybody likes having someone do for them, and you're good at that."

"Real good," Little Silas teased.

"Shut up," she said.

"Henrietta!" Nance called, and she hurried out of the barn.

"Coming."

"Nancy can teach you some things. She's been all over Europe," Henderson called after her.

"What do you know about ladies?" Little Silas laughed.

He is only nine, Henderson thought to himself, *why bother to answer him?* Little Silas walked over to the Bay and stroked his nose. "Mama said I needed to start asking Mister Bryant for more things. She said I was too quiet around him. What do you think?"

"I think you should listen to your mama and stop bothering me," Henderson said. "And get your hand off my horse. Old Paint is needing some attention if you must play with a horse."

"Can I ride Old Paint?"

"You can have him."

"Honest?"

Henderson nodded his head yes. Little Silas was a weird sort of a kid. He was related somehow, but Henderson wasn't sure how they were kin. He just knew they were.

Little Silas ran to tell Little Doe and saw Henrietta standing outside the door praying. "Lord, help this lady like me," she prayed. "I wanna keep living in Mr. Sherrod's house. He is the only family

I got. Don't let this pretty traveling woman come in and change things, please."

"Amen," Little Silas called as he ran by her.

Henrietta picked up a rock and threw it at him. "I hate you, Silas," she said.

"You don't do no such. Now get yourself in here and do your work," Helen scolded Henrietta, and she was ashamed.

BRYANT ACRES CHAPTER XIX

I Learned That My Children Are
the Only People Who Are Mine

Nancy Johnson worked hard at trying to settle into Bryant Town. She had four children during the four years she lived there. There was William, Phoebe, Catherine, and Nancy Elizabeth.

She was the first lady of Bryant Town. In the beginning, she took a great deal of pride in her position. Her house was beautifully decorated with artifacts and furniture imported from Paris. She had beautiful window hangings and matching bedspreads and tablecloths with fabric imported from England. Her clothes were custom made. The housework and garden tasks were done and supervised by Nance and Helen. Henrietta, whom she adored, served as her personal servant and nurse to the children.

Sherrod showered her with gifts of love and affection. He worked hard to increase business and provide a high quality of life at home and in Bryant Town. He built additions to his house and a special room for a secret school where Nance taught the children, slaves and free people alike. He fussed over and tried to please Nancy by granting her what she asked for, including special freedom. Against his better judgment, he allowed her to go to Nashville and fraternize with the white women there.

Nancy knew Sherrod was doing everything he could for her, but it didn't keep her from getting bored. After living and experiencing the pace and customs of Europe and Paris, Bryant Town reminded her of the hills and colonies she had worked so hard to escape. She began to feel as if she was moving backwards instead of forward. She took to leaving Bryant Town to go to Frederick Stumps Tavern on White's Creek. She began to spend more and more time there. Soon, she lost interest in the home, the children, and Sherrod. She was polite to him but refused to share anything intimate with him. His advances were ignored.

Stumps was not unlike Black Bob's, which Renfro closed in 1814 because he felt Stumps had robbed him of his business practice, his staff, and his menu. That is, all his staff except for Little Doe, who had returned to work at Black Bob's and had gone to live in Bryant Town when the tavern closed.

Because of Little Doe's relationship with the employees at Stumps, she was up on all the gossip, which she shared with Helen and Oscar. Free people of color were hard-pressed to socialize publicly with slaves or whites. White folks were punitive and uncaring and seemed to need to justify their abuse of African Americans by projecting their feelings of inadequacy and meanness onto the person or group of people that they were misusing. The slaves, on the other hand, shared a quality of life in Bryant Town with the free people of color who were building and living among them. Still, they envied the free status of their neighbors, and they were overzealous in their quickness to share negative information about their owners and their family members.

In Little Doe's case, she was jealous and wanted Nancy to be out as soon as possible. She discussed it with Nance, with Helen, and any other slave in Bryant Town who would listen.

Sherrod was aware Nancy was turned off by him. He tried to compensate by becoming more sensitive to her needs, but no matter what he tried, Nancy continued to be unhappy. He was aware of her insensitivity to the children and he asked Henrietta to fill in. It didn't take much encouragement on Sherrod's part. Henrietta saw the need and took the children to heart.

One night on his way home from the Donelson spread, he decided to pass by White's Creek to see what all the talk was about. Renfro had come to him several times to tell him how White's Creek had put an end to Black Bob's.

Sherrod was sorry Robert Renfro had let personal fears cloud his judgment and get in the way of business decisions. When Renfro heard Frederick was going to open the hotel and tavern, rather than feel motivated to take advantage of his experience, Robert felt pressured into going to Frederick and asking him if he needed his help.

"As a matter of fact, I do," Frederick had said. "You can send that Nigger cook of yours over here with the menu and tell Ava and Molly, if they know what's good for them, they will come and wait tables for me as well." Renfro was devastated by Frederick's response.

"I have done business in this town for twenty years. People know me," he told Stumps.

"And they like you," Stumps said. "But you're still a Nigger, an uppity Nigger at that."

"I just turned and walked away," Renfro explained to Sherrod. "It was either walk away, kill him, or kill myself. I have enough for me and my family," he said. "The way this town feels about people of color and how they're passing to keep us out of the marketplace is scary. I am not young or brave enough to force myself down these white crackers' throats."

"One thing white people understand is money," Sherrod said to him. "If you know how to make money in a way they don't, they will do anything to gain your knowledge. Stumps watched you make money, so he thinks he got the way you did it all figured out. When you went to him, he knew he had you. He knew he could steal what you had without any problems because you were running scared. What you could have done was upscale your business. Spend some of that money you're holding onto and come up with a new angle that would catch people's interest."

"That's all well and good," Renfro said. "If I was a young man, maybe I would try it. The way things are headed, white folks are even fighting white folks over Niggers. I don't feel like getting into it. I'm gonna get myself a little place and move me and my family back so far up in the woods everyone will forget who Black Bob is."

Sherrod smiled to himself thinking about the conversation. Nobody was going to run him out of business. White he wasn't, but smart, he was. As smart as anybody.

He came upon White's Creek and heard the music as it sounded through the trees. It was the end of March 1824. The sun had just set, and people were celebrating the beginning of planting time.

White folks from everywhere were going and coming on the trail leading to Stump's place. Some he knew, and some he didn't. He was just about to join the crowd when he saw Nancy walking arm in arm with Sam Lefler. They were coming out of the tavern and about to enter Sam's carriage when Sherrod pulled up on the reins of his horse and galloped to where Sam and Nancy stood.

A surprised Sam fell away from the carriage and Nancy hid her face in her arms as if she thought Sherrod was going to hit her.

"If you ever step foot in Bryant Town again, I will blow your head off," he said to her and rode off the way he had come.

When he arrived back on the trail, deep inside the woods, he let go of the reins and slid from his horse, falling to the ground. Anger lifted his chest and crowded his throat. A bitter-tasting substance rushed up from the bottom of his stomach and sent him heaving and crying into the grass. "Bitch," he cried and vomited. "Bitch . . . bitch . . . you bitch," he vomited and vomited. A flash of heat came over him, and he was done. He took the tail of his shirt, wiped his mouth, and blew his nose. He felt drained and his head hurt. Conflict raged in his mind, tugged on him, and wouldn't leave him. It kept going and going.

"You were too easy on the bitch," one voice said.

"You loved her," the other argued.

"She was a tramp. How were we supposed to know that?"

"Love . . . ha . . . You don't know anything about women."

"She was different when you first saw her. She was from a good family. You knew her all your life. How were you to know she wasn't that person you left in the woods?"

"She played you. Sent for you. She deliberately played you."

"You should have known better. Where did she get the money to go to Paris and buy all them fancy clothes?"

"Enough," Sherrod shouted, got up from where he had fallen, got back on his horse, and headed for Bryant Town.

On the way up the main thoroughfare, he saw the light flickering in Little Doe's cabin. He tied his horse to a tree and walked quietly to the front door. Little Doe opened it before he could knock.

"What are you doing here?" she asked.

"I need someone to be with," he said. "Is Little Silas asleep?"

"Wait a minute. I will walk with you."

"Who are you talking to, Mother?" Little Silas called from the back of the cabin.

"Daddy Bryant, Silas," Sherrod called in to him. "Your mother and I have some things to talk over. Is that okay?"

"Yes, Sir," Little Silas replied.

Little Doe stepped out and closed the door behind her.

"I have ignored the boy long enough," Sherrod said as they walked away from the house. "Silas is thirteen years old. It is time he becomes more involved with me and what I am doing in Bryant Town."

"What will others think?" she asked.

Sherrod moved in front of her and took her in his arms. "Have you ever known me not to act because I was afraid of what others would think?"

Little Doe looked back over her shoulder to be sure they were out of hearing or seeing distance. When she was satisfied they were, she raised her hand and slapped him. He pushed her away, surprised and startled.

She turned and started back towards the house. He called after her. "I caught my wife with another man about an hour ago, Little Doe." She stopped to listen to him. "I walked away without killing her. I am not sure how much more I can deal with."

"Is that why you here, trying to use Silas and me?"

"I am here because I need to be hugged. Can you give me that?"

The sight of him humiliated and hurt her and overwhelmed her with anger. She searched his eyes and his mouth and tried to figure out what to do.

He wanted to walk away, but his legs wouldn't move. Everything in him wanted to tell her how he didn't need her, how he was through with women, but his body was numb and his heart ached, almost as if she was feeling his pain and began to cry.

"I am not a throw-away, Sherrod Bryant."

"I know," he whispered and hugged her.

"Silas is not a toy. You want to play Daddy cause you need."

"Tonight, I learned that my children are the only people in life that are mine and always will be mine, no matter what."

She took his hand, and together they walked deep into the woods. "This time it is my hideaway that we are going to." They walked and talked and made love until dawn.

Little Silas woke up the next morning and found his mother's bed was not slept in. He went across to Sherrod's and pretended to talk to Henrietta a while. When he was satisfied Little Doe wasn't there, he went out into the woods to look for her and came upon her and Sherrod sleeping under a tree. He eased over, touched Sherrod gently on the shoulder, and whispered, "Mom catches cold easily. Will you wake her and send her home?"

Sherrod nodded that he would, and Little Silas left. When he was out of sight, Little Doe stirred.

"He try to preserve my honor," she said, and opened her eyes. "I left the reservation because of what some of my people said and called me."

"He is sure grown for thirteen," Sherrod said. He thought about what had just happened and added. "I will speak with Henderson as soon as I get back to the house. See if he has any ideas about how we best fit Little Silas into what we are doing."

She turned a deaf ear to what he was saying. She didn't want to hear his promises, out of fear they were just that, promises. She knew how easy it was to get her hopes up and before she knew it she would be thinking they were going together.

He was always fair with her. He always did everything he said he was going to do, and that was her problem. No matter what occurred between them, she had no influence in the relationship. She hadn't been able to persuade or change his mind in any way, and that hurt. It hurt to learn Henderson existed when she thought Silas would be Sherrod's first-born son. It hurt when he stopped by and told her about Nancy Johnson and going to Ohio. Now, because he was hurting, he found a use for her in his life.

Sherrod wasn't one to share his business, so when he told Little Doe about Nancy she was surprised. It was common knowledge around town there was some kind of a relationship between her and Sherrod because everyone in Bryant Town was either related to or owned by a Bryant. The confusing part was Little Doe's son was named after Sherrod's brother, Silas.

Sherrod and Little Doe were only seen together publicly when every now and then he stopped to talk with her when he saw her outside on the porch.

Henderson knew. He had learned about them when he was twelve years old. When he asked Sherrod if it would be okay for him to give Old Paint to Little Silas, Sherrod hugged him.

"Why you do that?" Henderson asked.

"Because you are accepting and generous," Sherrod replied. "I've been trying to figure out a way to tell you that Silas is your brother. I wanted to tell you before you found out some other way. I guess I am a little late."

Henderson looked at Sherrod strangely. "Do all grown-ups lie or is it just those in this family?" he shouted and ran towards the door crying.

Sherrod caught him before he could exit, grabbed him by the shirt, and held on to him. Henderson tried to struggle free. "I guess I spoke too soon, and I apologize for that. But, since I did speak, you are going to hear me out."

He forced Henderson to sit down in the closest chair. He stood prepared to block any escape attempts that Henderson made. Henderson continued to cry. When he finished, Sherrod sat down next to him and in a quiet voice said, "I know grown-ups' behavior appears strange to you sometimes, and I can't say it doesn't appear strange to me, even when I am the one involved in it."

Henderson stared straight ahead, without a reaction or response to what was being said.

"Silas is my son, Henderson, but not like you're my son." He tried to hug Henderson but Henderson shrugged away from him. "I didn't love Silas's mother. I haven't been involved in raising him. When your mother would come and leave me after a long stay, I would get lonely. Little Doe agreed to help me with my loneliness. We didn't plan or expect to have a child together, but we did. When you don't take a part in raising a child, feelings for that child are different."

Henderson continued to stare, and Sherrod started to feel frustrated.

"Love is usually what helps children come to be. Sometimes as a man and a woman come together out of loneliness and children are born because of their parents' need . . . What I am trying to say is that I love your mother. We were excited when we learned you were about to be born. We planned for your birth. Bryant Town is here because of you. When we learned you were coming, we knew we had to do everything we could do to make you safe.

"Your Uncle Silas and Aunt Sara, they helped Little Doe raise Silas. That is why he carries Silas' name. Everyone calls him Little Silas. Haven't you ever wondered about that?"

"Silas' mother stayed here. Mama Mary left," Henderson said.

"I never thought about it that way," Sherrod said. "I guess we have two half families."

Henderson stood up. "No, you have two half families. Silas is my brother. He will be my brother. I couldn't treat him like a brother before because I didn't know. Now I do know." With that, he turned and walked out of the house.

Sherrod knew he had been set out, and he was fine with it. Henderson was young and didn't know how hard it was to be part of a small group of people being inside a much larger group that categorized and abused you at every turn. He didn't know what it felt like to have to own people of color in order to gain enough credibility to earn a living. No, Little Doe was not his wife. He would be useless in the marketplace if she were. He had a family to lead, including Little Doe and Silas.

He was thinking about this conversation with Henderson as he walked his horse up the path to the house that March morning. He had been through an emotional wringer. For the first time, he agreed with Henderson about who the woman was, rather than what she was.

He entered his house calling, "Helen, Nance, Henrietta. Grab Mrs. Bryant's things, tie them in a sheet, and tell Oscar to come here. Nancy Johnson doesn't live in this house anymore."

The three women scrambled happily around the house collecting and seeing Henderson come in from outside.

"What's going on?" he asked.

Sherrod motioned him outside to the porch for a private talk. When his father told him how he had caught Nancy and Sam Lefler up at White's Creek, Henderson slammed his fist into his hand and said, "I heard it and didn't want to believe it." Then he cursed. "Damn. Damn, Damn, Damn her hide."

"We were too slow for her, Son. She wants a faster life."

"She is lucky she has a life," Henderson replied angrily.

Sherrod put his hand on his son's shoulder. "The Lord really blessed me when he put you in my life, Henderson Bryant."

Henderson hugged his dad. He felt like a man standing there beside him. His dad trusted him, and that meant they were friends. They stood there, the two of them, looking over Bryant Town.

Henderson saw Little Silas walking out on the path and called to him.

"Hi, Silas, Daddy Bryant's got a spare room over here if your mama makes you mad and you need some man talk."

"And have to put up with all those girls in your house?" Silas laughed and waved a no-thanks and went about his business.

"I am proud of the way you and Little Silas are getting along," Sherrod said.

"We're brothers, Dad."

"You're going to be seventeen next year. I've been thinking about helping you get some land of your own. Maybe you and Silas can start building out there in Rutherford County. In a few years, I will buy some middle property and extend Bryant Town. Right now, it is important to box ourselves across county lines and help people to want to sell."

Oscar approached them from around the side of the house. "You sent for me, Sir?"

"Take that pile of junk the women threw in the bed sheets and take it over to Sam Lefler's house. Tell him I sent it if you see him. If you don't see him, toss it up on his porch and come on back."

Henderson was amazed by his dad's calmness. Every time he thought he had him figured out, some crisis occurred and Sherrod seemed to step out of himself and become this unattached-to-the-incident kind of person who doled out responses that were right but unexpected.

Underneath, he knew Sherrod was hurting. He hated that Nancy did what she did because he knew his dad loved her and was all torn up inside. He didn't like that his dad was in pain and felt protective.

As for Nancy, as warm and friendly as she was, it had become harder and harder to be nice to her. She kept having babies and ignoring them. When she saw that the children found solace in Henrietta's care, she would call them away from Henrietta. When they wouldn't want to go with her, she would become angry and punitive, demanding things from everyone in sight.

He had learned not to trust her warmth. Several times she was in the middle of one of her tirades, abusing Nance, Helen, and Henrietta, when unbeknownst to her, Sherrod had entered. When she finally saw him, she immediately rushed to him smiling as if he hadn't seen or heard the commotion.

Henderson had anguished over whether or not to tell Sherrod about seeing Nancy going into White's Creek. Silas had told him several months before that he had heard a lady who worked at White's Creek talking to Little Doe about Nancy being there and how she was acting. It seemed the white people that frequented Stumps were taken by her airs, the way she dressed, the way she talked, and threw money around.

Henderson didn't believe Silas, so he followed her one night. Sure enough, White's Creek was where she went. He could almost say she met a man there but he stumbled over a bush trying to hide in the woods out of view, and by the time he got up, she had already gone inside.

He felt a little guilty about not telling his father. He was almost sure he had done the right thing. Besides, if he had told, he wouldn't be standing on the porch next to his father the way he was doing, letting his mind go and become flooded with all kinds of thoughts.

He remembered the joy he felt in the mornings when Sherrod came to take him horseback riding at the Coles, him sitting in front of Daddy Bryant, holding onto the reins like a two-year-old man. He remembered the joy in Sherrod's eyes when he greeted Mama Mary after a long trip and the tenderness he felt from Sherrod standing between his legs. He was a little boy trying to understand words his Daddy Bryant was using to help him accept the fact that he couldn't go back to live with John, Missouri, and Mary Ann.

He thought about Mary Ann, how pretty she was, and how she made him feel when he tussled with her on the ground. How she giggled when he called her name, how she smelled when they were up close, and how his privates stirred inside his pants, caught him off guard, and embarrassed him. He looked at Sherrod and was glad that he couldn't hear his thoughts. He was satisfied only he knew, and smiled. In a few months he would be going to Kentucky. Now that the General Jackson Steamboat was open to passengers on the Cumberland River, he was more than sure that is how he would be traveling. His mind told him to ask Sherrod, but he knew Sherrod was hurting, and he didn't want to burden him with anything new.

Sherrod took out his pipe and asked Henderson if he wanted a puff. Henderson looked at him, not knowing what to say.

"I figure you're a man now that you are about to take on new responsibility," Sherrod said and laughed. "That property that Gulledge has for sale out there in Rutherford. You do want it, don't you?"

"I certainly do," Henderson said, trying to sound grown-up.

"You certainly do want to smoke, or you certainly do want the property?"

"Both," Henderson wanted to say, but the word stuck in his throat. So when he said, "Both," it came out as a yell.

"I'm not deaf," Sherrod laughed. He gave Henderson a pipe and continued as if sharing a pipe was a normal occurrence. "After you return from your summer vacation with the Coles, we will speak to William Gulledge, and put the purchase in motion."

He waited, but Henderson didn't respond. He turned to Henderson who was standing there holding his breath. Sherrod took the pipe from his hand and, as if he had released a coughing spell, Henderson hacked and hacked and hacked. Henrietta, who had been watching the sequence of events, came running to the door with Nancy Elizabeth sitting on her hip and a glass of water in her hand.

"You trying to kill your son, Mister Bryant?" she said, giving Henderson the water. He grabbed the glass and tried to drink in between coughs.

Nancy Elizabeth started to cry. Sherrod took her from Henrietta. "It's okay, Baby," he said, and kissed Nancy Elizabeth, who was ten months old. "Your brother is learning the ways of men. He is going to be fine."

"The ways of men, my foot," Henrietta said. Henderson dashed her with the water from the glass. Sherrod laughed.

"Where are William, Catherine, and Phoebe?"

"Nance is reading to them. I believe Nancy Elizabeth is wanting to nurse."

"There will be no more nursing for Nancy Elizabeth," Sherrod said sternly. "Now, go inside and tell Helen . . . Never mind. I will do it," he said, jumped up, and went inside.

He was clearly irritated, and that confused Henrietta. She allowed Sherrod to close the door before she gave Nancy Elizabeth to Henderson and followed them inside, mumbling. "No man is giving milk to a baby in my care."

Henderson hugged the baby and kissed her on the neck. She laughed.

"Grown folks are strange, but don't let that bother you," he said to her. "I don't know if I want to be a man. Being a kid is less confusing, don't you think?"

The baby laughed and pulled his hair. "What did you do that for?" he said and buried his face in her chest. She laughed and laughed.

"Don't sound like she's hungry to me," a calmer Sherrod said coming back to claim his place on the porch.

Henderson knew Henrietta had run him out of the kitchen. It amazed him how fast Henrietta grew up. She was only two years older, but her sense of what she had to do was much further ahead of what he was thinking and doing. She was more his father's equal than she was his, and that was okay because his dad seemed to need her to fuss and do errands for him.

Henderson sat there beside his father holding the baby. His father now had six children and no woman. Silas was the only one of them who lived with his mother.

As he thought about Little Doe, he wondered how it felt to really like someone and have that someone accept those love feelings only when they felt like it.

There was something not nice about it, and it bothered him that his daddy was successful in every way except for keeping his children's mothers. He knew that the men on the road had chased his mother away. He had come to understand that it had to do with being white and rich and coming from an unkind family. But, with Nancy and Little Doe, it was like Nancy did to Sherrod what he did to Little Doe.

He thought some more about it and then said to himself. *Maybe there was a little difference. Nancy married Sherrod, but he never married Little Doe. Nancy married and she was supposed to stay married.* He was going back and forth with it in his mind when Sherrod spoke up.

"You are awful quiet," he said.

"Shhhshhh," Henderson whispered. "The baby is asleep." He rose to take the baby in the house and saw Oscar driving up in the wagon. He hastened his pace because he wanted to hear what Oscar had to say. When he returned from putting the baby to bed, Oscar was leaving the porch and Sherrod was smiling.

Henderson crossed to his chair and took a seat. He was hoping Sherrod would share what Oscar had said. When he saw that wasn't going to happen, he got up and went to the barn where Oscar was unsaddling the horses.

See what that dirt farmer does with your fancy ways, Sherrod thought to himself. He sure wished he could have seen the look on Nancy's face when Lefler told her to stay inside and to tell Oscar to keep her things. He laughed aloud. Nance and Helen were going to have a time in those fancy wigs and powder puffs.

"Henrietta," he called. "Bring me some ice cream. My sweet tooth is calling for some of your good homemade ice cream."

"As soon as these children are settled, I will bring all you can eat," she replied.

Sherrod laughed to himself. "I do say that woman sounds like she's running this family."

BRYANT ACRES CHAPTER XX

Me and My Sons

The 1820s were a building time for Middle Tennessee. It was a time when the cotton gin had taken hold and planters were trying their luck with larger crops. Cumberland and Stones Rivers, and the many creeks flowing through the area, had proved to be useful power sources for mills of all kinds. The soil was exceedingly fertile, and the native growth of timber was plentiful.

In many places, the ground was covered with stone. The white settlers who came to live in Davidson, Rutherford, and surrounding counties were industrious and they, like those before them, depended on Sherrod for his husbandry. He taught them the importance of rotating crops for improving the land, and how growing red clover for a few years would help them reclaim worn-out land that had been over-cultivated. Without a doubt, Sherrod had become a powerful fixture in the area.

There were some rumblings about free men fraternizing with slaves and filling their heads with notions of freedom. The Denmark Vesey insurrection of 1822 happened in Charleston, South Carolina, and was said to be directed by a free Negro. In 1825, David Walker wrote Walker's Appeal in four articles together with a preamble to the colored citizens of the world.

His first article described how the Negro was treated and the low regard his white Master held for him. The second article predicted the rise of a great Negro leader who he said would guide the Negro to freedom and independence. The third article discussed the consequences of the colonizing plan, which he wrote was based in the way Americans manipulated religion to justify their treatment of slaves. The fourth article discussed how Negros were justified in using force to acquire independence.

These articles, printed in Boston in 1829, were widely circulated incidents that drew the attention of Sherrod's white neighbors and supporters. They refused to see how what was happening outside of Tennessee would or could apply to him or them. They knew that Bryant Town was what Sherrod lived for. They watched him build it, and they took comfort in knowing everyone that lived there, including some of the slaves, were members of his family.

They were so sure of their relationship with him and Bryant Town they took to discussing some of the issues raised in the fraternization of free men and slaves with Sherrod.

"What do you think about this Walker fellow over in Charleston? I hear he was born a slave in North Carolina, but he now lives in Boston. He is getting a lot of attention. What do you think about him?" Donelson asked Sherrod one day.

"I don't have time to think about other people's business," Sherrod replied. "That family of mine is growing so, it is all I can do to keep them doing what they are supposed to do to eat and sleep."

"My thinking exactly," Donelson laughed.

When he walked away, Sherrod spit in the dirt. "If you know half of what I know, Cracker, you would be trying to blame me for what is being said about you white folks. Don't insult me by asking me such nonsense. What I think is you need me more than you need a fight."

He looked over the land where he stood and thought about the problems. He heard Nancy had married Sam Lefler the day before. Henderson would be leaving to visit the Coles in a few days, Little Doe was going to have his second child, and Henrietta was starting to reach out to him on those cold nights. These were the matters that needed his attention as far as he was concerned.

He thought about why Donelson had asked him what he did. "You let me know you were keeping up with it, didn't you?" he said aloud, as if Donelson were still present. Then he said, "David Walker, whoever you are," and tipped his hat. "I wish you well. Your war is important, and so is mine."

With that, he remembered that years ago he had promised Chavis he would reach out to colored people and get involved. He thought about where he was with that, and said to himself, "Right now I have six children and one about to be born. My brother, Silas, has three. William has four. That is three families and thirteen-and-half seedlings, two husbands, two wives, a pregnant woman, fifteen slaves, and me. Bryant Town has approximately thirty-three residents," he said and smiled. "Imagine that. Thirty-three."

"What's thirty-three?" Henderson called to him from inside the house.

This was the day he was to leave for Kentucky, and he was excited. It was the first year Joel wasn't coming back to travel with him. He would be traveling alone, and he was going on the General Jackson.

Sherrod argued with himself as to whether or not he should discuss with Henderson the negativity he could experience as a young colored man traveling alone on public vessels. He gave it a great deal of thought and decided against the discussion. He wanted Henderson to have his own experience and not be influenced by anything he might say or suggest.

Henderson had olive-colored skin, the same as Sherrod. He had Mary Polly's black hair and dark black eyes, making one wonder whether he was mulatto or an Indian.

The captain of the General Jackson was an acquaintance of Sherrod's. He welcomed Henderson as a passenger but was careful to let Sherrod know he could not be responsible for Henderson's well-being. He explained that many men that traveled the Cumberland River were strangers from neighboring states who were brokering the slave trade and at times were apt to be unpleasant to a colored sixteen-year-old traveling alone.

"Will you at least guarantee his safe arrival?" Sherrod asked.

"That I guarantee," the captain said. "Kentucky is our first stop. Henderson will have to weather whatever storm that rises between here and there."

Sherrod was nearly as excited as Henderson. He felt sure Henderson could handle himself. Joel and his family would be at the dock waiting when he arrived. Other than getting tossed overboard, there was very little else Henderson couldn't handle.

Henderson was trying very much to be the man. He was wearing a new dark-blue suit, a matching shoe string tie with a white shirt, and a dark blue hat. He looked so much like Sherrod it had startled him when Henderson first came out.

When he came out of the house, they walked together to the carriage they would be traveling in that morning. Willie was waiting for them. "You awful sharp this morning, Mr. Henderson," he said, and Sherrod laughed. "You are having an experience your old dad hasn't had. Do you think you can handle it?"

"I will handle it the same way I handle the crackers that run in and out of Bryant Town," Henderson said. His voice showed some concern, so Sherrod thought he'd better touch on the race issue lightly.

"I like the way you handle the business with white customers," Sherrod said. "You don't get chatty with them, and that's important. White folks love to start telling you something, so you will come forth with a comment they can use to attack or twist to their advantage. It gives them a chance to tell you what they wanted to tell you in the first place."

"You noticed that, too," Henderson said and added, "I have made up my mind. I am not going to say anything to anybody, be he black or white. I got myself this whittling knife and a piece of wood. Going to make Mary Ann a doll."

Henderson thought himself an expert on white folks. Most of the negative comments they made to him he didn't bother to share with Sherrod. He knew his daddy had to deal with them and didn't want to cause him trouble. Besides, if his own grandparents, Big Mary and Jesse, were against him, what could he expect from strangers?

He would listen to them talk as they shopped in the various businesses. Like his father, he figured their opinions didn't amount to much. Outwardly, when they said something out of the way, he would act as if what they were saying didn't apply to him. Meanwhile, he would tear them to shreds in his mind and then add an additional few cents to their bill to compensate for their bad manners.

Sherrod was satisfied his son's thinking was where it should be at his age. He couldn't think of a single thing else to tell him, so he became playful with him. "You are going to see someone else besides Mary Ann, aren't you?"

"John likes to trade information, so I will teach him all the new tricks I have learned. Missouri, I think she's my mother, so I will painfully sit and eat her cooking. And, Mama Sally, she can do all the hugging she wants. As for Papa Joel, he just wants to hear what you been doing." He thought for a moment and then added, "You don't mind if I don't tell him about your new baby, do you? He took your marriage to Nancy pretty hard. I don't want to complicate anything."

"I didn't know Joel had feelings about my marriage," Sherrod said, somewhat surprised.

"He knew you couldn't wait around on Mama Mary. I heard him and Mama Sally talking. He said it was hard, said he had so much to be grateful to you for. He don't want to lose you as a brother."

"I have a lot to be grateful for. Why, he and Sally practically raised you. Building a few barns and teaching him to expand and manage a farm is nothing compared to what he and Sally gave to you. He will never lose me, no matter what."

"Good," Henderson said. "Maybe I will tell him what happened with Nancy."

Sherrod laughed. "I guess I walked into that one." He hugged his son. When they arrived at the boat, they sat in the carriage and observed until everyone was aboard. The captain of the General

Jackson saw them sitting there and waved. When the last "all aboard" was called, Henderson grabbed his bags and ran aboard.

Sherrod sat and waited until the boat started to sail. He had carefully scrutinized every person who boarded the boat and there were only two men he was leery of. He etched details of their faces in his mind and warned Henderson to stay away from them.

Driving home he thought about Mary Polly and wondered how she was doing. The success of their teamwork was where he drew strength from when he felt pressured by events in his current life.

It was clearly time for him to set Henderson up, give him more responsibility so he could start preparing to make his own way. He felt good that he was keeping his promise to Mary Polly and was sad she had not been there to share her son's growing up years and see how well he had turned out.

He was more than sure Joel kept her aware of what was happening to Henderson. He hoped Joel told her often how grateful he was that she had been in his life. He had been careful to tell Henderson to let Joel know he was about to receive his first gift of property, as Mary Polly had instructed.

On the way home, riding down the main thoroughfare of Bryant Town, he saw a very pregnant Little Doe sweeping the porch. "Silas home?" he asked in the way of a greeting.

"This time of day," she replied, without looking at him. Then she sarcastically added, "You put him to work. I imagine that's where he is."

Sherrod got down from the carriage. "I know you are angry about the baby."

"I am angry about allowing myself to listen to you."

"As soon as the baby is born, I want you to give him or her to me. Let 'em grow up with his or her brothers and sisters."

"No," she said angrily. "We are going home. My family is disappointed in me. But they are good people. They will forgive."

"I'm sorry it turned out bad for you."

"Silas is happy. He will be staying."

"Is there anything I can do to help you move?"

"Silas will let you know when the baby comes."

"Thanks," he said, and took the reins of the horses and walked the rest of the way home.

He knew Little Doe was angry because he said he wouldn't marry her, and there was nothing he could do to change that. When he entered the house, he heard Henrietta in the kitchen with William and the girls.

"Henderson will be back in four Sundays. You all got that? Now, how many Sundays is four Sundays, Phoebe?"

Phoebe held up three fingers.

"No, it's this many," Catherine said, holding up four fingers.

"This," Nancy Elizabeth said and slammed her fist down on her bowl of mush turning it over on the tablecloth.

"Bad girl," Henrietta said, and the others laughed.

Sherrod entered and everyone turned their attention to him. "Daddy ready for breakfast? Daddy eat."

"Yes, Daddy wants to eat," Sherrod said to Nancy Elizabeth and picked her up.

"Henderson got on all right?" Henrietta asked.

"He's gone," Sherrod said, watching her dish food from the stove, the sun shining through her dress, silhouetting the firmness of her young body. "You're a good mother to my children, Henrietta," he said.

She giggled. "I love Mister Bryant's children. They part of Mister Bryant."

"Put the children to bed early tonight. We're going to have some talking time together."

"Okay," she said. "But I ain't much for talking."

Instead of responding, he started eating from the plate she had set in front of him, a sign she took to mean he was done discussing the invitation. She went on about the business of getting the children ready for their story hour with Nance. She was excited and that was her cue to be careful not to tell the others about the invitation, lest they be jealous and alienate her from the flow of gossip in town.

Sherrod finished eating and went over to the blacksmith shop where he found Little Silas. It was the first time he was singling Little Silas out to spend time with. While Henderson was away, he figured it was a good time to get to know the boy. "It's time we talked, Boy," he said, and motioned Silas outside to a tree stump.

Silas quietly obeyed. He was basically a quiet boy. He teased Henrietta a lot because she was the only woman near his age in Bryant Town. When he came out and sat, he looked up at his dad like the child that he was.

"I'm told your mom is moving back to the reservation to live," Sherrod said, starting the conversation.

"I'm staying," Silas replied without blinking an eye.

"Where you plan on living?"

"In my house."

Sherrod laughed. He liked the boy's spunk. The more he was around the boy, the more he saw that he liked. "Do you have anything you want to say to me about your mother or my treatment of her?"

"That's grown folks' business," Little Silas said. "She doesn't tell me much. It ain't got nothing to do with me."

I'm sure what she hasn't told you, Henderson has, Sherrod thought to himself. There was no acknowledgment of anything coming from Silas, so he continued. "I was thinking you would like to take a ride and look at some property Henderson's mother is buying for him."

"Do you think Henderson would want to live with me?" Silas asked, his mind still on his mother's leaving.

"I don't see why not," Sherrod said. "He could use a good man like you to help him build." Sherrod waited for further deliberation. When none was forthcoming, he got up and headed for the carriage. "You coming?"

Silas got up and ran to be with his father. It was the first time they had done anything together, just the two of them, in all of his thirteen years. He had always wondered what that would feel like. Now that they were alone, he had a hundred questions he wanted to ask but couldn't get up the courage. So, he sat quietly and rode the trail with his father thinking about questions he would like to have answers to. Answers to questions like, why white men hated Indians and Africans? What had people of color done to let the white man know they would accept the kind of treatment they were receiving? He knew his mother's people had lived for hundreds of years on the land, taking its resources the way one takes in the light of the moon, the rays of the sun, and the brightness of the stars, things that God gives to all life, to be used, shared, and cared for.

Little Doe had told him that the Africans came to America against their will. She said white men forced Africans to build, to do his work, build his homes, his farms, and to care for his children. She said Indians were nearly wiped out by the white man. Their lies and confusion had tricked the Indians.

He needed to know, because when he thought about it, it made him sad. He didn't want to feel sad. It was a happy day. He was with his father, and that was a good thing.

"If I cut my hair like yours and wear different clothes, do you think the white customers will stop calling me Injun and Buck?" He finally got up the courage to ask.

"I wasn't aware that anyone called you out of your name," Sherrod said. He thought about it for a moment and added, "The next time it happens, you tell whoever it is that your father, Daddy Bryant, said they are to discuss their reasons for treating you bad, with him."

"Yes, Sir," Silas said, and his sprits lifted.

When they rode through town, Sherrod took him into Nash's store and showed him a stack of clothes. "Grab yourself two pair of them britches there, a couple of shirts, some new boots, a belt, and a pair of long johns." Sherrod knew they had all that stuff back at the store in Bryant Town but he wanted to send a message to the white people that he was dealing with.

"What color?" Silas asked happily.

"You choose," Sherrod said. Silas didn't know what to choose first.

"Go on. I'll be right over here, talking to Mr. Nash."

"Who's the Injun?" Nash asked as Sherrod approached the front of the store.

"That lad there is my second son, Silas," Sherrod said loud enough for Silas to hear.

"I didn't know you had but one son."

"I have three sons and three daughters. The others are a little young. Silas here, you will be seeing more often." He picked up a tie back and threw it on the counter.

"He is trying to decide if he should cut his hair or not. He just turned thirteen; it's a big decision."

"Thirteen!" Nash exclaimed. "Silas, you're a man. Grab yourself a couple pair of them socks over there. From here on out, you're a full-fledged customer in this store." Silas chose two pairs of socks and put them on top of the pile he was carrying.

On the way from town, they stopped by the house of Sherrod's brother, Silas, and asked him to cut Little Silas' hair. He was amazed at how well Silas' children knew Little Silas. They hugged and climbed on him, laughing and teasing, making so much noise Big Silas had to speak out. "Y'all let that boy get his hair cut."

"We don't see Little Silas anymore since you put him to work, Sherrod," Martha teased. "And, as far as that go, Sherrod, we see less of you than we do Little Silas."

"We are on our way to Gulledge's place. I hear he has land for sale over in Rutherford County. They tell me parts of it even crosses into Wilson County."

Seeing Silas, Martha, and the kids was great for Sherrod. He saw them around town, but rarely took the time to sit with them as a family. Little Silas, he wasn't paying attention to much of anything once Big Silas cut his hair. He didn't see much of William Gulledge's place or hear much of the conversation. He was too busy standing over the water trough, trying to catch his reflection in the water.

It was hard for him to get used to how he looked with short hair. He was grateful for all that had happened to him. He couldn't wait to show his mother. However, he didn't feel like his reflection was his when he saw it. His eyes appeared larger, his face rounder, and his ears, he had never paid attention to his ears before. He wondered how his mother was going to accept his new look.

Thoughts of his mother moving away from Bryant Town crossed his mind, but he managed to push them away until he and Sherrod started up the trail to his house.

"Thanks for everything," he said, as he jumped from the carriage with his packages in hand.

"I am sorry we didn't start to do this earlier, when you were younger," Sherrod said.

"That's okay," Silas said, and ran into the house. *That's okay, Daddy Bryant,* he said to himself and hoped the next time he would be strong enough to say it to Sherrod. Maybe if he said it enough times.

"Daddy Bryant. Daddy Bryant," he repeated until he saw his mother sitting in the rocking chair by the door.

"Is everything okay?" she asked him.

"Everything is fine," he said. He didn't know about the baby, and she wasn't going to tell him.

"Daddy Bryant bought me some clothes."

"And talked you into cutting your hair," she snapped.

"That was my idea. You don't like it?" She didn't respond. He was excited, and he didn't want her to ruin his mood. "You should have seen us in Nash's store today. Nash gave me two pairs of free socks. Daddy Bryant told him who I was, and Old Man Nash nearly chewed up his lip."

Silas made a funny gesture with his mouth, trying to make Little Doe laugh. She was determined she wasn't going to get involved with Sherrod's activities, even if they involved Silas. She trusted Sherrod wasn't going to hurt the boy, but that was as far as she was willing to go.

Silas was determined she was going to be a part of his day. He took hold of his top lip with his bottom one, tried to talk while sucking his teeth. "You know how he do," he said. Little Doe ignored him. He grinned.

"Daddy Bryant wanted to laugh. I could tell by the look on his face. He knows how to play white folks. 'This here is my son, Silas,'" he said, trying to imitate Sherrod.

"Just like that?" a surprised Little Doe asked, trying not to appear too interested.

Silas smiled. He knew he had her. "Without any coaxing or anything. It surprised the devil out of me. Told him I was thirteen, and I needed a man's suit. Old Nash started smiling and grinning. He gave me these here socks. He said I could be a regular customer, anytime I liked."

"The same Nash that called you a heathen for accidentally bumping into his old wall fixture?"

"The same Nash," he said, proudly, taking his new clothes out of the bag to show her.

She looked at him and felt sorry she was being so irritable with him. *He is such a handsome boy. I certainly hope the new one will be just as handsome*, she thought.

"Well, what do you think?" Silas asked. He had put on one of the shirts.

"You are more handsome than Daddy Bryant," she said sarcastically.

He detected her anger. "You don't mind if I call him Daddy Bryant, do you?"

"No, I don't," she smiled and hugged him.

Later that night, long after she had gone to bed, Silas was sitting in the window watching the moon and thinking. If he were Henderson, he would have taken the stagecoach instead of the steamboat. But, no matter, he was glad Henderson was away. He loved Henderson, but there was no way he would have got to go around with Sherrod the way he did if Henderson had been home.

He decided it was time he got to know his other brother and sisters. He promised himself he was going to go over and play with William, Catherine, Phoebe, and Nancy Elizabeth.

Little Doe's leaving was going to bring about a lot of quiet. Even if Henderson moved in, he was going to miss Little Doe. He wished she would stay. It wasn't that she couldn't visit back and forth, because she could, but it just wasn't going to be the same. His eyes welled up and he started to cry.

What was making her want to leave Bryant Town all of a sudden? He had thought that after Nancy left, his mother was getting together with Sherrod. He couldn't understand what could have happened.

He cried some more and decided she was just as disappointed as he was it didn't work out. It was best for her to go back to the reservation, find someone to be with.

He was out checking fences with Sherrod the next day when he asked him, "Would it be all right if I called you Daddy Bryant like your other kids do?"

"It would please me a great deal," Sherrod smiled.

Silas waited a while and then said, "I was hoping you and Mama would get together so she wouldn't have to move."

"You are full of surprises," Sherrod said and stopped what he was doing. He called Silas over to sit with him in the grass. "What I am going to say is going to be hard for you to hear, but I want you to listen carefully. There are those of us in this town that are free men. What that means is even though we are people of color, we do not belong to white men like the slaves and Indians do. White people rule this country, Silas. You might as well say this is their country because they have the say over what is and what is not going to happen in it. If white folks don't like the way something is going, they will find a way to change it. Make laws to justify the change. Do you understand what I am saying?"

"I think so," Silas said trying to let Sherrod know that he was listening.

Sherrod continued. "Africans were stolen, traded, and bought like cattle in the homeland. Then they were forced to come to this country to be worked like animals, to keep the white man from having to pay wages.

"Free labor makes people rich. I have slaves, but they share in the profits. I hold the paper on them because it's the law. I am responsible for their upkeep, but they have rights in Bryant Town. Indians like me, who were fathered by white men, are borderline people. White folks haven't decided where we fit. Your mother is also free, but she is a marked person because the white men defeated her people in war and took Tennessee land away from her tribe.

"I am telling you all this to let you know that in spite of all that has happened, and is still happening, all of us have to live together as people in Tennessee, and we have to get along.

"White folks frown on free men marrying slaves, marrying Indians, and Indians marrying free men. It frightens them, and it brings trouble.

"I care a great deal about your mother. She is a Tennessean, and I am not. She understands she and I will never marry, no matter what happens between us. Until the night I came to call on your mother, I hadn't been with her since you were born. Now your mother is about to have another baby by me and . . ."

ANN L. PATTERSON EARLY

Silas' face went white. Sherrod realized he had misspoken. "She is having a baby?" Silas stammered.

"I thought you knew," Sherrod said. "I'm sorry."

Silas ripped his new shirt off his body, threw it at Sherrod, and ran for home. When he arrived at the house, he told Little Doe what had happened and asked if she was having a baby.

"Today I am going to talk to you like a grown-up and I want you to listen like one."

"I am tired of people telling me how to listen," Silas snapped.

"Then get out of my sight until you are grown enough to deal with the trouble that you started."

"That's real good," he said. "I'm responsible for being born."

She slapped him, catching him off guard. He put his hand to his face and realized he had better listen.

When Little Doe was sure he had calmed down, she looked him in the eye and in a quiet voice said, "Mr. Sherrod come to Nashville. People say he had no money. He don't have friends, he stranger to everybody, he young. Many people not brave like Mr. Sherrod. He proud too. Act like white man, know what he want. Make white man think. I want to know this Mr. Bryant, this smart Mr. Bryant who people want to know. Silas you work hard, be smart like Daddy Bryant. Then, white folks can see Daddy Bryant no tell fib. He say he come to reservation, he come. He Indian like Little Doe and Silas. He be careful and make a right move. He loves you and baby inside."

"Did you know about Henderson when you went with him?"

"Henderson is secret. Nobody see Henderson with Mr. Bryant."

Silas started to cry.

"Be brave," she said. "Little Doe is hurt when you're unhappy."

"I sure hate that we have to do all this hiding and caring about what white folks think," Silas said through his tears.

"You tell Daddy Bryant you sorry you tear shirt. I will stay here until new baby comes."

Silas laid his head on her lap. "Will it ever be any different?" he asked.

"Daddy Bryant build new town, town like big family; family makes difference."

Silas got up from his mother's lap and went off to find his father. *Mama has this way of talking that makes you believe her. I certainly understand Daddy Bryant giving in to her*, he said to himself, as he walked along the path.

When he apologized to Sherrod, Sherrod ruffled his hair on top of his head. "I am glad your mother decided to stay," he said.

The next time Silas went to Gulledge's house, Henderson was home. He, Sherrod, and Henderson rode out to the place on Nashville Turnpike. On the way out, they discussed the possibility of starting a slaughterhouse and a meat packing plant.

Henderson liked the tract of land, and they made Gulledge an offer. Gulledge accepted the offer, and Henderson took possession of his land in October 1825.

Henderson and Silas spent the first part of 1826 building a house on Henderson's land. When it was time for him to go for his annual visit to Kentucky, to everyone's surprise, instead of his going that summer, John and Mary Ann came to Tennessee.

Missouri had registered in a teaching school in Kentucky, and Joel and Sally were going to spend the month of June at Cole Manner. They decided to reverse Henderson's vacationing habits, so they sent John and Mary Ann to Tennessee to return home to Kentucky with them sometime in July.

The Coles told Sherrod and Henderson about their plans a week before John and Mary Ann were to arrive in Bryant Town. Little Doe had taken baby Robertson to the reservation for the summer so that allowed Henderson, Silas, and John to occupy her house. Mary Ann was put up in what was now being called the Big House.

Henderson and Silas had started building in Rutherford. The Coles' plans suited Henderson. He didn't have to leave his work and still got to see Mary Ann and John.

He was glad they had decided to travel to Tennessee. He had had a hair-raising experience traveling on the steamboat to Kentucky the year before and he was not looking forward to repeating it. Now that summer had arrived, he was having recurring nightmares about traveling. When he was awake, thinking about his experience on the General Jackson sent him back to that day in June.

As soon as he had run aboard the General Jackson that day, the captain had summoned him. He followed the man, and when he arrived, the captain and the two men Sherrod had pointed out to him were sitting and waiting.

The taller of the two threw a pair of large britches and a large work shirt in his direction. "Put these on."

"I have on clothes, Sir," Henderson said, and the other man grabbed him by the front of his shirt and pulled him up against his chest.

"We don't know who gave you the idea you would ride topside with good, decent white folks when your job is in the boiler room with the other Niggers. Do you understand? Am I clear?"

"I am a paying customer," Henderson mumbled. Before he could say anything else, the little, short, bad-smelling man slapped him across the face and knocked his hat to the floor; fear overtook him.

"Are you any clearer?" the man said through his teeth.

Henderson saw rage in their faces. Their eyes were clenched, their complexion red, and beads of sweat stood on their foreheads. Henderson's knees buckled and he felt sick to his stomach. He was having trouble breathing. He was so scared he was afraid to ask where the boiler room was. The men, satisfied their point had been made, left the room. The captain picked Henderson's hat up from the floor.

"I will keep this in here until we dock."

Henderson quietly slipped the britches and shirt over his suit.

"Why don't you take off the jacket and lay it over here with your hat?" the captain said kindly.

Henderson did as the captain said. He was confused, and he felt as if he had no voice. His mind was void of thoughts, most of all of anything that would be a danger to him.

The captain led him to a dark shed of a room, two steps down from the main run. As he passed the entranceway window, he caught a glimpse of Sherrod sitting in his carriage waiting for them to take off. His father sat only a hundred yards away, but it appeared to Henderson at that brief moment that he was on the other side of the world. Unknowingly, his daddy watched while white folks forced him to the bowels of the boat to work.

He wanted to cry out, but he knew, somehow, to do so would put his dad's life in danger. Instead, he put one foot in front of the other, ignored his weak buckling knees, and held fast until he reached the bottom step.

"Lem and Sam will tell you what to do," the captain said and left.

There was a large contraption and piles and piles of wood and coal, which two tall black men wearing pants without shirts were heaving piece by piece into the machine that dominated the space.

Henderson picked up a shovel and put it in the coal pile. As he dug in, he heard the captain topside.

"Moving out," he called.

Henderson peeped through a porthole on the side of the wall and saw his father ride away. He started to cry.

"It ain't so bad," Lem said. "Every colored man that gets on this boat has got to come down here to work. They will let you off when you get to Kentucky."

"You mean they ain't gonna try to keep me down here?"

Sam laughed.

"Everything is going to work out fine. Grab that shovel and do like you see us doing, and everything will work out." Henderson picked up the shovel and pretended he had volunteered for the job. He got between Lem and Bob and did whatever he saw them do. Sure enough, when the sounds of the city reached his ears, the captain came and called him out. He gave him a bar of soap and a pail of water to clean up.

"If I was you, I wouldn't tell nobody about this," he said. "It won't do anything but make your daddy mad and possibly get both of you in trouble."

Henderson didn't respond. He washed his hands the best he could, took his jacket and hat, and waited downstairs until he was sure everyone supposed to have left had left the boat.

When he got topside, Joel, Sally, John, Missouri, and Mary Ann were waiting for him. When the hugging and greetings were finished and they were preparing to leave, the captain called out to him and waved.

"Thanks for riding the General Jackson, Henderson."

God is going to punish you, Henderson thought, and pushed the experience from his mind until it was time for him to return to Nashville. He traded his ticket for a stagecoach back. So as not to be assaulted in any way, he volunteered to ride topside with the driver.

The driver was an old Indian scout who loved his job. He talked to Henderson about the Chickasaws, Choctaws, Creeks, and Cherokees. He told him how they once owned Tennessee Territory, how General Robertson, in 1794, came in with a troop of soldiers and camped near Black Fox Springs. They went to war with the Indians and fought them from Murfreesboro to Nicklejack.

When the war ended and the Indians were defeated, the parent state of North Carolina gave six hundred forty acres of land to the head of each family who knew how and why the battle of Murfreesboro was fought. He knew about Nicklejack and Fox

Springs, but he kept the information to himself, lest he said he had a brother who was Choctaw.

Henderson's silence was not just extended to the stagecoach driver; it was extended to Sherrod as well. He didn't tell Sherrod about his experience on the steamboat General Jackson. He told him the captain of the boat wasn't his friend and left it at that.

Sherrod figured the captain had made a disparaging remark that Henderson didn't like. More important was the fact that Henderson was grown up enough not to have to give every detail of his discontent. There was a great satisfaction in being able to send his son traveling alone on modern transportation. Any petty thing the captain may or may not have said was not worth thinking about.

What Henderson mostly talked about when he returned home were his interactions with Mary Ann. For weeks, every other word that came out of his mouth had her name in it. It was Mary Ann this and Mary Ann that. Finally Sherrod asked him, "Did you see any of the rest of the Cole family there in Kentucky?"

Henderson laughed and teasingly said, "Yes, but it is really Mary Ann I go to see. She's beautiful, she's nice, she's smart, she's funny, and she loves teasing me."

"Are you planning to marry her?"

Sherrod's question shocked Henderson. He knew he was going to marry someday, but he certainly hadn't considered which day or that the day was approaching. He wondered if that was why Sherrod wanted him to have the land in Rutherford.

"Do you think it is time that I married, Dad?"

"It's not what I think," Sherrod said, continuing to be playful.

"Then, yes. Yes, I am going to marry Mary Ann."

The thought of it excited him. It made him feel giddy and unfamiliar with the parts of him that reacted so strongly that he was embarrassed with himself. When he thought about being with her, and occasionally when he allowed himself to think about sleeping with her, he became fired up. There was involuntary movement in his pants, his palms became sweaty, and he started to feel like he didn't belong in his own body.

He had kissed her several times during that visit. The kisses were light and friendly, nothing heavy enough for them to talk about. Whenever it happened, however, they would become quiet and pensive.

It was funny that Sherrod had detected how he felt about her. He had never told anyone. He never even told her.

Missouri was going to delight in their getting together. She said she was his sister, and she meant it. He knew she meant it because she was always doing his work for him. Sometimes she did so much, Mary Ann would get jealous and they would fight.

He was sorry Missouri had decided to stay at school and not come with John and Mary Ann. He would have liked to see her. The good part, however, was that he would get to have Mary Ann all to himself.

Henderson had already told Silas he wanted him and John to help him put the windows in the house they were building. Silas said he would and was true to his word.

As soon as he and Henderson picked up Mary Ann and John in Nashville, they headed over to Bryant's Grove—that was Henderson's name for the place. He named it so because he wanted to distinguish his land from his father's and still have it be a part of Bryant Town.

Mary Ann remembered Bryant Town from her youth. She was surprised by how much it had grown with the addition of Sherrod's family, his brothers and their families, the businesses. It was a real town, with a store, a blacksmith shop, a lumberyard, a weaving shop, a carpenter shop, a gristmill, a barbershop, and now Bryant's Grove.

From the minute she saw the house at Bryant's Grove, she knew she was going to live in it. While Silas, John, and Henderson went around surveying the outside of the house, discussing the windows and doors, she stayed inside the house, decorating and deciding on colors. She started to measure the size of the front room when Henderson entered.

"What are you doing?"

"Measuring the room," she said, and went to the window and looked out.

He came up behind her and stood touching the back of her hair. "I love you, Mary Ann. Will you marry me?" She was overwhelmed by the unexpected question and didn't know what to say. "I know we are young, but we have known each other all our lives. Daddy Bryant is up the road if we need help, so your folks need not worry."

"I want a big wedding," she said, as the idea of marrying settled in. Then all of a sudden she whirled away from him and the window and danced around the room. "With people and relatives from everywhere. We will get married right here. Right here in front of this window, overlooking the orchard."

Henderson had never seen her prettier. He reached for her hand as she went by and gently pulled her to him. "I like your plan," he said. "But it will take at least a year to finish this house."

She kissed him, and for the first time he kissed her passionately. They stood there kissing and clinging to each other, discovering and taking liberties with a different aspect of their relationship.

Silas and John entered, stood, and watched, until Mary Ann felt their presence and pulled away shyly.

"Mary Ann and I are getting married," Henderson said.

"Who says?" John asked, somewhat surprised.

"I did," Mary said and walked over to the window. "Next June, a year from now, we will be standing here at Henderson and my wedding."

Silas looked at them both. He thought he knew everything there was to know about Henderson. "Are you serious?"

"You heard the lady," Henderson said proudly.

"Wow," Silas said. "We better work day and night to get this house finished, that and the barn ready for the cows."

"Then let's go," John yelled and ran out of the house. Silas followed him.

The news spread through Bryant Town like a wildfire. Joel and Sally were as happy as Sherrod when they heard. The excitement of the impending event lent a festive air to the town.

Joel and Sally began helping with Bryant's Grove, and before anyone knew it, everyone in Bryant Town was contributing. Even five-year-old William, four-year-old Phoebe, three-year-old

Catherine, and two-year-old Nancy Elizabeth toddled around the grounds carrying wood and sticks for one thing or the other.

The slaves got so busy running back and forth between Bryant Town and Bryant's Grove that Sherrod had to remind them that business was to be conducted as usual. Customers were not interested in what was going to happen to colored folks a year down the road. If there was time or a day left after business had been taken care of, it was okay to contribute to the making of Bryant's Grove.

There was so much ongoing activity that it kept Henrietta, Nance, and Helen cooking from sunup to sundown.

Joel and Sally worked so hard fixing and planning that before they knew it, it was the night before departure time. Henderson, Silas, John, and the older cousins begged the adults to let them spend the night at Bryant's Grove. Sherrod and Joel agreed on the condition that the adults would also stay.

That June night in 1826 became the official engagement celebration. The men made a big bonfire. Henrietta, Nance, and Helen cooked at home, and Henry, Vitch, Samuel, Oscar, and the others filled the wagons with pots and pans full of vegetables and fish of all kinds, pies and cakes, and jugs of fruit juice. Pints and gallons of homemade wine were also included in the menu.

William's boy, Felix, played the juice harp, Oscar scrubbed out notes on the washboard, Samuel fiddled, and Walter played the comb.

The older people talked, the younger ones danced, and the tiny ones chased each other until they were tired and fell asleep.

Mary and Henderson sat quietly watching the fire. "I will be making curtains and table cloths," she told him.

"The windows will be large, well finished, and waiting, the same as I," he said.

"We are soon to be wed," she giggled.

"I will be counting the days, and every time I come up here to Bryant's Grove, I will stop at this spot and remember how pretty you looked with the light of the fire shining on your face."

Neither of them was saying what was really on their minds. They knew it wouldn't be wise.

"Let your dad take us to the stagecoach tomorrow. Say goodbye to me tonight. It would be too hard to leave with you there."

Henderson took her hand in his. "Let me know if there is anything you need."

"I will," she said, stood up immediately, and called to her mother. "Mama, I feel chilled. Can we go inside?"

Her voice cracked and Henderson knew she was about to cry. He helped her to her feet and stood staring into the fire until she and Sally were inside. Once they were gone, he went around to the side of the house, sat on the ground, leaning against a tree, and bumped his head on the trunk.

Sherrod asked John and Silas to go sit with Henderson. Sherrod's brothers, William and Silas, and their families said their goodbyes and left. Some were carrying sleeping children; others were dragging themselves after drinking and overeating.

Henrietta, Nance, and Helen loaded William, Phoebe, Catherine, and Nancy Elizabeth in the wagon where they slept until they reached their house. Oscar, Henry, and Samuel followed them in one clean-up wagon. Vitch and the other slaves did the last bit of cleaning from the other wagon. Sherrod and Joel sat and watched the fire go out.

"Tell Mary Polly I am expecting her to come to the wedding," Sherrod said as soon as they were alone.

"I will tell her," Joel replied. "She won't be surprised. She told me Mary Ann had her sights on Henderson. She said it when they were little children, three and six years old. I asked her what made her think that, and she said she could tell by the way Mary Ann kept pushing Missouri every time she got near Henderson. I believed her because the girls have never squabbled over John, and they didn't know at the time that Henderson wasn't their brother."

"You are something, Joel. Henderson and Mary Ann are doing what your sister and I couldn't do."

"I am not Jesse or Big Mary, that's for sure."

They both laughed and Joel mumbled, "Mary Polly sure would have been better off."

"What do you mean?" Sherrod asked.

"Forget I said that," Joel said. "Daddy is sick. Big Mary, well, she is still herself. Robert, let's just forget Robert and Lavonia. Mary stopped speaking to them twelve years ago."

"And the cotton business?"

Joel stood up. "I try not to ask."

Sherrod didn't know what to say. He was dumbfounded by the news.

Joel saw that he was upset. He sat back down. "This is our kid's night. Let's not rake up old memories. You have done a wonderful job with Henderson. Mary Polly is grateful to you."

"I am grateful to her too. All of what you see was possible because of her," he laughed to cover his sadness. "I don't have to tell you, do I? Your wife nursed my child."

"And now my daughter is going to nurse your grandchildren."

"Yahoo!" Sherrod yelled and broke open a bottle of brandy he had buried in the dirt next to him. "My dad would be proud," he said. "He fled the hills of Virginia to get away from the hate and abuse that white men bestow on people of color. You have helped me uphold that tradition. Bryant Town is our legacy. Your daughter will be safe living here at Bryant's Grove. The good white people of Davidson and Rutherford counties are friendly. We Bryants have the things we need. They won't give us any trouble."

"You have done well," Joel said. "The only thing missing in your town is a church."

Sherrod smiled. "Our minds work the same, friend. I've been thinking about all the blessings God has bestowed on this family, and it is time we gave him his praise. Willie is a God-fearing man. I am going to ask Nance to teach him to read and help him with the Bible so he can start Sunday services here in Bryant Town. Some of these women have nice singing voices, real nice to listen to. Maybe Sara and Martha will help build a choir. Get William and Silas to help me build a church."

Joel smiled. "All is well, Sherrod."

Sherrod smiled back at him and the two of them sat quietly, neither of them daring to speak on the possible ramifications of a colored male and a white female getting married in 1827, just when slavery was starting to peak.

They sat together and stared into the flames until the fire went out and the brandy was gone. All was quiet, and it was time to turn in.

BRYANT ACRES CHAPTER XXI

He Was About to Become a Grandfather

Henderson and Mary Ann's wedding took place in June 1827. As planned, Mary Polly sent a present and apologized for not being able to attend. Sherrod was more disappointed than Henderson.

"You would think she would want to be here," he said to his son.

"Daddy, you don't know why she can't make it. Don't sit back and make idle judgments about her reasons. She loves me. I will see her."

Sherrod listened to his son and held on to his other thoughts about Mary Polly and her actions. Last time he saw her she was having jealous feelings about Henrietta. He wondered if she was afraid to see where his life had taken him. If the word had spread about her being the mother of Henderson and she was bearing the consequences like a martyr, he hoped Joel would have heard and she would have told him before now.

Two months before the wedding, on March 20, 1827, Sherrod acquired some adjoining acreage from the Charles Hall Estate. He didn't want Silas to feel he was being pushed aside by Henderson's circumstance. He bought the land and put Silas in charge of developing it. He wanted it established and settled, and that was the way a proud Silas approached his new task.

Silas was now sixteen and feeling like a man. He appreciated how Sherrod was beginning to give him more responsibility. Any jealousy he felt towards Henderson had very little to do with Sherrod's treatment of him. It had more to do with Daddy Bryant not recognizing Henderson was not as capable as he.

Henderson was upset Silas was being taken away. There were a lot of last minute details that had to be attended to on his and Mary's house, and he was overwhelmed with the possibility of having to plan and help the slaves with the work.

Rather than get into his reasons for sending Silas to the new property, Sherrod agreed to fill in for Silas. Up to that point, Henderson had managed everything on the property, and he didn't want him to think Silas was taking over because he was getting married. In actuality, Sherrod wanted him to concentrate more on Bryant's Grove and less on what Bryant Town was doing. He would always keep Henderson involved, but it was time he brought in some of the other children, help them determine their role and place in Bryant Town.

In January 1828, Sherrod's decision paid off. Henderson came to Sherrod and told him, "Dad, Mary Ann is having a baby."

Sherrod grabbed his son and hugged him, patted him on the back, and hugged him some more. When he finally let go, Henderson explained, "I am going to have to spend more time close to home. Running the meat plant and increasing the stud service is about all I can handle right now."

Sherrod knew his decision to take Silas away was correct. He was glad he hadn't tried to tell Henderson how to handle his new responsibility. He was grateful he had come to it on his own.

"I will miss having you ride the trails with me, but I understand. A man's place is at home. Particularly at a time like this," Sherrod said, and they hugged again. Then it hit Sherrod—he was about to become a grandfather. He wasn't sure how he felt about that. A forty-seven-year-old man wasn't old. It was about time he showed the family his best years were yet to come.

He geared himself for further progress, and by the time his first grandchild, Henry Watson Bryant, was born on September 7, 1828, he had acquired a lot at Seven College Street from Thomas Loving and an additional fifty-eight acres that pushed his property line further into Nashville from John Brit.

In 1829, another grandchild, William F. Bryant, was born, and in 1832, Jasper N. Bryant.

Sherrod liked being a grandfather. His own children were growing up and he missed having a baby around the house. From time to time, he would take each of his grandchildren on his lap and fill them in on the history of their family. Henry was a combination of Bryants and Coles. His large forehead and deep-set eyes were definitely Cole. His straight hair, high cheekbones, and little ears were Bryant traits.

"You appreciate this hair," he often teased little Henry. "It is mighty thin and won't last till you're my age."

He wasn't afraid to hug the children. He would kiss them under the neck and revel in their laughter.

"Stop it, Granddaddy, stop it," Henry would giggle. Sherrod would laughingly tickle his stomach. "You are Bryant Town's first preacher," he would say amidst the laughter.

"What's preacher?" Henry would ask.

"You will find out," Sherrod would tease and tickle him some more.

He played with William and Jasper too, but Henry was the oldest, and as was Henderson, Sherrod felt he would be the one to set the tone for that generation.

William had his own special place, however. He looked very much like Sherrod. His features were sharp, and the nose not as pronounced as Henry's. His hair was also straight, but it was full and long. Jasper was an infant. His skin was paler than the others. He looked like a white child, and that amused Sherrod.

I guess you are Jesse's sweet revenge, he thought as he held the child. Jasper was a happy baby, and it was he who made Sherrod realize how much he missed having a little one around. William was now ten years old, and Phoebe, Catherine, and Nancy Elizabeth, nine, eight, and seven.

Henrietta was very much a part of his family life. He never involved her in his business, but, as far as the children were concerned, she knew more about them than he did. She was a good mother, and he began to observe more and more how she coddled and spoiled everyone.

At the beginning of the year 1833, Alonzo Summer, a black barber Sherrod and his brother Silas were friendly with, started a school for coloreds in a local colored church on the edge of Nashville. As soon as he made the announcement to the community, a brother of Tom Cole and his outgrown sons broke into Alonso's home and beat him unconscious.

Sherrod heard the news and got mad. He called all the men, twelve and up, who lived in Bryant Town to a meeting at the Bryant

Town church. Forty showed up: his sons, Henderson and Silas, his brothers, Silas and William, and their six sons, and the twenty-nine slaves that helped to make up Bryant Town.

Sherrod explained what had happened to Alonzo. "A gang of local white crooks is trying to control our lives and the future of our children's lives. We cannot do much about the US government treating us like cattle, but we can do something about what is happening here." He pulled out a drawing very much like the one Mamie had made on a piece of wood with charred wood years ago.

"This here is the building we are in." He pointed to an X on the board. "As you can see, many trees surround us. No one can get back here to this church unless they pass several of our houses and cross many fences. The whites know we are back here, but long as we are just having a church, they are not going to bother us.

"What we are going to do is build ourselves a school under this church. We are going to use the same plan the miners used when they tunneled underground. We are going to move the preacher's stand aside and dig a room under the floor. The room won't have windows, but that's okay because like the Indian mud huts out on the reservation, the walls will be sealed and damp. The air will be supplied from up here.

"We will increase the width of the base of the preacher's stand and make it hollow. The only thing solid about that stand will be the top piece set up once a week for the Bible.

"The underground room will be damp and smelly. We will have to work hard to keep it clean. The way it is built will determine the odor. Steps leading from the base of the preacher's stand will give our children and Nance a way in and a way out. The room can be well lit because there will be no window and therefore no wind blowing in.

"Is anybody against the idea?" There was silence, so he continued. "Good. Willie, you and Samuel pick the men you want to help you and let me know when you are ready to start. Meanwhile, Nance will continue teaching at the house until we are finished here."

The new school gave Sherrod new life. He was sorry about Alonso and angry about what had happened. Even though the Bryant School was a way of letting colored folks know that the white folks are powerless over the progress of people of color, the school had to remain a town secret. Everyone living in Bryant Town knew it had to remain a secret. As much as they wished they could invite Mr. Alonso and other colored neighbors in, they knew they couldn't.

Everyone was aware that Sherrod was despised and envied for his family community and that it was the Bryant Town resources that kept its residents safe.

Free men and slaves living outside of Bryant Town envied Bryant Town's economic position and oftentimes tried to start dissension among the residents. Aware of these pitfalls, Sherrod held frequent town meetings and allowed everyone to vent their frustrations.

Most residents chose to stay within the confines of the town and remained close-mouthed about the plans and expansion ideas. Husbands and wives seldom discussed town business out of fear of the children overhearing and saying something in front of white customers that frequented the town.

When the school was finished and the children started to attend, Nance told them they were going to a playhouse and that was what the students called it.

Henrietta was happy to see Sherrod get involved on a large scale with education and religious issues. She often felt they didn't stop to consider how painful it was to be a slave, not that their master-slave relationship was bad or anything. It was just that sometimes he made her feel so special and other times he made her feel that she was there and took advantage of her presence. She had never discussed her sleeping with Sherrod with anyone because she knew at any time he could choose someone to marry and she would have to cater to them like she catered to that Nancy person he had married. She knew if she never discussed her personal business, she wouldn't have to struggle to save face when he needed a change.

Sherrod thought about Henrietta in the same manner he thought about Little Doe. They served a need. He treated them decent, and they were not a focal point of his or the town's existence.

Strangely enough, he began to think more and more about Henrietta. What a good woman she was, and how she was patient and didn't nag him about anything. One night, when he came in late, she had the old tin tub filled with warm water, poured for him to soak. He had been terribly busy trying to get the school built. Henrietta saw he was dog-tired and was neglecting himself somewhat, so she fixed the bath. He was so appreciative he invited her to bathe with him.

She did, and for months after, the baths became a nightly ritual. Henrietta learned she was pregnant. Mary Ann was also pregnant, and at the end of the year in 1933, Mary gave birth to a son. Two months later, in the beginning of 1834, Henrietta gave birth to a son.

Sherrod was pleased. The newborn made him feel as if he had a new lease of life. He named his son Milia and called him "Dollar."

Henderson was also pleased about the birth of his son, whom he named Joseph. He was shocked and dismayed by the impending birth of Joel and Sally's baby, Margaret Emily, and his stepbrother, Milia. He knew he lived at a time when a man was measured by the number of children he fathered. However, his children having to cross generational lines disturbed him. Poor Joseph would have to live with Margaret Emily and Milia as an aunt and uncle who were a few months younger. Unlike his older brothers, he would also have to compete for his grandparents' attention.

Mary Ann was okay with the birth of her new sister, and she tried to tell Henderson that Sherrod was like the men in the Bible. He was full of life and he believed in procreating, and as long as he lived, he would probably father children.

As Mary Ann said, Sherrod continued to have children with Henrietta. In 1836 a son Jno was born, in 1839 a daughter Sarah, in 1840 a son George, in 1841 a daughter Ailsie, 1843 a son Zoneigg, in 1844 a son Lauranzee, and in 1846 his last child, a daughter Mary Ann was born.

Henrietta told Sherrod she wanted to name their last daughter after Mary Ann because she was like a sister to her. Mary had four additional children around the same time as Henrietta. James K. Polk was born in 1838 and named after President James K. Polk. A son, Henderson, was born in 1841, a daughter, Missouri, born in 1848, and Sherrod Riley born in 1849. The uncles and aunts and nephews and nieces shared clothes, toys, and at times, furniture. Henrietta loved her kinship with Mary Ann.

In 1837, amongst all the births, education, and new businesses, Bryant Town was booming. Silas moved with his family out to the Britt property Sherrod had purchased. His brother, Robertson, was now eleven years old and a big help in his jewelry and hardware businesses.

Sherrod felt pressured to expand the town. His brothers, William and Silas, began to relinquish his land and make purchases of their own, but that didn't satisfy his need. He wanted to be sure all his children and grandchildren would have enough land to establish themselves when the time came. So, in 1844, he purchased a tract of land from the Carter Estate and fifty-two acres from his neighbor, William Donelson. In 1846 he purchased an additional forty-three acres on McCreary Creek from Benjamin Rogers, and in 1852 he purchased twenty-nine-and-half acres in Davidson County from John Grey. In 1854, seven months before his death, he purchased another eight acres on McCreary Creek from William Scott.

In 1848, two years after he purchased the forty-three acres on McCreary Creek, Joel came to town unannounced. Sherrod was sitting on the porch holding his infant daughter, Mary Ann.

Joel and a woman and a young child he thought to be Sally and Margaret Emily drove up in a carriage. Sherrod took the baby and ran out to greet them before the carriage could roll to a complete stop. "What are you doing in Davidson County?" Sherrod exclaimed. "You are such a welcome sight."

Joel jumped down, and they hugged. Over Joel's shoulder, Sherrod caught a glimpse of the woman sitting there, and he realized it wasn't Sally. He stuck his head inside the carriage and the woman smiled. The memory of her flooded his senses: the face, the eyes, that nose, that head of coal black hair.

"Hello, Secret Friend," Mary Polly said. Her voice sent chills through him. His heart leaped, and he was afraid to respond, afraid that he was mistaken.

"Mary Polly?" he finally asked, searching her face. "Mary Polly, is that you?" She smiled and a peace came over him. He gave the baby to Joel and took Mary Polly's hand and helped her out of the carriage. She looked frail and weak, and he knew something was wrong. When her feet hit the ground, she reeled forward and he caught her, swooped her up in his arms, and carried her to the porch. For the first time, neither of them gave a thought to who was watching or not watching.

"I can walk," she laughed, enjoying his response to her being there.

Sherrod was walking so fast, with her cradled in his arms that Margaret Emily had to run to keep up.

"Where is my sister?" Margaret asked. She was coming to spend the summer and Margaret was excited.

"She doesn't live here in this house, but that is her namesake," Sherrod said proudly, pointing to the baby.

"Children always did take to you," Mary Polly laughed.

"Vitch . . . Vitch," he called. Vitch came from around the side of the house running. "Run and get Henderson. Tell him I want to see him and don't tell him we have guests."

"Yes, Mr. Bryant," Vitch said, and started off.

Sherrod looked at Mary Polly and changed his mind. "On second thought, Joel, why don't you and Margaret Emily ride with Vitch? I will bring Mary Polly as soon as I settle the baby with Henrietta."

"Is that all right with you, Sis?" Joel asked Mary Polly.

"That will be fine," she said.

Sherrod took the baby from Margaret Emily, who had taken her from Joel. "And don't tell Henderson she's here. We will surprise him."

Joel and the others left, and Sherrod took Mary Polly's hand and led her into the house.

"Are you sure it is okay with the missus?" she asked him.

"I don't have a missus," he said.

She liked his excitement. As soon as they stepped inside the house, she started to cough. He let go of her hand and gave her room to care for herself.

"Are you all right?"

Mary Polly grabbed her stomach and waved him and the baby away. Henrietta, who had been watching from the other room, came out, took the baby, and went back inside.

Mary Polly caught her breath. Beads of perspiration wet her bow. Sherrod could tell she was in pain. He asked her again, "Are you all right?"

"I am now," she said and smiled weakly.

Henrietta reappeared with a glass of water. Sherrod took it and gave it to Mary Polly.

"Thanks Henrietta," Mary Polly said.

"You welcome Ma'am," Henrietta said, and disappeared back inside. Sherrod watched her go through the door. It pained him to see her being so nice about everything.

Mary Polly watched him watching her. "I did not come here to cause any trouble, Sherrod," she said. "I needed to see my grandchildren. It's why I came."

Her statement irritated him.

"Well, I can help you with that all right," he said and then turned and led her to the carriage parked under the tree.

For a long while they rode in silence. Sherrod was pouting. He didn't want to hurt Henrietta, but Mary Polly was sick. He could tell by the way she held herself when she moved, the way she turned her head. Besides, he hadn't promised Henrietta anything. He was good to her, and that was all there was. Right now, the children were both theirs, and he hoped she appreciated them as much as he did.

Mary Polly was scared. She knew Sherrod had a mess of children. Joel had told her that. Her excuse had been she couldn't let that keep her from seeing her son and grandchildren. The truth was she thought she was up to seeing Henrietta more than she was. She knew she didn't have the right to be jealous. But she was, and there was very little she could do about that.

After a while she turned to Sherrod. It so happened it was at the same time he was turning to her. They looked at each other and without a word or thought, they fell into each other's arms, kissing and hugging and kissing and hugging. When he caught himself starting to heat up, he said, "Would you like to see the rest of the town?"

She said she would, and he took her to the ridge and showed her all the property he had bought.

"I saw bits and pieces of Bryant Town as Joel and I drove out. This view is magnificent. From here, it looks like you own all of Nashville."

"You can never have too much property," Sherrod said.

"You have your town, Mr. Bryant," she smiled.

"I couldn't have done it without you, Missus Bryant," he said and smiled.

"How many Missus Bryants do you think you will have in your lifetime?" she smirked.

He took her arm. "Don't start."

She playfully punched him in the ribs. "Just wanted to see if you still had any fight in you."

"Our baby is a father many times over," he said.

"I know," she said and thought about it for a moment. "I wish I had had the courage they have."

"They can afford to have courage. You and I paid a price for their courage."

"Thanks for saying that," she said. "Sometimes I feel so guilty about not trusting we could have done it together." He hugged her. "Well, I guess we better get on," she said quietly walking away. "I want to see this Bryant's Grove that I have heard so much about."

He took her hand, and together they walked back to the carriage.

BRYANT ACRES CHAPTER XXII

You Are Who I Thought You Were All the Time

By the time Mary Polly and Sherrod arrived at the house in Bryant's Grove, it was almost dark. The table was being set and everyone was preparing for dinner. Mary Ann saw the carriage approach and she hurried to the door.

"Hi, Grandpa Bryant," she called, "Who is that you have with you?"

She saw it was Mary Polly and rushed back to get Henderson.

"Come here," she said and snatched Henderson's hand away from the stove, pulling him outside.

"What is wrong with you, woman?" he protested, until he saw Mary Polly.

He rushed out to where she stood and hugged her. He buried his face in her neck. The smell of her ripped into him. Like a little child, he began to cry. "I missed you, Mama Mary . . . I missed you."

"I missed you, too," she managed to say as her throat muscles began to constrict and bind.

He walked with her to the porch, and they sat there crying and holding each other while Sherrod tended the horses and watched from afar. Finally, she took his hand, and Mary Ann went back inside. She helped him to the set beside her.

"I am thirty-eight years old, a father with six children," he said through his sniffles. "What will they think with me here bawling like a baby?"

"I am seventy plus years old," she said, "and for the first time in my life, I don't know what to say."

Henderson smiled at her. "Start by telling me what's wrong."

"I can't seem to digest my food. I got real cold last winter. Ruben and his family did everything to make living easy for me, but I just became disoriented somehow. Went out in the rain one night. Next thing I know, the doctor was standing over me and said I had been out of my head with delirium for three days. I haven't had much appetite since then."

"How long have you been with Joel?"

"Since last month. He came to Ruben's and got me."

Henderson stood up. "Well come on in and meet the family."

Mary Polly was delighted and overwhelmed by their grand-children. "Boys must run in the Bryant family," she laughed.

"It does seem like you have to have a mess of children before you have a girl around here. Henderson and I, we gone keep on trying, Aunt Mary."

"You are quite a lady, Mary Ann," Mary Polly said to her niece, and they all went in to dinner.

Henderson was so grateful for his mother's presence that he volunteered to say the blessing rather than deferring to Sherrod as he usually did.

Before he prayed, he told everyone at the table how grateful he was that they were his family. Then he began . . .

"Lord, thank you for allowing me this time with my family. My mother has returned, as you know. She isn't in such good health, and I need you to give me the foresight to make decisions that will nurse her back to health. Mary Ann is the best wife a man could ask for. She has given me six beautiful, healthy children, and for that I am grateful. My daddy and father-in-law are in the house tonight. I want you to know how grateful I am for their guidance. This Bryant and Cole family are special, and I am asking you to bless them. Bless the food we are about take for the nourishment of our bodies and bless those who also lovingly prepared it. And, Lord, when it comes time for those of us who are traveling to depart, help us convey our love or those who are leaving. Help them have a good visit and a safe journey home. These things I ask in Jesus' name."

There wasn't much adult talking going on at the dinner table after this blessing. The children chattered idly. Sherrod, Joel, Henderson, and Mary Ann kept their eyes on Mary Polly who had very little food on her plate and wasn't eating any of it.

Instead, she was sitting and wondering if she had been too quick in her decision to come and find Henderson. Except for the occasional present she sent to Bryant Town, there had been no contact between them the past twelve years. Mary Polly sat there thinking, Henderson was so overcome with emotion, would he wake up and resent her tomorrow?

After dinner that night, Sherrod was preparing to go home. He was saying his goodbyes to the children. Mary Polly quietly asked Joel, "Do you think I did the right think coming back here?"

"You have been thorough a lot. Your heart is in Bryant Town. Trust your decision. Lots of rest, proper care, a will to live, and you will be up and around in no time." A rush of love for her brother came over her. "Look at Henderson and answer your own question," he continued as he took her hand. "Our children are married. Of all the people in the world, I love you most. Our kind of love breeds happiness. Henderson and Mary Ann are blessed."

"I am not angry at Big Mary. It is Daddy that I can't forgive."

He put his finger to Mary Polly's lips and stopped her. "There is no need to discuss that now. It will only bring on one of your spells, and making yourself sick won't help the pain."

"You're right," she said, knowing she could never give the details of what happened. Sherrod couldn't handle it.

When Sherrod came to find her, he automatically assumed she was coming home with him, and she didn't dissuade him. He said goodbye to Joel and then picked her up and carried her to the carriage. Henderson came out the door as he carried her down the steps.

"Tell your dad that I am not an invalid," Mary Polly said smiling.

"There is nothing I could say that would convince him to do anything except for what he is doing," Henderson said, enjoying the dialogue between them. He felt like he used to feel when she came to visit. She looked older and weaker, but next to Mary Ann, she was the prettiest woman that he had ever seen.

Mary Polly felt his warmth. Her chest hurt a little less than it had been. All that had happened to her over the past thirty-three years flashed quickly through her mind, and for the first time, in that setting, she knew why she had endured so much pain.

Sherrod and Mary Polly were riding towards Bryant Town. All of a sudden, she felt very tired. She settled back. "Home at last," she thought, and fell asleep.

Sometime between sunset and daybreak, she heard a noise, opened her eyes, and saw Sherrod climbing into bed where he had put her.

"It's only me," he said, and she reached for him.

"Hi, me."

"Hi," he said, and they lay together holding and touching, each in his own thoughts, not saying a word.

The rooster crowed, and noises of people stirring in other parts of the house could be heard.

"What do you want to do today?" he asked.

"Make love to you," she said.

He lifted her gently in his arms and brought her to rest on top of him, and for the first time they looked at each other, let their eyes meet, and search for all the told and untold passages of time that carried stories of their experiences.

Keeping the tenor of her mind in place, she began to stroke his hair, let her hands follow the outline of his face. She touched his lips with her own. Slowly, ever so slowly, she allowed herself to feel the warmth of his body beneath hers.

She relaxed her knees on each side of him, straddled him in a way that allowed room for his erection. It commanded attention, and she gave it willingly. She wanted to pleasure him, and she did. The fight was over. The secret that began in the woods at Cole Manor no longer existed, and she wanted him to know.

The passion that sparked the relationship between the inden-tured slave and his Mistress forty-six years before in Virgilina, Virginia, was alive and willing to be dealt with.

After breakfast that first day, Sherrod introduced Mary Polly to all of Henderson's brothers and sisters: Silas, William, Catherine, Phoebe, Nancy Elizabeth, Little Robertson, Milia, Jno, Lauranzee, Ailsie, Sarah, and Mary Ann.

Joel had kept her apprised of Sherrod's life and the births of his children. She expected to be jealous, but instead, she delighted in how much they loved Sherrod, their racial mixture, and their phys-ical appearance.

For the first time, she began to appreciate the teachings of Sherrod's father. She remembered that day when she challenged his belief in the human race and the good of man rather than the racial and ethnic make-up of the person. She knew now that she had used that belief to seduce him. She was ashamed but not sorry.

Sherrod strolled with her through Bryant Town and showed her all that had been accomplished in her absence. She marveled at the many businesses, the stores, homes, church, and school. She was overwhelmed by the layout and the respect shown the slaves and their families.

She met Nance and Helen. She had already met Henrietta, whom she knew to be the mainstay of Sherrod's existence. Henrietta graciously moved aside and accepted her as she had accepted Nancy into the household. The pain of her separation from Sherrod was never touched on in private or in public. She continued to care for the children and the household. Mary Polly remembered Sherrod's description of her when he had first acquired her. She remembered how jealous she was and how Sherrod teased her, but she never mentioned it.

There were things Mary Polly had to tell Sherrod, but she decided to wait. After that first night at the Big House in Bryant Town, she knew she was going to move to Bryant's Grove to be with her children. Spending the night with Sherrod was her way of finding out what was going on between them. She didn't like disrupting Henrietta, but she felt she had longevity and that gave her rights.

Sherrod was surprised when she told him that she was moving. He told her he was disappointed. She took his face in her hands and gently explained. "I love you, Sherrod Bryant. I can now say it. I don't expect to pursue any type of new understanding in our relationship at this time, because you and I have a lot to talk about. Inasmuch as this visit is about our son, I need to be with him as much as possible these first few days. I have missed many important events in his life. He has top priority. Us? We have weathered many storms. Let's do what we have to do." She smiled and said, "Court me. I would like that."

Sherrod laughed. "You are who I knew you were all those times when we kept missing each other in our efforts to be close. My job now is to get you well. I asked Nance to cook up some of that brew she's been reading about in them fancy books from England. She said she would have it for you by nightfall."

By late spring, Mary Polly wasn't feeling well when she got up in the morning. Without her knowledge, Henderson rode over and told Sherrod he was concerned about her.

Sherrod suggested he go back home and look after her, and as soon as he felt ample time had passed, he would be over. He didn't want Mary Polly to feel the two of them were colluding to get into her business in any way. He tried hard to convey that Mary Polly deserved her privacy and everyone needed to respect her right to it. If she didn't want to tell what was causing her illness, it was her right not to.

His curiosity was at an all-time high, however. On his way over, he decided he would do everything to get her to tell him what was going on. He would be subtle, of course. He prided himself on his ability to extract knowledge from others, making them think they were sharing voluntarily.

He and Mary Polly had been spending Sundays together since she arrived in town, mostly having picnics on the ridge where he had taken her on the first visit, talking about their time together at Cole Manor. Somehow, she seemed more comfortable with the past.

She hadn't seemed any sicker, but she wasn't getting any better either. She still held her body when she walked, and she stiffened her neck and held her head as if she was afraid for it to bend.

As much as he wanted to ask what was wrong on those days, he couldn't bring himself to do so. He told himself she would tell him when she was ready, and he waited.

When he arrived at Bryant's Grove, she was sitting on the porch swing dozing. The sound the horses made as they approached awakened her.

She looked up, still dazed from sleep. Sherrod spoke, "Hi, friend."

She laughed, clearly delighted. "Come sit here beside me. It's time we spoke."

He did as he was told, but not before he picked a handful of flowers from the patch growing beside the front steps.

"I always like flowers," she said, smelling them. Then she laid them on the swing opposite to where they sat. Sherrod made a mental note to remember to put them in a vase before he left.

He reached for her hand and saw an erratic muscle movement of the mouth and throat began to occur. She tried to speak, but her voice was constricted by the spasm that was occurring. The upper part of her chest and head stiffened. She started to gasp for air. He reached for her, but she pushed him away. He sat helplessly watching her.

After a moment or so, she calmed herself. "I don't do well with help during these spells," she said.

"I noticed," Sherrod replied, somewhat put off by her.

"I have a damaged throat muscle, several broken ribs, and the side effects of a severe blow to the head."

"What are you saying? How? What happened?"

Mary Polly moved over and put her head on his shoulder. Then, with that faraway look of pain in her eyes, she went into her pain with the hope that this would be the last telling.

"Tom Cole never visited Virginia, but he wrote a letter responding to an inquiry that Lavonia made about me. Tom told Lavonia that I had a black bastard child living with Joel in Rutherford County. He said he had met this child on the road one morning, heard him call me 'Mama Mary'.

"At first, Daddy didn't believe Lavonia when she came to him with the story. Then Joel moved back to Kentucky, and Big Mary convinced Daddy that that was the reason why. Daddy sent Jesse to visit Joel and Sally. Without Joel's knowledge, Jesse talked to the children about Henderson and about you. Daddy was so mad when Jesse confirmed what Tom said. He had Robert drag me out of bed in the middle of the night.

"He told Robert I had been had by a black heathen and he was to go in my room and take me. Use whatever means he needed but take me like I have never felt the likes of. If I fought back, he was to use whatever force he needed to get what he wanted." Mary Polly gasped. Sherrod squeezed her hand and she continued, "He said," she gasped again, "he said he would be outside the door to make sure I understood the consequences my type of behavior brought.

"I had been back at Cole Manor almost a year when this happened.

"Robert . . . Robert . . . He awakened me from a deep sleep. I didn't know what was happening. Robert tore off my gown, and I slapped him. I knocked him up against the bedpost.

"Daddy heard the noise and ran into the room. 'Take the slut,' he yelled, and handed Robert his rifle.

"Robert hit me upside the head with the rifle butt. Cracked my head open. Pain shot through me. I fell dazed across the bed, blood trickled down my face, shot everywhere. I kicked Robert, and he grabbed hold of my throat. I could see Daddy looking on. His face was twisted and strange looking.

'Fuck her,' Daddy said to Robert when he saw me looking at him. 'Fuck her,' he yelled again . . .

"Then . . . then . . . as if Robert wasn't doing a good enough job, Daddy . . . Daddy . . . He pushed Robert aside, dropped his pants, and mounted me himself." Mary Polly started to cry. Sherrod put his arms around her and held her.

"He banged and clutched and pawed me until I passed out. When I came to several days later, I was lying in the slave camp. Mamie and Marie were bathing my face and throat with cool damp rags.

'You gonna be all right, Mary Polly. You gonna be all right,' Marie kept saying.

"'I don't want to be all right,' I tried to say but couldn't speak. I reached up and touched my burning throat. There were deep gashes underneath. Mamie explained they were fingernail wounds, infected and oozing. Inside, my throat was spastic. I could barely breathe. It was the pressure Robert ad Daddy applied that caused the lack of air; it still sometimes affects my speech.

"My eyes were little more than slits. They were swollen to where I couldn't see anything but images, and my chest was tightly wrapped.

'If you don't eat, you will die,' different ones kept saying.

"Again, I tried to tell them that dying would be okay, but the words wouldn't come. I slept and slept. Off and on, I slept for weeks. Finally, near dark one evening, Big Mary appeared at my bedside.

'You have disgraced us, Mary Polly,' she said. 'Your father is unbending in his disowning you. So, I have no choice but to tell you that as far as we are concerned, you are dead. Your possessions and your position in this family and the town no longer exist. I have instructed Mingus and Cato to take you to the Carolina border and leave you. Your father said if you are not gone by weeks' end, he will kill you like he does the rest of the vermin on this farm.'

"With her piece said, Big Mary stormed out. The first, and I presume the only, time she acknowledged the existence of a slave camp on her property."

"Why didn't you ask Mingus to contact me?" a dumbfounded Sherrod asked.

"And get the both of you killed?"

Sherrod realized he had spoken out of turn. He became quiet again.

She continued, "Mingus had permission to help me, and that's all he needed. He bundled me up as soon as Big Mary cleared the door. He rode all night and all the next day and night until we arrived at Ruben's.

"Tisha rode with Mingus. She knew I needed more care than Mingus was able to give. She wasn't afraid Daddy was going to punish her in any way. She boiled roots, ground plants, and used bat wings and insects to make salves and compresses. She used chipped tree barks to make tea.

"Ruben and Mary sent Mingus and Tisha back to Cole Manor as soon as we arrived. They told them that they were never to mention where they left me. If asked, they were to say some religious camp in the woods had agreed to take me in.

"I lay around for over a year at Ruben's house. One day, Joel showed up. It seems Jesse felt guilty about what he had done and contacted Joel.

"Joel wanted me to go back to Kentucky with him to live, but I couldn't. I knew that you were doing all you could for our son, and I wasn't going to move to the vicinity and contaminate that in any way."

"Damn your self-righteousness," Sherrod said. "You were afraid even then to be with me."

"Stop trying to be so noble. You would have been useless, and you know it. I like the alibi Ruben had created, so I used it. I was prepared to die but rather than kill myself, I went and joined the Quake Church. I was without money, position, or family, and that was perfectly suited for the position of recruiting. Christian white people around the country who were against slavery and were willing to assist the Quaker's mission group in their efforts to help slaves escape to Canada.

"The Quakers understood I was ailing. They exchanged medical care and lodging for small chores. Once I was stronger, they hired me to be North Carolina coordinator for the church's plan of freeing slaves and building an underground railroad that would help slaves escape to Canada.

"Sherrod, I have lived intimately with African Americans, some smart ones, educated, and not educated, and some not so smart ones. Their trust of me came with me sharing my story. Each time I shared it, I became stronger. Until last fall, I got caught in a rain storm and the muscles in my throat had problems fighting the cold I contracted.

"I saw a doctor. He said it wasn't just my throat. He said I had constrictions throughout my body, that I would never be well again, and in time I would die from the wounds. He didn't say how long I had. I don't think he knew."

Sherrod's grip on her tightened. She turned and looked up at him. "What I am saying is I don't know how long I have to live."

He hugged her and hugged her. Then, without warning, he called out, "Henderson, Mary Ann, get yourselves ready. Your mother and I, we are going to get married. Go get Silas. Tell him to ride ahead, help Vitch and the others to get things ready."

Sherrod swept Mary Polly up in his arms.

"Put me down, crazy man," Mary Polly argued.

"You have had your say; now it is my turn," he said and kept holding her.

Henderson appeared in the doorway. He saw their struggle. "Dad, what are you doing?"

An embarrassed Sherrod set Mary Polly down. She laughed. "Your dad proposed marriage and mistakenly picked me up to carry me over the threshold rather than get down on his knees."

Henderson walked over to where she stood and hugged her. "Daddy wants to do right by you, Mama."

She smiled. For the life of her, she couldn't remember either Sherrod or Henderson being this handsome.

BRYANT ACRES CHAPTER XXIII

"Look Around You and Be Proud"

Sherrod and Mary Polly's marriage was almost anti-climactic. A peace settled over the couple. Sherrod did what he always did when he felt motivated. He made plans for increasing the size of Bryant Town. The town was twenty five plus years old and he was afraid that everyone was becoming complacent.

Most of the early children born before 1825 were grown, and the second generation of Bryant Town were fast heading to adulthood. Henderson's first son, Henry, was already fifteen.

Sherrod was sitting and enjoying the brightness of the day, when Mary Polly entered from the bedroom carrying Missouri, her youngest grandchild.

"You must admit she was pretty good last night," she said and smiled.

"I'm surprised Henderson let her out of his sight," Sherrod laughter. "Mahalia said when she told him it was a girl, he was so happy that he went to running off at the mouth, fighting every man in Bryant Town off of her before she was even cleaned up good."

"I don't know what you said to Henry but every time I see him he is walking around with a bible."

Sherrod laughed even harder. "Better than a lot of other things he could be walking around with."

"Oh, you," Mary Polly said, and hit him on the arm.

At almost that time, Mary A. arrived sitting in the back of the carriage. Willie was driving her. Mary Polly stood up, Missouri clinging to her with both arms around her neck.

"Don't tell me. Henderson sent you for the baby."

Mary A. laughed.

"Don't blame him. This little angel was hard to come by.

Mary Polly kissed Missouri on the cheek.

"See you later, Pun'kin, she said, and held her out so Sherrod could kiss her.

When Mary A. and Missouri rode away, Mary Polly stood and watched until they were out of sight.

"Our grandchildren are such a combination of Bryant and Cole. I hope the have the best of both families." She thought about Jasper who appeared whiter than any of his siblings. Everything about him looked White. He favored Jesse and that made her sad.

Big Mary and Jesse could love him, she thought and became sadder still. She quickly admonished herself for allowing either of her parents to come into her consciousness. To think that they still had value was more than she cared to know.

Sherrod carefully watched her without saying a word.

"Get a hold of yourself," he said.

She turned to him and asked, "Do you think children love their parents no matter what? I think about Henderson's treatment of me and I wonder."

Sherrod knew she was talking because she was thinking about her parents. Even though he believed love was possible after the hurt passed, he wasn't going to let Jesse Cole get away that easily... or Big Mary Cole either, for that matter.

"Your parents are vermin," Sherrod said. "Look at them. From the beginning of your birth, your mother loved another person's child because she was afraid to deal with you."

"Not one of her children lives in close proximity. You tried and look what happened. Your dad was always no good. First, he violated Tisha, her daughter, and then you. His sins are murderous. You and I represent what they had enjoyed in secret all those years, and he couldn't tolerate it."

Sherrod took her hand and gently held onto it.

"You have touched many lives, not only here in Tennessee, but across the country. You may not be here to see all the good work, but that Underground Railroad you told me about is going to be invaluable. Generations to come will benefit; Your son's children, their children's children, and so on. You are a noble woman. Look around you and be proud."

Mary Polly took his words and hung on to them. She moved about Bryant Town touched base with each of its residents. She sat down with Henrietta one day and told her how grateful she was that she had cared for Sherrod and his family.

SHE apologized for any hurt that she had caused and told Henrietta that she was to look at her as an intrusive visitor on her way someplace else.

Henrietta hugged her and told her she was sorry she was ill, she belonged in Bryant Town, her presence was bigger than any regrets she might have, and she was glad she had come.

Mary Polly awakened that last day and said to Sherrod.

"Today is our day together… No work for you today. I need you to help me to let go."

He had watched her grow weaker, and he knew it was a matter of time so her words didn't come as a surprise.

"Have you spoken to Henderson?" he asked her.

"I have," she said. "Let's go on a picnic. Go to the ridge… take in some peace and quiet."

Henrietta packed a lunch and off Mary Polly and Sherrod went. The ridge was where they had gone her first day in Tennessee and it seemed right that they should return on that day.

She was not capable of getting down on the ground to sit so Sherrod put the top down on the carriage and spread a blanket between the seats. He helped her down and the walked hand in hand.

"One of my greatest losses this past year was not being able to feel you inside of me," she said.

He tightened his hand on her grip and they kept walking.

"I can't tell you how many times I have thought about the night you arrived in town; the dinner was long, the conversations were long. You were sick, and all I could think about was making love to you. You fell asleep and I carried you into the house, afraid to go to bed, knowing that I would have to contain myself. When I finally got up the courage, I was overjoyed by your response.

"I want to pleasure you, she said,"

His voice broke…

"All that you had been through, the beatings, the violation of your body…and…and, you still found enough caring to visit that place for me." She let go of his hand and fell against his chest. "I want to make love, Sherrod Bryant."

He held her… helped her struggle to the edge of the cliff.

There they stood together and watched Bryant Town, Bryant's Grove, and all they owned laid out before them.

Mary Polly began to cough and shake. Sherrod heard a rattle in her voice.

"Bryant Acres," she whispered.

"Bryant Acres, " he repeated, and she slumped.

He caught and held onto her. He buried his head in her neck and held on until the she breathed her last breath.

A cloud hung over Bryant Town with her passing. Town residents had come to realize that Mary Polly Cole was truly the first lady of Bryant Town. The funeral was simple. Joel and Sally's family came, along with Jesse and Mary Polly's younger sister, Missouri.

Sherrod created a cemetery on the banks of McCrory Creek. There he buried Mary Polly, the first person to be buried in the Bryant Town Cemetery.

HRH and Mary A. invited the family back to Bryant's Grove after the funeral. Sherrod went home to his quiet, empty room. He had gotten used to having Mary Polly around. Even when she wasn't around, he knew she was out there somewhere and he could find her if he had to. Her dying brought feelings in him that was strange and new.

SHE was his partner; that had been decided long ago. When she was married to Nancy, he often wondered what would happen if Mary Polly showed up. He had always known that one day she would return and that they would be together. Bryant Town was hers as much as it was his, and even though he knew that to be the case, it wasn't until after he married Mary Polly that he felt that she was really in his life.

The hours that they sat and talked helped him appreciate the strength of her belief in him. He realized how angry he had been at her all those years; how he had blamed her for the relationship, and how he had hated her for being White.

All of a sudden he felt old.

"I am sixty seven years old." He thought. "The best I can do is to make sure my children and their children have enough to go around."

He didn't have much conversation for Jesse and Missouri, as far as he was concerned, their show of family was a little lame. He was careful not to influence Henderson or Mary A's feelings in any way, however. He felt that would limit the chances and stifle their senses of family. He politely asked to be excused to mourn in private. There he was, sitting and crying in silence.

Long after he went down for the night, he tossed and turned in his sleep. At one point he cried out,

"Mary Polly… Mary!"

Henrietta went in to see about him.

"Are you all right? She asked.

"Come and sit with me," he said.

She pulled up a chair and quietly watched him until he was asleep. Once or twice she tried to quietly leave the room. By the time she got to the door, he would ask her...

"Where you going?"

"Nowhere, Sir," she would reply and sit back down to sleep in the chair. She stayed there until the sun came shining through the window waking them both.

He started to stir and she sneaked out of the room, not wanting him to have to address his needing her to stay with him. He withdrew into himself and became less talkative with everyone. Pain showed in his face. His only spark seems to be the younger children. He would sit for hours and tell the stories about their home community. How it came to be and why it was necessary.

Sometimes Henderson would try to sit and listen and Sherrod would ask him to leave.

"These are the third generation of Bryant's," he would say. Their rule will make or break Bryant Town. They need this time alone with me."

In 1849, he once again became the grandfather of a newborn son. Henderson wanted to honor his father so he named him Sherrod Riley.

That same year, Joel sent word that Jesse Cole had killed himself, Robert had taken off for places unknown, and Big Mary had gone crazy. Sad as it was, Sherrod felt vindicated somehow. He tried to support Joel however, sent messages of condolences, and asked if there was anything he could do?"

Joel wired back and said,

"God has a way of taking care of things that need to be taken care of." He said that Big Mary had to be taken in by her sister Lavonia. He, Jesse Jr, and Missouri were selling Cole Manor and sending all the slaves to Bryant Town to him. He also said Henderson would be receiving Mary Polly's share of the proceeds from the sale."

Old man Jesse must be turning over in his grave, he thought, reading the wire.

He ran out to find Henderson. Old man Benjamin Rogers was thinking about selling land adjacent to that parcel he had purchased outside of Nashville. He thought Henderson should make Rogers an offer.

In 1850, little two year old Missouri died from diarrhea. Henrietta grieved almost as much as Mary A. and Henderson. It was the first death among the children in Sherrod's immediate family and everyone was overcome with grief.

Henderson cleared a lot of land and created the Bryant Grove Cemetery. Missouri was buried there. Henderson and Mary A. were so shaken by the death of their little girl that Sally sent Margaret Emily to live with them.

Little Missouri's death exposed the need for medial assistance. Her illness had gone unattended by professionals because none was available. The White doctors on hand were busy attending to the White sick. The few Blacks that called themselves healers were about as competent as Helen and Nance were with their home remedies.

Sherrod called the family together and spoke of the need for medical training and health knowledge. Illness frightened everyone. It made them feel helpless.

"We may not be able to get to the doctors," he said, "but we can get to the books. I promise you, I will order medical books from Europe."

And, that is what he did.

Mary A. was distraught without little Missouri. She questioned herself over and over about the care of her baby girl… What she could have done and didn't do. She asked herself was she a good enough other.

Henderson reassured her, and Sherrod reassured her, but it was her oldest son, Henry, who put in into perspective.

"It was God's will, Mom," he said to her one day. "God gives us what we need. He didn't give us any more than we can handle."

"How do you know all of that?" she asked him.

"I pray a lot, he said. "When my sister died I was ready to give up reading the bible. Then it came to me. My Grandmother died. My great grandfather died, Missouri is in good company."

Mary A. was proud of her son. She still thought about little Missouri, but she didn't worry quite as much. In 1852, she had another baby girl. This one she named Mary Polly.

Sherrod went back to taking an active role in the day-to-day decisions of Bryant Town. He asked Henrietta to marry him and they became man and wife.

Henrietta was happy that she had never discussed her relationship with any of the other girls. Because when Mary Polly came, she was able to contain her anger of Sherrod's choosing the White woman over her. When it was all said and done, she thought Mary Polly was a likable person. If she had been as sick as poor Mary Polly, she would probably been back in Bryant Town much sooner than Mary Polly was. Besides, she was younger than Mary Polly and she was sure to outlive her and that would give her another chance to be special in Sherrod's life.

And special she was. No one could ever replace Mary Polly. Sherrod knew Henrietta understood that. Henrietta was more like the mother he never knew. She loved nurturing him, having his babies and being the mother of his children.

To celebrate his marriage, Sherrod talked Benjamin Rogers into selling him the 29 ½ acres of land outside of Nashville. Robertson and William had struck out on their own, and he wanted them to have plenty of room to set up their businesses. Little Silas had married Tabitha Fogg the year before Mary Polly returned. He as satisfied with the property he was on. William could share part of the land that he got from the Carter Estate. The girls he wasn't concerned about. If they didn't marry well, he would then consider what should be done.

On December 12, 1853, Sherrod's grandson, Henry Watson, married Margaret Emily Cole. Sherrod was seventy two. He found himself getting tired. The wedding brought back memories of ME. What was happening day-to-day held his interest less and less. He had seventeen children of his own and twenty grandchildren that he knew about.

The population of Bryant Town was way past a hundred. He promised himself that one day he would take a head count. But, he

resigned himself to sitting on the porch and taking about the past...
and forgot.

Right before the holidays in 1853, Sherrod decided it was time
he made a Will. He hadn't been feeling well, mostly old age pains of
stiffness in the back, legs, and arms. It felt more and more like it was
time for him to let Henderson take the reins. Every time he mentioned it, however, Henderson wouldn't hear it. He helped out every
way that he could, but he didn't want his father to stop working.

As Sherrod promised himself he was going to do during the
last part of 1853, he went over to the Buchanan household and
asked James Buchanan to witness his Will. James and his wife,
Addison, complied.

Sherrod spelled out his wishes for each of his seventeen children. He didn't consider the grandchildren. His philosophy was
that each parent was to provide for his own.

In May 1854, he decided he wanted to extend his property on
McCrory Creek near where he was to be buried. He went to William
Scott and asked him to sell him an additional eight acres, which
Scott did.

Sherrod's health began to fail after that. He seldom left the
house anymore. Out of caring and love, Henderson began to take on
more and more of the responsibility. Silas was very involved with his
own business. He knew very little of what was going on at the house.

Sherrod sat on the porch long hours, ordering his life in his
mind. He thought about those times when Henderson was about
to become a father and remembered them fondly. Even though
he himself was awaiting the birth of another child, Henderson and
Mary A.'s first born was awaited with greater anticipation.

Joel and Sally had come up from Kentucky. Mahalia had take charge of Mary A's prenatal care and Henderson spent a lot of time in Sherrod's company.

As he sat of that porch looking back, he played his and Henderson's talks over in his head. He could almost hear Henderson's voice saying,

"Now that I am about to become a father, I really understand what those horseback rides that I used to take with you when I was little boy were all about. Becoming a father is scary. Its like a part of you is separating, and you don't know the direction or the course it will take."

Sherrod smiled. He could hear his own voice equally, as well. "All you can do is be there to listen and to share, make sure as best as you can that there is enough of you to go around, so that your children can love each other and won't have to fight to exist. We people of color can't afford to fight to exist. Because when we do, the White man has us. This country only sees the White man. Colored people are invisible… to them. You remember that."

He liked who he was and he sure did miss Mary Polly.

"Those eight acres are for you and for me, Miss Mary," he would think to himself and laugh.

There came a time that anyone who spoke with him was perceived as someone from the outside who interfered with his thoughts, and it would take him a while to respond to what it was they were saying. Henrietta came to realize this about him and tried not to interfere.

Meals, dressing, and sleeping became the largest concern between them. Once in a while he would ask about the children and the neighbors.

On August 5, 1854, he got up and told Henrietta that he was going to take a ride out to the ridge. She asked if he wanted anyone to go with him, and he said he didn't.

Henrietta and the people he saw on his way out of town were the last people to see him alive. He died at the top of the ridge sitting and looking over Bryant Acres the same as his former life partner, Mary Polly Cole.

EPILOG

Today, more than one hundred sixty four years after Sherrod's death, a monument that attests to his morality and his character stands in the squalor of the uncapped grounds of the Bryant Town Cemetery. Mary Polly, who was buried beside Sherrod, has no marker; her name and death information are conspicuously absent, a mark of the times.

The author hopes this book, Bryant Acres, will serve as a testament to Sherrod and Mary Polly's lives and what she sacrificed when they shared a life together.

Mary Polly, a wealthy white woman dared to fall in love with a young free man of color and have his son. As a white woman, she paid a high price to help her lover and eventually her husband's people (free men and slaves) live and thrive in a climate of political and institutional racism that was and continues to be a part of this country's reality.

Seven generations ago, Sherrod Bryant and Mary Polly Cole lived, planned, and built a town on Bryant Acres. Two subdivisions of Bryant Town also came into being. Validating Sherrod's dream that all people can marry, live, and love together as one people. Sherrod and Mary Polly's son, Henderson Bryant, developed Bryant Grove. Henry Watson Bryant, Sherrod and Mary Polly's grandson, developed Bryant Hills. He was Henderson's oldest son. Henry was Big Mama's great-grandfather.

All of these men married white women. Henry's daughter, Big Mama's mother, Paralee, married a white man, and then the civil war happened. The Ku Klux Klan sprang up and Big Mama, her children, and her children's children were besieged by racism and hate. Their legacy was oppressed and pushed underground.

Today, vestiges of Sherrod's belief that white and black man can live, work, and worship together are too real. Some family members, both white and black, are defying society and honoring their fathers and mothers on both sides of the racial poles.

To those of you who are unaware, Henderson, Henry, and many of his siblings and their wives and children, lay in squalor of uncapped grounds at Bryant Grove Cemetery. The adjacent property, which was once a part of Bryant Acres, is now owned by the State of Tennessee.

This writing is an acknowledgment of Sherrod and Mary Polly Bryant's life. It is the beginning of a record of their love, their family, and their deeds and accomplishments in the antebellum South.

Bryant Acres existed and in part still exists.

Visit Long Hunter State Park. It is located on the boundaries of Rutherford and Wilson County in Tennessee. The park includes fourteen thousand acres at J. Percy Priest Lake and hundred acres at Churchville Lake. Bryant Grove sites are situated around a central parking area. It provides Lake Shore access with an adjacent recreation field. It has a launch ramp used for fishing, pleasure boating, and waterskiing. Walk the nature loop and the point trail at Bryant Grove. Then visit the longer Bryant Grove Trail that connects Bryant

Grove recreation center to the Couchville recreation area. Visit and listen; you might hear the voices of Sherrod and Mary Polly Cole. For it was they who bought, planned, and developed those acres where free men and slaves could live life in an environment where status, treasured resources, and productivity outweighed the color of a person's skin that oftentimes meant life or death.

Anyone who's ever been to the hills and countryside of Middle Tennessee will be willing to tell you of its beauty and the peaceful quietness of the fields. During one of my visits, my mother's seventy-six-year-old cousin volunteered to take my sister, Mosetta, and me to Bryant Grove Cemetery. Artha, like my mother, is from the sixth generation of Bryants. She still lives in the area.

I wanted something concrete to show me that he existed. Sherrod was listed in the Census as early as 1810 and Henderson, his son, as early as 1840. I wanted to see their resting places, so I was told I needed to visit two cemeteries, The Bryant Grove Cemetery and Bryant Town Cemetery.

My cousin, John Martin, said he'd go with me to Artha's house. Artha was familiar with the Bryant Grove Cemetery. Your great-grandfather Henderson, her grandfather, Sherrod Riley, and her father, Zenas, and a host of uncles, aunts, brothers, and sisters are all buried there. The hollowed woods, full of briar patches and sticker bushes, were overgrown with worn grave markers, Indian signs, wooden cradles, and large sunken-in spots where tombstones used to be. There is a tall monument with the names of Henry Watson Bryant and Margaret Emily Bryant, our great-grandfather and great-grandmother.

We read the names of uncles and aunts and tried to figure out some of the names that were partially worn away. In the midst of our search, two golden tabby turtles with red jewel-like spots on their legs and neck and large red eyes crawled across my foot and went down into the clover. They covered themselves with the many flowers that were in bloom. I felt a kinship with the turtles, and I wanted to take them home but the State of Tennessee had a different idea. Security at the airport informed me taking wildlife out of the state was illegal. My cousin Jonny Martin took them back to the cemetery long after I had gone home to California. He put them back to rest and live amongst the Bryants in the Bryant Grove Cemetery.

I guess I was destined to experience my ancestors, because my friend Dorothy and I went back to Tennessee that following spring. It was our time to find Sherrod's gravesite in Bryant Town Cemetery. We learned Bryant Town is now called Donelson, after William Donelson whose property was adjacent to Sherrod's. They were neighbors and business acquaintances.

Dorothy had her camera and had volunteered to take pictures that day. Cautiously, we walked among the clover, careful not to fall into the sunken graves. Some were open and easy to detect' others were masked with branches and fallen trees.

We found tombstones of aunts, uncles, and cousins, and then a strange thing happened. I came upon a non-descriptive tombstone covered with moss and mold. The name was worn, and in the place, where an inscription once appeared, were dented marks of wear and tear.

For some unknown reason, I found myself standing and staring at the stone. Dorothy, unaware of my fixation, continued to search for Sherrod's tombstone. When she found it, she called to me. When I heard her call, it appeared like a strange noise far off in the distance. She called again. I wanted to respond but instead I stood transfixed, staring at the stone. Finally, she came over to where I was. When she saw what was happening, she said, "Ann, there is nothing on that stone. What are you doing?"

Without answering her I picked up a stick and started to clean the mold from the stone. "I just wanted to see what is here," I heard myself say. Dorothy got down on her knees and took a picture of the stone. "There," she said when she was done. Then she laughed and asked, "Now will you come?" I was still somewhat befuddled because she had to explain it to me.

"Sherrod is whom we came to see, is he not?" I followed her to Sherrod's burial spot, walked behind it out of fear of being disappointed. Dorothy laughed. She was standing in front of the tall, thin monument identical to the one that marked Henry and Margaret's graves in Bryant Grove. She began to detect how overwhelmed I was. "Come on" she said, "I will take your picture with it." Something in her voice gave me courage to walk around to the front of the stone. When I saw Sherrod's name, I started to weep. Tears welled up in my eyes and flow down my cheeks. I tapped the stone lightly with my head. "Sherrod, you're about to get your do," I said. Then, I turned to Dorothy and asked her, "Do you think he knows?"

Dorothy nodded and smiled. I began to feel light-hearted and energized. I wasn't sure where the feelings were coming from, but I felt strangely spontaneous. "Let's say a little prayer," I said. Dorothy bowed her head and I prayed. It was very unlike me to want to pray outside the privacy of my environment, especially standing in the open the way we were. But it felt right, however, and it commanded me and gave me feelings of peace and well-being.

"I felt Sherrod's spirit back there," I called to Dorothy. Dorothy laughed. "You were surely acting strange. Something was definitely happening." I laughed, and we put the experience out of our minds until two weeks after we arrived back in San Diego.

I was browsing through the pictures and came upon the picture of the tombstone Dorothy had lured me away from. There imbedded in the stone was an image of Big Mama's mother, Paralee, and an inscription bearing her husband's name, James Watson Hammons.

Paralee died in childbirth in her early 30s. The image in the stone appeared to be around that age. That image is the same as that in the picture I have of Paralee when she was alive.

Dorothy and I were so enthralled by the image in the picture; we had it enlarged and reduced to see if the image of Paralee would change. Not only did the image remain constant but the more I studied the photograph, pictured at the end of this book, the more family members I saw. Paralee's husband, Grandpa Hammons was there. Paralee's father, Grandpa Henry. Paralee's twin sister, Tennessee, and one of the triplets Paralee died giving birth to.

I can also see images of others in the picture that are not as clear as Paralee's image, but they are there, the welcome party that came to participate in this—our—family outing. And so I say to all of you readers and to you, Big Mama, that hundreds of times since your death, I have either thought or visualized how right you were. I wish I had listened to you more and had asked more questions. You used to say we were going to miss you when you were gone. You were right; I have to appreciate how much you gave. Without your influence and your perseverance, I would have missed the opportunity and the experience of the gravesite welcome party, the family beginnings, their struggles to survive, their courage, and their passion for living. And more importantly, I would have missed the journey you so meticulously laid out for me. Thank you for loving me when I was too young and immature to recognize it. Thank you for caring when I didn't have the capacity to understand your education and that the lessons you were trying to teach me would give meaning to the world and my place in it.

I love you, Big Mama. Thanks for being there.

Your granddaughter,

Ann Lee.